GOING TO SEED

ESSAYS ON
IDLENESS,
NATURE &
SUSTAINABLE
WORK

KATE J. NEVILLE

TEXAS TECH UNIVERSITY PRESS

Copyright © 2024 by Kate J. Neville

All rights reserved. No portion of this book may be reproduced in any form or by any means, including electronic storage and retrieval systems, except by explicit prior written permission of the publisher. Brief passages excerpted for review and critical purposes are excepted.

This book is typeset in EB Garamond. The paper used in this book meets the minimum requirements of ANSI/NISO Z39.48-1992 (R1997). ∞

Designed by Hannah Gaskamp
Cover design by Hannah Gaskamp

Library of Congress Cataloging-in-Publication Data on file.

ISBN: 978-1-68283-203-5 (paperback)
ISBN: 978-1-68283-204-2 (ebook)

Printed in the United States of America
24 25 26 27 28 29 30 31 32 / 9 8 7 6 5 4 3 2 1

Texas Tech University Press
Box 41037
Lubbock, Texas 79409-1037 USA
800.832.4042
ttup@ttu.edu
www.ttupress.org

*For lynx and caribou and lake trout,
to sage and ravens and fireweed,
for all my feathered and quilled, leafed and rooted,
hoofed and finned and winged neighbours
—may we hold up your work and create more space for wildness,*

and

*for Dr. Erich W. Damm, who is deeply missed,
and for those in every stage of grief, for so many kinds of loss
—may love hold us all.*

In any case, it is very important to be idle with confidence, with devotion, possibly even with joy.

RAINER MARIA RILKE

CONTENTS

INTRODUCTION:	In defense of idleness	3
CHAPTER I:	Grasshopper songs: On creativity	21
CHAPTER II:	Bear pauses: On rest	39
CHAPTER III:	Beaver blockades: On resistance	53
CHAPTER IV:	Fir deferrals: On slowness	67
CHAPTER V:	Salmon migrations: On detours	79
CHAPTER VI:	Willow roots: On restraint	95
CHAPTER VII:	Owl observations: On attention	113
ROCKY CONCLUSIONS:	On paradox	131
ACKNOWLEDGEMENTS		143
NOTES		149
REFERENCES		201
INDEX		231

GOING
TO
SEED

INTRODUCTION

IN DEFENSE OF IDLENESS

Fur. Small feet. Watershed. Virginia Woolf. Toads. Seeds. John Maynard Keynes. Idleness and approximate synonyms. Greek poets. Japanese monks. Morality. Anarchy. Anti-tyranny. Spring weeds. Golden kites. Cicero. Illegibility. Incommensurability. Time. Other nations.

At first, it was a tuft or two of black fur tucked in the corner. Maybe it had drifted there, I told myself, shed by my Labrador Retriever in his seasonal molt. It was a warm spring, a little windy. The days were growing longer, buds on the shrub birch and willow emerging in the warmer weather. I swept out the watershed and closed the doors. That night, I ignored the scurrying noises, the sound of small feet through the screened-in window not quite drowned out by the creek's steady murmur. Outdoors was fine, that was where small animals belonged, I mused sleepily. They fed the owls, the lynx, sometimes the wolves. In the morning, though, when I went to get milk for my coffee from the fridge, the clusters of fur were back—this time interspersed with tiny pieces of chewed-up foam insulation.

The fridge takes up much of the lower level of "the watershed," a four-foot-by-eight-foot stick-frame structure tacked onto the back of the roughly 200-square-foot, one-room log cabin where I live with my partner. The insulated top holds a small water tank open to the inside of the cabin, providing gravity-fed cold running water to our

INTRODUCTION

kitchen sink through a coil of hose. When the grey water drains out through a barrel buried in the ground, it filters through the rocky soil to the creek, which flows downstream into a glacial lake that feeds the Yukon River; over 3,000 kilometres from here, it pours into the Bering Sea. This boreal landscape of lodgepole pine and trembling aspen and spruce is tied by the sinuous thread of the river to the reindeer lichen and sphagnum moss in the wetland tundra of that distant coastline. We're always connected to somewhere else; some places just remind us of that more vividly. Our cabin is about fifteen kilometres or so outside a small town, on the unceded territory of the Taku River Tlingit First Nation in the northwest corner of British Columbia. As the raven flies, we're closest to Juneau, Alaska, which is just over an icefield; by road, two hours from Whitehorse, the capital city of the Yukon. Mostly, we're among mountains and trees and kind neighbours. We moved to the town while I was still a PhD student, a quiet spot from which to write a dissertation, and for my partner—a freelance writer—a book. We bought this cabin once I graduated and started a postdoctoral fellowship, my research focused on emerging energy debates in the Yukon. When I landed a professorial job in Toronto a few years later, I spent teaching terms in the city and the rest of my time back at the cabin. Until March 2020; when the pandemic hit, I returned westwards. A year of online teaching and then a sabbatical meant more than two years of full-time cabin life.

Our cabin is off the grid—that is, we're not on power lines, there's no plumbing. We have solar panels and batteries, a few LED lights, a propane stove for cooking, a wood stove for heat. The bottom of the watershed, fully enclosed with doors that open outside, holds the fridge. This is powered by our batteries in the summer, and in the winter we unplug the system and use it exclusively as a freezer, kept cold by the subarctic temperatures outside. The shed doors, in spite of our best efforts with wood and wire and spray-foam insulation, leave tiny gaps through which, it turns out, mice can squeeze their elastic bodies.

It was undeniable: mice had moved in. This nest they were building looked soft and warm, a mess of dog fur and foam. I could see they were dedicated to their new home-in-progress. A weeks-long standoff ensued: I would dismantle the nest and clean the corner; the mice, undaunted, would rebuild. A battle of wills—a battle of work. Eventually, my partner pointed out the fire risk posed by the mice given the exposed power cord of the fridge, and we resorted to traps.

Was it then? Was it later? Memory can be fickle. In any case, not long after my standoff with the mice, I picked up my battered copy of Virginia Woolf's novel, *To the Lighthouse*. In it, Woolf writes of a house that "was left like a shell on a sandhill to fill with dry salt grains," having been abandoned by its occupants.[1] The world turned, dispassionate, on the empty house. In previous readings, I had accepted the house as desolate, a corner of the world gone idle. The novel's philosophical preoccupations are with perception, weaving in deft and unflinching studies of gender roles, of the strictures of social status, of life in upper-middle-class England in the first half of the twentieth century, and I had focused on these, with the rest receding as backdrop. "It was too much for one woman, too much, too much,"[2] Woolf wrote of the housekeeper's efforts to restore rooms gone to ruin, to sweep out dust and decay.

But why was this building too much for one woman to maintain, let alone to recover from neglect? Was it just a big home, endless large rooms? I revisited that section on the ramshackle house by the sea: "The saucepan had rusted and the mat decayed," and later, "the plaster fell in shovelfuls; rafters were laid bare."[3] Breakdown. Decay. Just as I remembered. I had long read Woolf's domestic scene as one of decomposition and disrepair. We describe such ruin colloquially as *going to seed*. To "deteriorate in condition, strength, or efficiency,"[4] as the dictionary tells us of this expression: something shabby or unkempt, evidence of a lack of care and effort. "Past one's prime," I've heard it described for people. Lives dispersed and now idle.

But then, as I reread Woolf's account, idleness seemed to give way to something else: "Toads had nosed their way in."[5] Amphibian challenges:

this seemed trickier for the housekeeper than rust, suddenly the rooms were less empty in this shell of a house. And next: "rats carried off this and that to gnaw behind the wainscots."[6] Oh, I knew of rodents and their gnawing. I kept reading of other lives taking over, vivid accounts of thistles and poppies, swallow nests and artichokes. Things no longer seemed quite so steady and quiet. Then this exuberance: "Tortoise-shell butterflies burst from the chrysalis and pattered their life out on the window-pane."[7] Burst from chrysalis! This was not the barren, desiccated house I recalled. The birds and the flowers had filled the spaces left by the absence of humans and their ceaseless cleaning.

We humans aren't the only ones who try to make a home of a seaside house—or of a log cabin. Over the years, my partner and I have plugged cracks with steel wool and caulked windows and stuffed insulation into gaps to dissuade the forays of ants and wasps and, one year, insectivorous tundra shrews. Sometimes it was indeed too much for one woman, or even two. I had imagined the house in *To the Lighthouse* left unoccupied for many months, but as I removed yet another fluffy fur-and-foam bundle from the watershed, I realized it might have been days, maybe only hours. *Gone to seed?* I reconsidered the phrase. We learn so much about ourselves from our idioms. As a gardener friend of mine protested, this shouldn't be an expression of disintegration; the seed phase, she reminded me, is a time of so much activity. Plants send out compressed packets filled with the energy and nutrients needed to sow new life—a beginning, a *becoming*. They aren't following our instructions, of course: those seeds floating off into the air or falling to the ground don't fit our commitments to orderly rows and efficient production. Poppies sowing themselves among dahlias, and carnations among cabbages: these are not under our control. A casting off of the goals and aims of humans, maybe, but certainly not done with the business of being and doing as they pour their energy into the future.

And so what if we reread these tales of abandoned houses and gardens not as idle and unproductive, but instead as shifts in occupancy? The absence of the activity of some beings—namely us, as is the case in the house in Woolf's novel—makes space for the flourishing of others. Moths unfold elaborate dust-covered wings, molds erupt into extensive colonies. Any time I left the watershed alone, the mice saw their chance. When human activities pause, even temporarily, there is a fluid shift to a world of different labour: the exertions, replication, and activity of the other-than-human lives that are usually excluded from our built and settled spaces. What might these dynamics mean for different conceptions of work, then, and, centrally, for work's *absence*?

When we consider work in our political debates, we tend, along with Woolf and her Bloomsbury counterparts—including economist and utopic hopeful John Maynard Keynes—to think in human terms: which people engage in what kinds of work, where and when and under what conditions? In 1930, Keynes offered a fifteen-hour work week as a route to a thriving economy and society;[8] this was not so different from a plea made almost fifty years earlier by the revolutionary socialist Paul Lafargue, Karl Marx's son-in-law, for a three-hour workday.[9] Such debates are part of a response to industrialized life, and the exploitative conditions that accompanied its rise from the nineteenth century onwards. Technology in the modern world, suggested philosopher Bertrand Russell in 1932, so diminished the need for labour to achieve material gain that it was foolish to continue valorizing overwork.[10] Reorganizing work forces, job guarantees, shortening working weeks, installing new technologies, and implementing a universal basic income are among the many proposed routes to a future of sustainable work.[11] These discussions probe the distribution of labour, the motivations for work, the use of people's time if they are freed from necessity. The conversations vary depending on one's assumptions about human nature and ideas of progress: what forms of economic redistribution might enable the conditions of dignity for all, for instance, or what regulatory systems could rein in exploitation without crushing motivation, and what rewards are reasonable, and in which realms, for effort, intellect, innovation. In all these debates over the future of work, our attention is focused on how to direct and organize our efforts more efficiently, more effectively, more productively, and, sometimes, more equitably. We might turn to questions of the distribution of labour among and across peoples, where systems of inequality press certain bodies into certain forms and domains of work and overwork, for inadequate or absent recompense. These are pressing matters, of course: in a flurried and flustered world, the lines between waged work lives and home lives are blurred, there is unevenness and exploitation in the labour of caring for children and elders and the ill, and even creative and passionate pursuits are thrust into entrepreneurial gain. A pause or slowdown in work is needed, in such accounts, to make space for other endeavours.

But the environment, in these accounts, is so often just a backdrop. In these conversations, we tend to sidestep what we really mean by *work*, and what that work achieves.[12] We evade consideration of the labour done by the myriad inhabitants of the world beyond humans, and especially the activities they undertake that seem not to benefit us. *Going to seed*, then, remains just an expression, instead of a recognition of the fundamental work of life unfolding. Further, we rarely spend time attending to what kinds of work should—or should *not*—be part of the future. What kinds of labour shouldn't just be shunted to automated processes and machines, but should be abandoned completely? What should we value and valorize, and how should such efforts be rewarded? And while we pay some attention to the potential that shorter waged work weeks might enable for leisure and for self-realization—relaxation and socializing, say, or study and creative pursuits—rarely do we laud the reduction of work as the opening of space for undirected activity, or for the absence of human activity altogether. Maybe I need to stop sweeping out the watershed.

WE TEND TO POSITION WORK AGAINST A SERIES OF opposites. Some of these are lauded, or at least tolerated: leisure, play, meditation, contemplation, rest. But one of the antonyms of work is, in most accounts, something of more dubious value: *idleness*. Apathy and a lack of care; laziness and slothfulness and inaction; indolence and shiftlessness; sluggishness. The synonyms are plentiful, and they take us from stasis and immobility to slow, languorous movement, and from a distracted kind of absentmindedness to undirected activity with no set intentions. The expenditure of energy with no identifiable benefit, as in a car idling, or the dispersal of thought with no specific direction, as in idle daydreaming. In all these versions, idleness is something for upstanding citizens and responsible adults to studiously avoid.

Exhortations towards work as the path to truth, meaning, virtue, and salvation suggest the contemporary valuation of work is—although not universal—more than the legacy of a single cultural tradition. In the Greek poet Hesiod's epic poem *Works and Days*, written in the eighth century BC, we learn that "When you work, you will be much better loved by the gods."[13] Even in the Garden of Eden, "where there was no neede of labour," we are told by the English rector John Sakeld in the 1600s, "God would not have man idle."[14] It wasn't a material imperative, but a spiritual one, something existential. This was not just a Judeo-Christian tradition: work was also *"the Way"* for seekers of enlightenment in Japan in the 1300s. As explained by the monk and poet Kenkō, "it is a wicked thing to allow the smallest parcel of land to lie idle." He listed the things that should be planted—food and medicine—as he recounted the teachings of a lay priest who chastised him for his unkempt garden, urging more productive uses of the land.[15]

Some thinkers and writers have interrogated the meaning of work over time: it may seem self-evident to many, as historian Andrea Komlosy writes in her genealogy of the term, something we all intuitively understand. But "[u]pon closer inspection, . . ." she clarifies, "work proves to be quite the linguistic chameleon: everyone has their own, nuanced definitions, which themselves are in constant flux."[16] In her project, tracing a thousand years of changing understandings of work, she offers a sweeping definition that ranges from activities for survival to cultural expression to securing luxury and status, from subsistence to market exchange to the exertion of power.[17] A wide-ranging term, then, that brings us beyond waged industrialized work. Komlosy's project aligns with scholar Cara New Daggett's extensive history of the changing meanings of energy, where she tracks how we arrive at contemporary perspectives that equate energy with fuel, and both with work.[18] The widespread uptake of the science of thermodynamics, with its history in the Scottish Presbyterian world of Glasgow in the 1700s, drove a particular understanding of energy that took on social as well as pragmatic industrial significance, Daggett explains. There is a clarity of sorts in a vision that equates fuel with energy and work, and work with productivity, employment, and morality. Work is understood as the central tool to survive, to prevail, and to succeed in a world that tends to entropy and dissolution. With such a view, opting out of these equations is to reject progress itself, embracing a form of shiftlessness and even depravity.

But what to make, then, of this counsel from the writer Mark Slouka *against* filling our time with work:

> Idleness is not just a psychological necessity, requisite to the construction of a complete human being; it constitutes as well a kind of political space, a space as necessary to the workings of an actual democracy as, say, a free press.[19]

Slouka expands on this claim in a provocative essay, calling idleness "unconstrained" and "anarchic."[20] He suggests that idle time provides people with the chance to reflect on their values, beliefs, commitments to justice, and strategies for enacting change. Far from an embrace of sin or a dodge of responsibility, idleness is recast as a political project, and an unsettling one for those in power. "All manner of things can grow out of that fallow soil," Slouka writes, with indeterminacy at the core of his point. That fallow soil of our imagination, that undirected energy of our independent minds. At rest, yet restless; unoccupied, yet invigorated. Citizenship, for Slouka, especially a democratic version, requires time and unclaimed intellectual space in which each person can consider what they see as necessary for a flourishing society. Being constantly occupied, whether in waged labour or in commercialized forms of leisure, leaves no space to form our own values and views and ethical judgements, and so leaves us ill-equipped to contribute to a collective social and political life. Instead, we are too harried to mount any challenge to inequity, servility, creeping authoritarianism or even its fully fledged version. Idleness, then, might be a crucial emancipatory project.

A FRIEND FROM THE SOUTHERN UNITED STATES, WITH the self-proclaimed "deep anti-tyranny roots" befitting someone raised in Virginia, once gifted me the anarchist Emma Goldman's three-volume autobiography.[21] Goldman was born in Lithuania in 1869, then part of the Russian empire; she fled to the United States to escape the pogroms against Jewish people of the 1880s that followed the assassination of the czar.[22] She became a garment factory worker in New York, and, soon after, a labour organizer and a staunch anarchist. Anarchy is an oft-maligned term, at least in its misinterpretations. It is regularly understood as chaos, as randomness, as carelessness or violence, as selfishness and self-interest and even nihilism. But these angles offer little insight into a political concept that, at its core, eschews hierarchy as its organizing principle. For Goldman, anarchism paired a fierce belief in the value of the individual with a hopeful account of collective harmony. There was no tension between these, in her account, "any more than there is between the heart and the lungs"—two essential elements of social life that allow for individuals to thrive.[23] Although the language she uses of purity in her work may unsettle readers in the twenty-first century, given the legacy that such ideas carry, her writing was not in service of nationalism or a racial order. The path to harmony, she explained in her pamphlets, was to do away with religion, property, and government: a trio of problematic forces that dominate mind, body, and spirit.[24]

What rules are meaningful and valuable; which ones perpetuate inequality? At what point do we substitute deference to authority for our own autonomous consideration—and what might emerge if we were to choose our own, distinct path? To hone our capacity for independent judgement, political scientist James Scott urges a daily practice of "anarchist calisthenics," a form of small-scale rebellious actions that cut against the grain of authority; he envisions minor acts of law-breaking, in cases where this would not endanger others or undermine social well-being.[25] Hierarchies that bring with them pogroms and violence, oppression and exploitation are not easily overturned: such recognition of the stability of unjust systems requires him to "confront the paradox of the contribution of lawbreaking and disruption to democratic political change;"[26] law-breaking is needed to break the stranglehold of unjust rule. In Scott's assessment, "Most of the great political reforms of the nineteenth and twentieth centuries"—among which he describes those for racial equality and civil rights—"have been accompanied by massive episodes of civil disobedience, riot, lawbreaking, the disruption of public order, and, at the limit, civil war."[27] But in societies defined by hierarchy, how do we develop the skills for anything else? Scott advises carefully chosen confrontations with imposed laws to assert and practice independence and autonomy, without inflicting harm upon others.

Anarchism—or what scholar Marina Sitrin calls the "anarchist spirit," noting the ideological diversity of anarchic ideas[28]—can involve a vibrant social life, with fundamental operations that rely on collective care emerging without force and coercion. Far from a rejection of society and relationships and care, this understanding of social life suggests that order can arise not from following mandates set by higher authorities—monarchs and dictators, militaries and rulers, or even elected officials vested with enforceable powers—but instead from voluntary, cooperative agreement, continually renewed and renegotiated. Individual judgement is needed to enable this consensual collective. As socialist scholar and ever-hopeful activist David Graeber wrote, "one cannot know a radically better world is not possible,"[29] and anarchism, at least in some forms, can offer a path to that reimagined world. Idleness as anarchic, then, suggests a kind of self-determination. Slouka proposes that *undirected* consciousness is crucial for being in community as a meaningful political citizen, an engaged social participant—and, perhaps, an engaged participant in the wider world.

In our definitions and debates, we tend to consider the work and the absence of work, or idleness, in human terms. When Kenkō, amidst essays on aesthetics and commentary on the lives of his compatriots in the fourteenth century, extols the virtues of a garden of "useful crops,"[30] he fails to reflect on what else is growing in those untended beds. His idle land, among the "spring weeds," likely hosted a thriving neighbourhood of hardy wildflowers and mosses, shrubs and lichens, visited by all manner of insects and songbirds.[31] His distaste for caterpillars is palpable in his writing, as they infest the late-blooming cherry trees.[32] But how does he know that none of this is useful to the golden kites and giant crows circling above or to the roots of the wisteria and irises and five-needled pines that he so admires?[33] We know so little of the needs of others. Beyond the human, self-determination describes the riot of life that erupted in Woolf's imagined English drawing room, empty of human industriousness. In abdicating the conventions of a society that valorizes work above all else, the anarchy of human idleness leaves space for other relations to unfold. If idle time is needed to awaken our political selves, as Slouka suggests, it must be crucial to considering what citizenship might mean in a broader sense, beyond just a human context. The undirected attention that idleness allows can leave space for other relations, for other politics, for other ways of being.

Idleness has long unsettled powerful political figures, not least because of its temptations and pleasures. Historian Thomas Biggs writes of the tensions, during the wars of the third century BC of the Roman Empire and in the subsequent texts of Roman historians, between pastoral regions as places of necessary rest—part of military strategy—and as places of problematic escapism.[34] Campania, an agricultural area in Southern Italy of what Pliny called "blissful and heavenly loveliness,"[35] was not only a region of fertile production with its pastures and fields, but, according to Cicero, one of "indolent and slothful *otium*."[36] The Latin *otium*, akin to the Greek *skhole*, translates loosely to idleness, but context adds subtext, with the term varyingly evoking contemplation, a release from political life, virtuous human pleasure, freedom from practical activity,[37] or, less virtuously, "leisure and retreat from public duty."[38] What the statesman Cicero and his contemporaries worried about were later described by historian Titus Livius as the "excessive pleasures of the region,"[39] Abundance came too easily in Campania. The wine, the bathing springs, and the music of reed pipes might tempt Roman armies, and even their leaders, to abandon their military obligations. They undid discipline and moral character.[40] Of course, in the accounts of these Roman writers, the labours of shepherds and musicians, wine-makers and farmers, and especially the fertile fields themselves, go unnoticed or at least unmentioned.

MOSTLY, THE WORK OF NONHUMAN ENTITIES—ANIMAL, plant, fungus, mineral, element—remains illegible to us. This is not for lack of effort: ecologists and physiologists and statisticians map territories and count offspring and track mates, overlay mealtimes and prey densities, measure brain activity and body fat and stomach enzymes. The result is ordered groups and categories of activity, confidently enumerated and named and labelled in terms of productivity. Least flycatchers engaged in aerial acrobatics to snag insects on the wing is sustenance, from this perspective, not entertainment. Wilson's Warblers hopping in the shrub birch branches, munching on little green inchworms, are engaged in functional foraging and not gustatory pleasure. The spruce grouse my black lab flushes from the woods is fleeing for survival, not searching for solitude and hermetic peace. But are we really seeing these lives in their entirety? The porcupine trundling along the trail; the lynx with its unhurried paces along the road; the moose, when *not* browsing willow, *not* surveying for wolves, just standing in the brush looking out at the mountains?

When we think we understand the imperatives of the world, we constrain the possibilities for deeper understanding. Our interpretations of the actions of others reflect our own judgements; we observe what aligns with our expectations. When we hold this confidence, we act as though we can rule and organize the lives of those around us. What is lost in that certainty is both the autonomy of the lives of others and space for their self-determination—for their anarchy, in both idle and productive forms. Legibility, after all, is the condition for power. In James Scott's critique of state-based versions of these impulses, he writes, "A legible society is one that can be controlled and manipulated."[41] This compulsion to gain control is not always destructive in intent. In a time of damage, it gives us a strategy for undoing the harm we've wrought: if we have more information about these ecological interactions and these multispecies systems, there is hope we can remake and repair them. Organizing our trade-offs accordingly, we fool ourselves that we can evade the costs of expansion, of growth, of the march, so to speak, towards progress, which is typically understood as technological complexity and the fulfillment of all imagined desires. And so we manipulate genes to bring back long-extinct species or to stave off invasive ones; we swap out one wetland for another, confident these exchanges preserve the ecosystem services we need; we offset one harmful activity through another positive one, planting some trees in atonement for cutting others, sure that we can sequester the same carbon, house the same species, maintain the same overarching balance.[42]

We persist with this optimism about our own understanding even when we continually discover how little we know. For years, North American forest managers replanted trees on logged lands, clearing out underbrush to reduce competition with the new saplings. But these new plantations were fragile and stressed, exhibiting little of the resilience that characterized the forests that they replaced; only later, and reluctantly, did mainstream Western forest scientists consider that underground fungal networks link trees across species and ages, redistributing nutrients and sharing resources through linked root systems.[43] This hoped-for equivalence of ecosystems, places, and lives is the logic both of contemporary restoration efforts and of mobile capital, a world governed by the fungibility of everything. One place exchanged for another; one tree planted for another felled; one stock sold for another purchased—the specifics of the materials can be blurred when the prices alone signal their worth. But as philosopher Jean-Luc Nancy asserts, we need to recognize "the inestimable singularity of living beings and things."[44] Complex systems, as Scott reminds us, so often remain inscrutable from the outside—and in this irreducibility and incommensurability, political autonomy is possible.[45] The integrity and complexity of the other beings with whom we share this planet remain beyond our grasp, beyond our control.

In my earlier readings of *To the Lighthouse*, I paid attention to the dissolution of order, and a portrayal of human industry battling against the ravages of time—Time, for Woolf, capitalized.[46] It seemed human labour could only temporarily stave off the inevitability of loss and decay. There is a melancholy tone to the account of that house overtaken by poppies and thistles and swallows. But as I deconstructed yet another mouse nest in the watershed, I realized that Woolf herself recognized and celebrated the work undertaken by her nonhuman characters. "Let the wind blow; let the poppy seed itself and the carnation mate with the cabbage," she exhorted.[47] Her writing signals a kind of triumph of that larger sweep of eternity. When human industry moves on, it leaves the anarchy of the spiders, beetles, flowers, the dust itself. The voices of the rest of the world—the "hum of an insect, the tremor of cut grass"[48]—can again be apprehended, and, after that, silence.

THE SEVEN ESSAYS THAT FOLLOW CHALLENGE THE EASY categories of work and idleness, offering instead a circumambulating look at what ideas and ideals might be needed to imagine a radically different world of creation and repair, recovery and connection. "Grasshopper songs: On creativity" asks what Aesop's insects might invite us to consider about art, possibility, and undirected time. "Bear pauses: On rest" questions the dichotomy between rest and production, and reflects on respite, renewal, and silence. From there, we push back: at the core of "Beaver blockades: On resistance" is the acknowledgement of contradictory orders and infrastructures. Some work undoes other work; this essay considers, too, the limits of human work in restoring our damaged world. Beyond full stops, and as another form of resistance, we might just slow down. Reflections on a less frenetic pace are at the core of "Fir deferrals: On slowness." In exploring strategies of survival and the costs of convenience, it asks what must change in our hyperconnected industrialized life—and what work is offered by our nonhuman neighbours—to make other speeds possible. "Salmon migrations: On detours" takes us off track into unruliness, submerges us; here, we follow a set of diversions that never happened, finding our way upstream. "Willow roots: On restraint" circles back to the relationships between certainty and possibility, separation and connection, and how holding back can enrich us and the world around us. Still, surrounded by so much devastation and injustice, we might understandably despair; "Owl observations: On attention" offers reflections on tenderness and love in grieving, and in rebuilding out of the losses of the world. In the final chapter, "Rocky conclusions: On paradox," we return to the inextricable entanglement of our lives with those of others and consider how sometimes we only know something in its dissolution; in it, too, we consider stillness and walking, and, finally, how idleness might be a form of responsibility, rather than delinquency.

In all these essays, am I trying to convince you, the reader, of something in particular about idleness and work and the great art of loafing about? The playwright Hanif Kureishi reminds me that "there should neither be footnotes nor much information in an essay; as a form, it is a meditation rather than an act of persuasion."[49] So, notes and sources aside (even with Kureishi's advice, it's a hard habit for an academic to break), this is what I strive for in these pages: a meditation, an act that itself occupies an unsteady place between work and idleness. Different from distraction and daydreaming, meditation is a concerted practice; yet, at the same time, the goal of it is a release from doing, striving, or reaching. It is an act of being, entirely and completely. In letting go of the self, we come to know it better; or perhaps the self is only illusory, and what we come to know is the world. In any case, on everything from speed and slowness and creation to restraint and abandon and grief, I have less to declare and more to consider, and little to impart but lots to question. Uncertainty abounds—as it should. The writer Stacey D'Erasmo observes, "Doubt is like a divining rod; it begins to tug when it nears something fertile and fluid and underground."[50] And perhaps that is the crux of the need for idleness: the chance to reflect, and wonder, and imagine; the space to relax our self-assurance and invite doubt.

This collection is not a "how-to" guide on slowing down. Leaning out, leaning back—these are not appropriate or ethical strategies in all cases. Reducing one's individual work can be an excuse to offload responsibilities to others, at least for those wealthy enough to do so. This displacement of labour creates layers of planetary injustice, as we substitute various fuels and bodies for our own efforts, upholding energy- and materials-intensive ways of life through extraction from and of the lives and lands of others.[51] This is not a call for self-care, or a simple admonition against (or urge for more!) technology, or a vehement manifesto against work. Labour can give us meaning, dignity, independence, connection. We can take care of others through our work, we can find our place in the world. But don't mistake this for a clear defense of work, either, an instruction to find a mission, a purpose, a true calling through labour. The claim that you'll never work a day in your life if your occupation is your vocation, as it is sometimes said, is in my view dangerous: a siren song of how to turn passion into profit. This can become a political strategy, as Graeber suggests, of underpaying workers by fostering resentment against those whose work is meaningful, whether care-workers and custodial staff or teachers and artists.[52] It becomes justification for the poor compensation and precarious employment conditions for those in fields that might bring nonmonetary rewards. Work, that slippery term, is absolutely necessary—for us and by us—and we must reckon with what this means.

Work and idleness are neither as antonymous nor as dichotomous as they might at first glance seem. We are quite comfortable acknowledging the politics of work, even if debates rage about productive and reproductive work, forms of labour relations, supply chains and financial models and economic transitions. The interrogation of idleness must likewise be seen as a serious political undertaking, embedded in the study of work. We need to think about both what kinds of work and what kinds of suspensions of work are needed moving forward. More boldly, we must search for a more creative and expansive vocabulary that lets us imagine and articulate a radically different world.[53] A less restrictive understanding of how we might spend our time. A more sweeping account of not only the activities of humans, our labour and our rest, but also of those around us, whose lives on this planet are so often shaped by our own. Through these meandering pieces, I ask, over again and in different ways, not "should we work or be idle," but rather, what work is needed, when, by whom, for whom, and at whose expense. And in concert with these questions, I explore how some of us, at different moments, can pause, slow down, fall silent, refrain, and hold back to support a thriving, flourishing world.

In these essays, animals and plants—terrestrial and aquatic, avian and fungal, mobile and sessile, life beyond the human—are not just enlisted as metaphors and tools of writing and tricks of rhetoric. Although fables feature in these pages, they are not merely animal characters for human moralizing. These are other beings, worthy of our attention, of our greatest concern. For animals, as Henry Beston writes—and plants, too, I would add—"are not brethren, they are not underlings; they are other nations, caught with ourselves in the net of life and time, fellow prisoners of the splendour and travail of the earth."[54] *The travail of the earth.* The French *travail* means work, although the English etymology is darker, the Latin translating to something like instrument of torture. Whether torturous or not, the earth's own work needs attention, and is often inhibited by our own. When human productivity is the cause of so much damage, why is it so often presented as a solution for salvaging the planet? What is sustainable work in and for a shared future? These questions have no straightforward answers. And so, this book of essays is my attempt to practice anarchist calisthenics, my effort at going to seed: a wandering, rambling, meandering look at the role—no, the vital *urgency*—for the idleness of some to enable the lives of others.

CHAPTER I

GRASSHOPPER SONGS: ON CREATIVITY

Ants. Grasshoppers. Aesop. Field mice. Production and manufacturing. Poiesis. Sand mandalas. Fernando Pessoa. Phaedrus. Muses. Moralizing. Victorian workhouses. Welfare. Coercion. Accumulation. F.I.R.E. Generous bees. Rotting grain. Serviceberries. Abundance.

A river of ants streams past the garden bed, distinct reddish-brown bodies moving as a coherent whole. One year, they invaded the roof of the cabin; another year, they moved into the garden, competing with the kale. Mostly, though, the colonies choose from an abundance of fallen trees and old stumps, and we leave them be, even if not everyone in the neighbourhood does. Some hummingbirds, I've learned, feed on ants—along with bees, spiders, and other arthropods—as do ravens and robins and flickers.[1] Black bears overturn logs to uncover nests, picking up wriggling torsos with their dexterous tongues. The risks are high on these summer days, but the ants flow on.

In many versions of the famous fable of the "Grasshopper and the Ants," a hungry grasshopper, having spent the summer fiddling, seeks food from a group of industrious ants in the winter. A translation from 1912 by V. S. Vernon Jones offers this exchange between the insects:

CHAPTER I

> Presently up came a grasshopper and begged them to spare her a few grains, "For," she said, "I'm simply starving." The ants stopped work for a moment, though this was against their principles. "May we ask," said they, "what you were doing with yourself all last summer? Why didn't you collect a store of food for the winter?"[2]

In some of the interpretations, the ants offer up a little sustenance alongside their moralizing. In others, such as Jones' translation, they are impassive to her pleas, denying the ragged, long-limbed insect's requests and sending her off empty-handed into the cold night. A cautionary tale about the value of hard work and future planning, this fable has been adapted and revised over centuries, in verse and in prose, in Latin and French and English, with and without excerpted lessons. It has sometimes been attributed to the Latin Avianus in the fifth century AD, but usual credit for the original takes us back to the seventh century BC with the Greek Aesop.[3]

But the popular account of a leisurely grasshopper whiling away the summer as the diligent ants store grain for the hard winter ahead sits alongside more ambiguous versions of the story. "I was not idle," protests the grasshopper in Thomas James' rendition from 1848, having "kept singing all the summer long."[4] And returning to the exchange told by V. S. Vernon Jones, the grasshopper explains, "I was so busy singing that I hadn't the time" to gather grain.[5] Singing and fiddling are hard work, keeping the orthopteran musician occupied through the long summer days. Is this music-making a diversion from work, or itself a form of labour?

The 1967 children's book *Frederick* by Leo Lionni offers a similar parable of an artist, this time with field mice instead of ants and grasshoppers.[6] As his companions store up grain for winter, Frederick roams the fields: daydreaming and idling, lounging in the sun, looking pensively at the sky, meandering with empty hands. The textured images show Frederick alone in his stillness, the other mice on the move, bearing sheafs of grain, stockpiling nuts and mushrooms. While not directly rebuked, he is questioned "reproachfully" by the others. But when winter days are long and dark and cold and grey, and supplies wear thin, Frederick's turn comes. He shares lyrical descriptions of the dazzling colours of the summer that he has stored up in his mind, reminding them with his words that plentiful days would again return. He is celebrated for this performance, having boosted morale in ways that a few more grains of food could not achieve. "But Frederick," the other mice exclaim, "you are a poet." In the final line, Frederick blushes, takes a bow, and answers, "I know it."[7]

An eight-year-old friend of mine observed, after his first reading of this book, that "the ending could be stronger."[8] Although the final rhyming couplet is glib, and a little too self-congratulatory, there is something hopeful in this turn to art as sustenance. Gathering impressions of summer sunshine is not compatible with constant gathering of grain, we see in the soft brushstrokes that illustrate the story's pages. Creative effort, at least for Frederick and for Aesop's grasshopper, leaves little time on the edges for other forms of labour. Imbibing colours and generating melodies supplant other forms of accumulation and production.

AZURE, CERULEAN, TURQUOISE, CYAN; BURNT SIENNA, ochre, umber, mahogany; flaxen, golden, lemon, amber. These words can be seen, even tasted—they invoke earth and sky, birds and trees, fields and flowers and fruits, a world awash in colour. These are the hues and shades around us, and also within poetry, at least for some readers and writers. In an interview on the craft of writing, the poet and novelist Ocean Vuong recounts that in Japanese aesthetics, poems have colours—or moods and tones; part of the work of a writer, then, he says, is finding them.[9] To do this, he continues, "takes sometimes weeks, months—years, really—to develop."[10] For so many artists, creative output requires stretches of what might appear to the observer as unproductive, undirected time. Reflecting on Vuong's observations, I wonder now if the problem with Lionni's ending wasn't the flippant phrasing or the metered verse of the book's last lines, but instead a deeper problem with the story's resolution. Frederick's creative work is justified, in the end, by the outcomes. His undirected summer days are made worthwhile, we understand, by the product of his efforts; rendered visible to his neighbours through performance, his meandering is finally understood as work, and he is recognized as a productive member of his society. But what if Frederick's words did not bring comfort and inspiration to his fellow mice to persevere and endure, and instead reminded them of the fleeting nature of all life, the futility of striving, the depths of loneliness that can be experienced? And what if his poetic colours weren't realized in a single year? What if it wasn't weeks or months of gathering that fed his creative spirit, but years? If Frederick had continued his daydreams through the lean winter months, and into summers and seasons of the future, with no visible returns?

This may be the missing depth of Lionni's account. In art, the outcome—a song, a painting, a poem—is by no means guaranteed by concerted efforts towards those ends. And when results emerge, they might be entirely unintended—not the product envisioned by the artist, but something distinct and unexpected. The word *production*, explains the scholar and critic Piotr Schollenberger, originates in the Latin terms for "bringing something forth" and "drawing something out."[11] Although it has come to mean something akin to "manufacturing," he continues, earlier understandings of production were closer to the idea of *praxis*—action with a goal of making a specific object. But art requires separating its outcome from its process, moving away from praxis and towards *poiesis*—an activity, Schollenberger clarifies, that "does not have its end in itself."[12] That is, to make art, one must forgo the expectation of the outcome of art; though the former is needed for the latter, the reverse is not true. A vivid illustration of this is the creation, in Tibetan Buddhist monastic traditions, of intricate mandalas from sand—the painstaking and laborious placement of each grain, and, at the end, the design washed away by flowing water, leaving no trace.[13] A metaphor for, and tribute to, the impermanence of life; an undertaking of pure commitment to the beauty held in a process.

The Portuguese poet Fernando Pessoa is said to have had dozens of heteronyms—alternate artistic identities with every one of them, in his own account, possessing a distinct style and voice, leaving their own legacies in verse and phrase.[14] Each had a unique biography, history, life details which differed from Pessoa's own. There is an anonymity to this form of writing. A signed poem, from an invented creator. This is no falsely universalizing gesture—not an omniscient gaze on the world that suggests some form of objective remove—since the pen names acknowledge that the words arise from a situated perspective; yet, at the same time, the unbinding of the poems from Pessoa himself releases the products from their tethers to the producer. He offers up the art, not the artist, as the thing in the world. A form of humility, perhaps, a privileging of the wholeness of art over the legacy of the individual. In one poem, under the name Ricardo Reis, Pessoa writes:[15]

> To be great, be whole: don't exaggerate
> Or leave out any part of you.
> Be complete in each thing. Put all you are
> Into the least of your acts.
> So too in each lake, with its lofty life,
> The whole moon shines.

For Pessoa, then, perhaps each heteronym is itself a lake, and he is the circulating water. A transformation from self to other; a recognition of the connectivity of the elements of the universe; a release from the ego. Impermanence as a person, even though in this case, unlike the mandalas, the art continues on.

In Plato's dialogue between Socrates and Phaedrus, as the two men sit by the banks of the Ilissus river, Socrates waxes eloquent about the sweet summer breeze and the "chorus of the cicadae," later described as the "grasshoppers chirruping" in the midday heat. The loose translation in the English version I've read is somewhat unclear to me—cicadas and grasshoppers are not just different species, but from different taxonomic orders entirely. Cicadas are more closely related to aphids and water bugs than to grasshoppers, as different from grasshoppers as from earwigs.[16] But regardless of classification, the story is intriguing. Socrates recounts to his companion the origin story of the singing insects: before the time of the Muses, humans had no songs; when the Muses arrived and brought with them music, the humans were so enchanted that they forgot to eat and to drink, and so perished. In return, the Muses turned them into grasshoppers. Myth diverges from ecology here, as grasshoppers and cicadas both do eat—leaves and sap, respectively—but these people-turned-grasshoppers in Socrates' account were creatures with no need of sustenance, capable of spending their lives singing without hunger or thirst.[17] Was this punishment or mercy? We could read this as a warning against being lulled into the neglect of the self through song—doomed by a love of music to future persistent hunger and thirst. I'd rather take this as a story of benevolence and redemption: art sweeps you away, and, through transmutation and metamorphosis, leads to a life of fulfillment.

As the writer Casey Cep observes: "The fables of Aesop and the myth of Socrates testify to our willingness to look for morals everywhere."[18] Maybe these insects never were humans, maybe there is no lesson to be learned from analyzing cicadas or other insect orders by a riverbank, or exchanges between ants and grasshoppers, or metamorphosis across evolutionary clades. The creation of art might need more than undirected time, it might need receptivity to the unexpected; as the writer Annie Dillard says, "writing a first draft requires from the writer a peculiar internal state which ordinary life does not induce."[19] The suspension of everything related to our usual, quotidian lives, of our sense of certainty. Suspension in the grandest metaphorical terms—here again from Dillard, on allowing ourselves to exit our ordinary lives:

Every morning you climb several flights of stairs, enter your study, open the French doors, and slide your desk and chair out into the middle of the air. The desk and chair float thirty feet from the ground, between the crowns of maple trees.... Birds fly under your chair.... Get to work. Your work is to keep cranking the flywheel that turns the gears that spin the belt in the engine of belief that keeps you and your desk in midair.[20]

Perhaps we don't need the moralizing of Aesop or Lionni; let us surrender to the flywheel, to reflecting the moon in still waters, to the artistic moment itself, at least for one clear night.

EVEN NOW, THOUGH, I CAN'T QUITE LEAVE ASIDE THE philosophizing about how we might live, perhaps because some of these lessons have such traction in social life. Fiddling is not accumulating for the future, in most accounts. This improvidence is not just an individual failing, according to these stories, but a social burden. Dominant Western traditions around work position the idle and the slothful as taking advantage of others, lazing while others toil. As philosopher Brian O'Connor explains, one argument against idleness is that it is exploitative, where the leisure of some is only possible because of the labour of others.[21] This view has emerged not just in moralizing children's stories, but more palpably and viciously in practice, from the justifications of the Victorian workhouses of the 1800s in England, to the work-for-welfare schemes of the 1990s in the US, to pushback against the social programs and payments put in place during the Covid-19 pandemic in Canada.[22] Those who choose punitive over supportive measures to address poverty and precarity declare that anyone who can work should work, that anyone who shirks their duties is unfairly burdening others who must sustain them. The myth of meritocracy: if you're struggling, you just need to work harder.

These systems are at odds with work as dignity, a principle embedded in the United Nations Declaration of Human Rights. Article 23 of the Declaration, as developed in 1948, sets forth that: "Everyone has the right to work, to free choice of employment, to just and favourable conditions of work and to protection against unemployment."[23] The *right* to work, instead of the *obligation* to work—this offers a different angle on what work might be. Freedom in labour, suggests the development studies scholar Guy Standing, requires the ability to choose which occupation to take up, but this choice is impossible if it's unclear how you will meet your fundamental needs.[24] We can imagine other options for understanding work: as chosen and self-directed, as insubordinate and defiant, as collaborative and sustaining. The guarantee of a job is so readily adopted as a goal in society and a metric of a well-functioning government—ensuring and creating jobs, reaching close to full employment, incentivizing hiring. These goals seem laudable when they allow for people to pursue the lives they wish to lead, but less meritorious when they increase the number of workers toiling in exploitative conditions. Standing proposes that to truly protect the right to work, there must already be a guaranteed basic income.[25]

Work is so often coerced and compelled. The uneven terms between workers and employers may be obvious. But the asymmetry of power can also be achieved under contracts that seem to promise flexibility and autonomy. The arrangements might be "zero-hour contracts," where employers do not promise any set number of hours to their employees, demanding workers' immediate availability without the security of guaranteed work. Similarly, gig economy positions, where jobs are linked to specific tasks (or "gigs"), are both flexible and unpredictable and come without established benefits like health care and sick leave. These can be forms of unfree labour.[26] Turning again to UN conventions, Standing considers the International Covenant on Economic, Social and Cultural Rights, which recognized "the right to work," where that work is something "freely chosen."[27] Uncoerced, autonomous decision-making is central to this right. He acknowledges that there is stigma and shame associated with joblessness, but we see from his analysis that these negative social outcomes are the product of a system where unemployment is required for the economy to function.[28] That is, unemployment provides incentives for labour mobility, for excellence in work performance, for competitiveness of industry. Stigma and shame are built-in elements of the system, not accidental by-products or preexisting conditions. Standing suggests the system could be different. The value attached to work can be shifted, in his account, if it is decoupled from survival and worth.

Now, Standing's arguments make us think back to those from 130 years earlier, as laid out by Paul Lafargue in his provocatively titled essay *The Right to Be Lazy*.[29] In it, Lafargue offers a rejoinder to the idea of a right to work, declaring it a repressive goal. Those who have accepted such a concept, he declares, have betrayed the revolution. He quotes Jesus on the lack of toiling, and thus the splendour, of the lilies; he points to the contempt of the Greek philosophers for labour, with their respect, instead, for a contemplative life; he sees the lauding of the nobility of work as a strategy of rulers to control and subdue their subjects, pointing to Napoleon's 1807 assertion that "The more my people work, the less vices they will have."[30] It is dangerous to those in power, explains Lafargue, for workers to see themselves as autonomous. He points to the warnings in a pamphlet on "trade and commerce" from 1770: "Laborers ought never to look on themselves as independent of their superiors." That author, a champion of early capitalism, inveighs against workers: "It is extremely dangerous to encourage such infatuations in a commercial state like ours, where perhaps seven-eighths of the population have little or no property."[32] Lafargue laments that such views are not only held by the powerful but absorbed and believed by the oppressed, too. The shame and stigma of not working is, for Lafargue, a tool of the bourgeoisie to keep the proletariat in line, and the proletariat seemed to have agreed to their own subjugation.

CHAPTER I

WHETHER IN THE 1700S OR THE 2000S, STORIES AND philosophies have not settled the question of the morality of accumulation. Back to Aesop and subsequent spinners of fables: the ants are positioned as upstanding, hard-working invertebrates in some of these tales. But are these gatherers of grain really so autonomous and self-sufficient? Other accounts doubt the virtue of the ants and the improvidence of the grasshopper.

One ant's challenge—"Why did you not store up some food for yourself, instead of singing all the time?"—is countered, in Ambrose Bierce's 1899 telling, with the grasshopper retorting, "So I did; but you fellows broke in and carried it all away."[33] The singing grasshopper, having dutifully gathered her stores of food, still found herself empty-handed come winter. In other stories, those ants were previously men, transformed into insects as punishment for having stolen their neighbours' grain—Roger L'Estrange's 1692 fable tells of the Roman sky god Jupiter (Zeus, to the Greeks) punishing a man "that secretly filch'd away his neighbour's goods and corn and stor'd all up in his own barn" by turning him into an ant.[34]

Not all exploitation involves outright theft. In his 1932 essay "In Praise of Idleness," for instance, Bertrand Russell characterizes two forms of work: one of direct physical labour, and the other of instructing others to undertake such labour.[35] Both are compensated, but not equally so: "The first kind is unpleasant and ill paid; the second is pleasant and highly paid."[36] This managerial role has remained part of discussions of work and leisure for centuries. If one desired wealth, suggested the Greek poet Hesiod, hard work was required; there were "no shortcuts to riches," so the translation goes.[37] But classics scholar Hans van Wees clarifies that the work of which Hesiod wrote in *Works and Days* was not quite the heavy toil of farming itself, tilling the soil and plowing the land—Hesiod was instead extolling the virtues of tireless *supervision* of the labours of others, in this case, of enslaved workers in the fields.[38] This oversight would ensure ongoing productivity, providing surplus to be reinvested into expansion.[39] It was "a powerful acquisitive drive," not a love of sweat and toil, that was being advocated for, suggests van Wees,[40] and this could be satisfied by directing the efforts of others.

The management of fields and their bounty for maximum wealth is not limited to the management of workers, but of the grain itself. That is, some accumulation relies less on further extracting from others and more on suppressing their own development. Ants—regardless of whether they have human origins—have long known this, at least according to accounts from the 1300s. The Italian poet Petrarch muses on the activities of ants, inferring their intelligence from their careful arrangements of wheat supplies. If the grain "has become mouldy" they "fear that it will rot and become inedible" and so bring these stores to the surface.[41] Even more, "they prevent the germination of their stored wheat," eating away at sprouting shoots to stop the wheat from going to seed.[42] An act of consumption that prevents the fundamental creative work of the wheat—nibbling ants stopping the grain from seeding its future.

Through arrangements of management and subservience, and through curtailing the lives of other species—not just those working, but those worked *upon*—work can produce deeply unequal outcomes, even absent the full brutality of slavery. These accounts suggest that accumulation and toil are irrevocably intertwined. And this always must be true, although there are other ways of accumulating that are harder to define as work at all, where the labour that enables accumulation is more hidden.

START YOUR F.I.R.E. PLAYING WITH F.I.R.E. QUIT LIKE *a millionaire. Your money or your life. House F.I.R.E.* In recent years, there has been a flood of books on strategies for "Financial Independence; Retire Early," an acronym that is also a movement. Pitched as manifestos, how-to guides, and even philosophical disquisitions, these texts offer plans and rationales for frugal living, concerted saving, and strategic investing, all in service of a plan for early retirement—where "early" looks not like just a few years before a senior's discount kicks in, but in one's 40s or even 30s. The goal is to reach the point where one can pursue activities for pleasure and fulfillment, not necessity. This could involve time with family, in study, in recreation, in creative pursuits—the usual activities we might associate with retirement; but among F.I.R.E. pursuers, this also can include ongoing paid employment or entrepreneurial activity, just in areas of one's passions.[43] Such outcomes might appeal to Lafargue, who does admit that a little work in life might not be intolerable—work might be useful for society but, crucially, "only when wisely regulated and limited to a maximum of three hours a day."[44]

Beyond cutting coupons and ruthless budgeting, these guides suggest the key to a long, prosperous retirement that enables the pursuit of passion is to pair high-earning jobs with strong returns on investments. Blogs and advisors and social media accounts proliferate, with advice on how to save half or even three-quarters of one's income. That surplus can purchase index funds, for instance, which generates further income.[45] In retirement, then—which is planned to last for many, many decades, often more than half a century—the funds that sustain this leisured class comes from the interest earned off the stock market. Retirement funded through lucrative investments is not a life of work-free wealth—it's just that those who accrue the wealth are not the ones working. Such a path requires being comfortable with one's sustenance deriving almost entirely from work done by other people: people who don't have the same choices. The capacity to accumulate such savings is impossible to imagine, for instance, to those spending a third or more of their income on housing, or who are burdened by education and medical debts or extended family obligations.[46] Early retirement seems a rewriting of the aristocracy, where some people luxuriate while others toil in precarity, under the guise of meritocracy, hard work, and careful savings.

Beyond the artificial idea of self-sufficiency—no one is entirely independent, and we always rely on the work of others—there is something particularly unsettling about this version of individual success. A movement for independence and fulfillment seems compromised when the release from waged work is achieved by the exploitation of the freedom and well-being of others. These concerns about investments and financial accumulation are not restricted to private portfolios—this is also a fraught question for those with public pensions at the more usual age of retirement (in places where, and for people for whom, such things exist), and in the uneven accumulation of national wealth. Still, the tension gains particular poignancy at the individual scale when age differences between workers and retirees collapse or even invert, and when a life of early "F.I.R.E." leisure is celebrated as personal triumph.

From a planetary perspective, there are further frictions. Fire, after all, is no trifling matter. Combustion consumes fuels, turning the physical world into heat and light and smoke; it rearranges the world in dramatic ways. Fires of biotic fuels are forces of creative destruction, environmental historian Stephen Pyne suggests, part of ecological systems and their cycles of seasons and expansion and contraction and renewal. But what Pyne describes as fires of lithic landscapes—meaning from fossil fuel combustion—are conflagrations that unhinge the planet. These lithic fires release ancient carbon, creating further instability in an overburdened atmosphere. Although the financial tools used to succeed with F.I.R.E. are abstract, the material basis of the economy remains firmly in place: growth in investments derives from continuous production and consumption, and so relies heavily on continued extraction and discard. F.I.R.E. is a haunting acronym, then, when the same investments that enable early retirement also destabilize the planet. Are the grasshoppers really the ones creating burdens on others as they spend their days in pursuit of musical joy and self-directed creation?

CHAPTER I

LET'S IMAGINE THAT THE ANTS PARTICIPATE IN NO oppression of others. Consider Aesop's ants as upstanding citizens, taking nothing from their neighbours, toiling in the fields themselves for their own future use, saving diligently. In such a case, the ants might not be hypocritical in their judgements; still, lessons beyond cold-heartedness might be gleaned from the Greek tradition. The usual moral of the tale—that it is one's responsibility to cache and hoard for the future—is not the only one held in this story. Turning away from the heartless ants and toward more compassionate insects, Jacques-Melchior Villefranche offered a sequel in 1851 that tells of misfortune striking the judgmental ants, who lose their winter stores of grain. When those destitute ants turn for help to the bee, they are scolded by the honey-producer for their earlier miserly behaviour. But this is no moment of simple poetic justice and retribution: after the lecture, they find a generous and forgiving host—one who shares food, and who has already offered refuge to the hungry grasshopper.[47]

In his account of the benevolent bee, Villefranche, as far as I've found, does not specify the cause of the ants' sudden impoverishment. But in this time of extreme weather and accelerating climate change, I wonder about the integrity of those grain stores the busy ants collected, and whether wet weather might have undone their careful work. One summer, atmospheric rivers in British Columbia washed out roads; a few months later, South Sudanese farmers watched floodwaters inundate cropland and Ecuador experienced its heaviest flooding in two decades.[48] The next year, floods in Pakistan submerged a third of the country.[49] Grain rots when it is damp. Large stockpiles might not be available to solve hunger in the lean months of production, it turns out, if those stored supplies aren't dry. The Ministry of Consumer Affairs in India, for instance, reported that between 2011 and 2017, over sixty thousand tonnes of food grain were damaged in warehouses in the country, in spite of a dedicated agency responsible for managing emergency supplies and distribution.[50]

Political scientist Sarah Martin describes the biophysical characteristics of agricultural products as producing "frictions" of consumption:

the storage, flow, and digestion limitations in the easy transportation and conversion of certain grains to other places and other products.[51] Martin is looking specifically at distillers' grains, the byproducts of the conversion of corn to ethanol. She tracks how the grain and livestock industries collaborate to overcome the challenges of the initial sodden, heavy outputs, and, even when dried, the difficulties in transporting and using them as animal feed.[52] Although her work reveals the specific frictions of an industrial byproduct, her points offer insight more broadly into our accounts of prudence and preparation for the future when it comes to material goods. Wheat and rice and millet, for instance, hit up against the rest of the physical world, subject to its vagaries of water and oxygen and heat and fungus.[53] Those storing these grains work to constrain and outwit biophysical characteristics, but there are limits to these strategies. Unlike the money of those aspiring F.I.R.E. seekers, grains held in reserve are not growing and expanding; at best, they are holding constant or, too often, becoming depleted. What if, instead, the grain fed hungry bellies in the moment, and food security arose from strategies other than centralized stores of a handful of staple grains? This might mean diversifying agricultural systems and supporting small-scale rural and urban gardens, where more producers and production strategies—not stockpiles—lead to greater resilience.

As for the grasshopper, she may have known the vulnerabilities of summer grain through a hard, wet winter. And beyond the vagaries of the weather, she might, too, have run up against a lack of space for personal accumulation. Perhaps the grasshopper turned to music rather than grain collecting because no matter how many bushels of wheat she gathered, she had no safe place to store her food supplies. We know she was a musician, but the stories say little of her home life: whether she was unhoused or precariously sheltered, spending a night here, another there. If she was wandering in the fields, excluded and dispossessed from the properties of others, unable or unwilling to participate in the accelerating enclosure of land. If she managed to find cover from the elements, but only in a place where her rations were subject to pilfering by rodent visitors. The virtues of self-sufficiency and future security that underpin the F.I.R.E. movement are predicated on peculiarities of certain forms of ownership and individualism that so often are unattainable, especially in a variable and unsteady world. If you have the inclination and aptitude for music, it might make the most sense to fiddle away the summer.

ABANDONING ALL THOUGHT OF THE FUTURE IS ONE option—generative for art, perhaps, but difficult for continued life. There are other options, though. A social network, a safety net, an offering up of care with no possibility for equal exchange and no guarantee of future rewards. Villefranche's story centred a kind bee, generous of spirit—and this might in fact be a common representative of the world. The lessons we glean depend on the stories we encounter: returning to those miserly ants, we must look beyond Greek philosophers and fabulists to understand what we can learn from insects. Hopi, Diné, and Inde stories, it is said—though I only know this from outsiders' interpretations and the specifics aren't mine to know[54]—tell of Ant People as rescuers and world-builders, offering their ancestors refuge from catastrophe. In these accounts, ants, not just grasshoppers, are socially-oriented and creative beings, perhaps with songs of their own.[55] For those of us who have been handed down traditions that invoke a stark dualism between nature and humans, we might do especially well to suspend our judgement and consider other possibilities. In the wider world around us, we so often see sharing, giving, and nurturing across and among species, within and beyond communities. Evolution is so often presented by Western scientific authorities—and Western literary traditions—as a competitive affair, a fight for survival, something that is ever antagonistic. But this is just one series of stories about species changing and adapting to a dynamic world. There are other metaphors than battle that can guide our interpretation of the interactions that unfold around us. The botanist and writer Robin Wall Kimmerer offers a picture of the world that is, instead, best summarized by the term *abundance*.[56]

Following the serviceberry, or Saskatoon berry—as its red and deep purple berries are eaten by cedar waxwings, its branches munched on by deer and moose, and its surfaces offer space to tiger swallowtail butterfly larvae—Kimmerer outlines the exchanges of gifts in the botanical and zoological world. It is an economy predicated on giving away, not storing up. Scarcity is not the driver of exchange relations, but rather a surplus that is freely shared. The response to abundance, she reminds us, need not be accumulation, but instead gratitude, reciprocity, and a willingness to share. In an unpredictable world, the safest policy might be to give back to the world at every turn, never knowing when you, too, might need such generosity.

More than ever, the bonds of relationship, of communal care, and of the sharing of abundance that Kimmerer observes in the world of berries and birds and butterflies seem diminished in a social world increasingly defined by inequality and damage. This is not to say that there aren't human traditions and communities where these exchanges thrive, only that they are too often undermined by acquisitive approaches. As Kimmerer writes, "How we think ripples out to how we behave. If we view these berries, or that coal or forest, as an object, as property, it can be exploited as a commodity in a market economy. We know the consequences of that."[57] The consequences of such thinking are all around us. An alternate perspective is both necessary and possible. We can learn from the serviceberry; we can learn from the bees.

We ought to be cautious in taking our lessons from children's stories and philosophical dialogues. But I think again of Cep's remarks on how avidly we seek revelations and divinations from the nonhuman world,[58] and wonder if this really is a problem. Our trouble might not be our search for guidance on how to live; it might just be that some of us are reading the wrong translations, listening to only a certain lineage of stories, one that insists that cicadas are grasshoppers, and that ants

CHAPTER I

are stingy. Now when I see the ants around the cabin in those busy summer months, shuffling along with their burdens, I imagine a few soft notes rising amidst the shrub willow leaves, above the concentric ring of fireweed flowers and the thorny stalks of the wild rose. Louder now, picking up the tempo, the ants shift their pace, lift their legs a little higher. They start to keep pace with the 4/4 time of a reel or the faster 6/8 of a jig rising up above the fields; it is impossible to stay still or be unmoved by the beat. The ants are held in the music around them, as they gather gifts of grain from the plants. And the grasshopper, preoccupied by the melody, is too busy to worry about the winter to come, fully immersed in *poiesis*—that moment of creation.

CHAPTER II

BEAR PAUSES: ON REST

Camera traps. Constellations. Denning. Spadefoot toads. Hummingbirds. Metabolic extremes. Audiobooks. Life hacks. Defiant indolence. Pirouetting. Companionship. Carpathian Mountains. Paul Celan. Exile. Antarctica. Telephones. Narwhal. Sycamore bark. Huge silence. Transformation.

A wood-and-wire weir, held down in the water's flow by large rocks, spans the width of the Nakina River. In the only gap between stakes, offset from the river's centre, is a metal box with a narrow cable snaking out of it, strung up into the spruce trees lining the bank. In the box, a motion-sensitive camera snaps a photo each time a fish swims through, or when other activity triggers its flash: bubbles from fish thrashing against the current, bear paws moving through water, sticks floating by. In the middle of the night, no one is out on the river, though the salmon still slap and struggle in the clear waters laced lightly with silt. Overhead, a sky flooded with stars, the seven brightest in Ursa Major—the Great Bear—pouring out the Milky Way.

This is still unceded Taku River Tlingit First Nations territory, though it is far from the cabin: the road ends in Atlin, and the rest is a roadless watershed that flows out into the Pacific Ocean near Juneau. The weir, operated by the First Nation's fisheries department, is set up to assess salmon runs in the tributary of the Taku River, informing management decisions and providing long-term monitoring data in the watershed. The camera box is part of these efforts, tracking migration numbers, which are mostly in decline. The fisheries crews usually fly in and out by helicopter now, but the traditional Tlingit trails through the watershed—to this and other camps and fishing spots along the river—are still walked in most years; more recently, the hiking journeys are intertwined with language revitalization efforts. Unintentionally, as it gathers spent salmon shedding scales as they drift downstream after spawning, the weir also provides a popular fishing site for grizzly bears, who return year after year, over generations, to this bend in the river. The weir is where mothers teach their cubs to scoop sockeye from the river, with bald and golden eagles circling overhead.

Ursus arctos horribilis in Latin, a harsh name for such regal beings. Other languages offer sounds both solid and soft—*xóots* in Tlingit, *sahcho* in Dene, *khoh* in Tahltan[1]—more suited to these behemoths of fur and muscle and sinew that meander through the forest. Ursine paws relocate nutrients from water to land, dragging disintegrating fish carcasses into the forests where they feed the insects, mosses, fungi, the trees themselves bearing the traces of salmon.[2] They are unhurried and at ease, these linchpins of the riparian ecosystem. The bears are at once practical and mythological; we tell of their power and danger, their strength and fierce nature—but also, too, of their lengthy disappearances, their idle winters.

Readying themselves for near-constant dark and cold, hushed surrounds muted by snowdrifts, with heartbeats and breaths slowed,[3] these bears first consume the energy of the oceans brought to freshwater in slippery bodies, whatever is left after the salmon's upstream journey to its origins. After golden days of subarctic summer light spent turning berries into flesh, the bears fill their bellies with fish before heading to alpine dens to settle in over long winters. Hibernation is a symbol of rest, of the seasons turning. But is this the truth, these winters of slumber and idyll? And what do these pauses enable?

BEAR PAUSES: ON REST

IN THE SPRING, GRIZZLIES—ANOTHER NAME FOR NORTH American brown bears, their colouring ranging from cream to nearly black—emerge from their dens, leaner by far than when they entered them in the late fall. In parts of Alaska, female grizzlies spend more than seven months in dens, leaving their winter lodgings with only a third of the body fat they started with.[4] Their counterparts in southeastern British Columbia and in Montana and Wyoming's Yellowstone National Park lose less of their heft over the winter, but also spend a month and a half less in dens.[5] This is a hungry time, a long fast, with the initiation and duration of denning dictated by food availability, weather, and altitude.[6] These bears survive the lean winter months by slowing down radically: dropping their body temperatures by a few degrees, their heart rates by as much as 80 percent, and their metabolic functions to just over a quarter of their non-hibernation rates.[7]

At the lower reaches of Arctic tundra, boreal forests encircle the globe—these are landscapes of grizzly bears. Bears possess what writer Ellen Meloy describes as "metabolic extremes,"[8] though when she wrote this, she was describing creatures of the US Southwest, specifically spadefoot toads. The "dormant slumber and brief, frenetic activity" of the burrowing desert amphibians, says Meloy, matches the desert's own rhythms.[9] And such wild fluctuations are echoed in unexpected places: in the snowdrifts with the bears; underground with the toads; in the air with the birds. Take the hummingbird, for instance, if you can hold it still long enough. In a tender essay on vulnerability, the writer Brian Doyle observes that a hummingbird heart beats ten times each second in spite of its tiny size.[10] This is no exaggeration—some species have heart rates of twice that speed, hitting 1,200 beats per minute when in flight.[11] Iridescent and mostly in motion, we tend to think of them hovering and diving between sips of nectar. But Doyle recounts that in the face of cold nights or near starvation, these birds enter into a state of torpor, with their "hearts sludging nearly to a halt, barely beating."[12] Torpor is a sort of sped-up version of hibernation with metabolic drops that last only for a single circadian cycle.[13] Some hummingbird species in Peru can drop their body temperatures by as much as 30 degrees Celsius overnight, a survival mechanism for the extreme environment of the high Andean mountains.[14] The black metaltail hummingbird, *Metallura phoebe*, for instance, is found at elevations that range from 2,700 to 4,300 metres—from nearly 9,000 to over 14,000 feet—and lower their heart rates to as low as forty beats per minute in a nocturnal near-death experience that makes it possible for life to go on.[15]

At a friend's birthday party a few years back, I found myself in the midst of a discussion about books with a few tech entrepreneurs I had just met. For someone who has fallen into a scholarly path, literature wasn't an unusual topic among my friends and acquaintances, but at this party, the conversation took an unexpected turn. It wasn't the choice of texts that took me aback, but the medium and delivery of their intake of words. This curious and creative group was so hungry for information, and so pressed for time, that they listened to their chosen text as audiobooks, at *twice* the usual pace. They listened to these sped-up versions while they commuted to offices or ran circuits for training or vacuumed their apartments, each moment fully spent. They did this too, I learned, when watching videos and lectures, taking in a barrage of information. Such an approach was particularly striking to me, as I had recently listened to a podcast at a regular speed, and still found myself stopping and backing it up regularly, repeating some sections three or four times. I kept this experience to myself at that gathering, having learned from Mark Slouka, in his essay *Quitting the Paint Factory*, that a dinner party revelation about his preference for eight or nine hours of sleep was taken by that crowd as an affront.[16] No doubt I would have had some sidelong glances, had I revealed my relaxed, even sluggish, listening. I wasn't thinking about hummingbirds at the time, but later, when I remembered that party, I saw a room filled with wings, zipping backwards and forwards, a dynamic hovering of constant motion.

Urban start-up culture isn't alone in its hunger for speed. The doubled pace of media intake fits right in with the outcomes of any online search for ways to increase efficiency. Strategies—or "life hacks"—proposed for the harried employee and the overstretched worker include options like waking up ever earlier to fit more into a day, hyper-organizing one's kitchen to reduce time spent searching for breakfast spoons and mugs, adopting preprogrammed email responses to reduce correspondence time, and deploying the "Pomodoro technique" of working in short, timed bursts followed by short, timed breaks.[17] In all these enthused, enumerated strategies for heightening focus and increasing output, breaks are encouraged because they enable continued, even increased, work. More needs to fit into these time-bounded pauses from work, and we see entertainment following similar accelerated trends—sped-up pop music on the video platform TikTok, for instance, has viral appeal that reinvigorates hit songs even a decade or more after their release. The velocity of relaxation matches that of work itself: a certain kind of idleness in service of more production.

None of these self-improvement lists ever suggest listening to the same material twice, or rereading a passage, a page, an entire book. Slowing down our information intake, our pace of work, our movements through the world is usually seen as troubling, a signal of inefficiency or illness. Rest can be virtuous, but only, it now seems, if it restores us to productivity—that is, a staccato rush of punctuated intensity, not a leisurely, unhurried ramble through ideas, blurring the lines between fast and slow. In our frenzied industrialized lives, rest is offered as an undertaking that enables renewed activity, a state of temporary torpor to set us up for the next burst. Saving energy in one moment to rededicate it to work the next: for the metaltail hummingbirds, to drink from 500 or so flowers each day;[18] for us, to efficiently make or convert or extract or produce or do whatever it is we do.

AN ARTICLE IN THE *NEW YORK TIMES* ADMONISHES THAT "Idleness is not just a vacation, an indulgence or a vice; it is as indispensable to the brain as vitamin D is to the body. . . . It is, paradoxically, necessary to getting any work done."[19] The article was interpreted by some readers as a justification of breaks in service of productivity, an exhortation to efficient work,[20] but that seems to me unfair. The writer, Tim Kreider, admits to his own "resolute idleness," in service not of a specifically productive life, but a *rich* one, situated "somewhere between [his] own defiant indolence and the rest of the world's endless frenetic hustle."[21] Perhaps this is idleness neither as productivity enhancement nor as defiance, not as strategy or confrontation or contempt, but instead as a kind of delight; recognizing that so much around us warrants our attention at any given moment offers up possibility. "Doors slam; water rushes. Here is another day, here is another day, I cry, as my feet touch the floor," effuses the character of Jinny in one of the dream-like sequences of Woolf's extended prose-poem *The Waves*, a novel woven from overlapping soliloquies.[22] She considers the impositions of the world. "It may be a bruised day, an imperfect day. I am often scolded. I am often in disgrace for idleness, for laughing," she admits, but then can't be held by the strictures of society for too long in a world with so much wonder, for

> even as Miss Matthews grumbles at my feather-headed carelessness, I catch sight of something moving – a speck of sun perhaps on a picture, or the donkey drawing the mowing-machine across the lawn; or a sail that passes between the laurel leaves, so that I am never cast down. I cannot be prevented from pirouetting behind Miss Matthews into prayers."[23]

Joy and distraction, disgrace and enchantment, something other than preparation for production; instead, Jinny revels in simply being in this unexpected world.

When we think of the grizzlies nestled in dens, it's hard to tell which of the versions of pause they embody in hibernation: rest as repose; rest as endurance. In either case, we imagine they are alone and undisturbed, self-sufficient and self-determined. The bears might have inspired Michel de Montaigne—to whom the essay form is attributed, this French writer of the 1500s—who, in a short reflection "On Solitude" exhorts, "Now, when we undertake to live alone and to do without companionship, let us see to it that our contentment depends on ourselves; let us cut loose from all ties that bind us to others; let us win from ourselves the power to live alone in good earnest and thus to live at our ease."[24] Perhaps ease is not an accurate description of this time of fasting and sludging hearts, but still, these bears undertake a solitary path in the mountains, we tell ourselves.

But winter is a season of "deep and often unseen nourishment," observes the writer and community organizer Jess Háusti. [25] For many female bears, the loss of body fat over winter is not just the result of a long fast. Denning is a busy time, when bears give birth and nurse their young. Along with dropping their metabolic rates, and forgoing food, water, and excretory functions, female brown bears spend much of their hibernation time gestating, birthing, and lactating.[26] Efforts invisible to us humans, undertaken in private by these denning mother bears. More extreme, even, than the activities of brown bears are those of polar bears (*Ursus maritimus*). In the summer and fall, females engage in a "walking hibernation," fasting when the absence of sea ice prevents them from hunting marine mammals, and in the winter, with cubs, they spend two-thirds of the year in a den without food.[27]

So much for "without companionship" and "undisturbed." The reproductive effort that takes place during denning leaves female brown bears emerging in spring with a cub or two in tow, and, though rarely, as many as six have been spotted.[28] Rather than Montaigne's cutting "loose from all ties that bind," these bears entangle themselves further in relationships of caretaking during the quiet hungry months. Montaigne, too, offered contradictory advice on solitude. Although he extolled the necessity of it to ensure self-possession and equanimity even in the case of loss—of family, wealth, health, and such—he still turned to the Roman Pliny for guidance on "complete and idle seclusion," recalling that statesman's direction "to leave to your servants the base and sordid domestic cares, and to devote yourself to the study of letters."[29] Complete seclusion, apart from the servants. A life of the mind, with the needs of the body taken care of by others. But here the bears and the French essayist diverge: the former do not place domestic cares on others even in their winter seclusion, but instead devote themselves to both the idleness of the dormant winter and the nurturing of their altricial young.

THIS SLEEP OF THE BEARS—ALTHOUGH DISRUPTED BY cubs, for some—is accompanied by visions of a silent winter night. The silence that descends when the noise of the humming, industrial world is abandoned. We flee to the woods, to the mountains, to the poles to escape that ever-constant noise. Polar traveller Erling Kagge writes of an expedition in Antarctica, "At home there's always a car passing, a telephone ringing, pinging or buzzing, someone talking, whispering or yelling. There are so many noises that we barely hear them all. Here it was different. Nature spoke to me in the guise of silence."[30] It was not just his surrounds that needed silencing, but himself, his inner thrum: he continues, "The quieter I became, the more I heard."[31] And with vision, too: what initially seemed both blank and silent resolved itself, with the sound of the wind, into a rich and textured land. "I began to notice that nothing was completely flat after all," he says. "The ice and snow formed small and large abstract shapes. The uniform whiteness was transformed into countless shades of white."[32]

It isn't so much that there isn't sound outside of our own human activity, but more that respite from noise of our own making is needed for that of others to be heard. And this is true not only for the whistling winds in Antarctic deserts but for the quiet murmur of other beings in places thronging with human sound. The journalist Ed Yong examines the "acoustic lives" of plants, for instance, pointing to recent studies that suggest plants both make and hear noises, using sound to communicate with insect pollinators.[33] While much of the research remains in early stages, it makes intuitive sense to those scientists, reports Yong, that plants might send and respond to airborne vibrations, just as they use chemical signals for defense.[34] As Yong observes, it's not that fields of flowers are truly silent—we just don't usually pay attention.[35] The writer Barry Lopez, too, writes of the sounds of others that we only barely understand, have only recently begun to perceive. In his expansive book *Arctic Dreams*, he writes of the spiral-tusked narwhal: its limited vision; its nearly imperceptible—to human hearing, at least—range of sounds; its ongoing impenetrability to scientific understanding.[36] With so little we truly know about these deep-water cetaceans, Lopez suggests an attitude of humility is needed: "the taking of a respectful attitude," he enjoins, "toward a mystery we can do no better than name 'narwhal.'"[37]

And if we don't pause from our ceaseless noisy labours, our making and taking underwater and aboveground, there may soon be nothing left to hear. The writer and scientist Rachel Carson evoked this eerie silence in the 1960s, not long before she died from metastasizing breast cancer that was spreading through her bones.[38] After a trio of books about the sea and its edges, Carson paused from the writing she most wanted to pursue to take on the damages being wrought by pesticides on the world around her. I am haunted still by her opening passage in *Silent Spring*.[39] "There was once a town in the heart of America where all life seemed to be in harmony with its surroundings," she starts, sketching the outline of this town and its outskirts of "fields of grain and hillsides of orchards, where white clouds of bloom drifted above the green land." Streams of trout; ferns and wildflowers lining roadways; a "flood" of migrating birds—this was a land alive with life. But then:

> ... one spring, a strange blight crept over the area, and everything began to change. Some evil spell had settled on the community; mysterious maladies swept the flocks of chickens, and the cattle and sheep sickened and died. Everywhere was the shadow of death.... And there was a strange stillness. The birds, for example—where had they gone?

The whole book—first published in serial form in the *New Yorker*—is a meticulously documented, scientifically backed case against a chemical assault on the Earth. But in her early paragraphs, we most vividly see Carson *the writer* at work. Those first lines in *Silent Spring* speak directly of silence: Carson asks us to pause, as Kagge does, to really listen; when we do, there is no sound—this "was a spring without voices." She moves us with her accounts of deserted skies and forests. And we don't just miss avian songs in such a spring: there would be no cicadas distracting Socrates and Phaedrus; no grasshoppers fiddling away the grain-collecting days. This isn't just the quiet cold before the hummingbirds return from their overnight torpor. This is spring, when grizzlies should emerge with growing cubs, when pollinators should be conversing with the flowers. A barren sort of silence, an empty world.

While Carson's was a fictitious town, she knew that we feel absence all around us. She warns the reader that even though "I know of no community that has experienced all the misfortunes I describe," still, "every one of them has actually happened somewhere in the world, and many communities have already suffered a substantial number of them." Decades before her book was published, and across an ocean, Eastern Europe was stripped of ursine life. In the 1930s, brown bear populations crashed in the region, especially in the western Carpathian Mountains, where only a few dozen bears survived the pressures of hunting and the loss of their habitat.[40] On the eastern side of the mountains, several hundred bears persisted,[41] although later in the century their numbers also plummeted.[42] It wasn't just the bears that suffered in those decades. Born shortly after the First World War to Jewish parents in the contested region of Bukovina, now split between Romania and Ukraine, the poet Paul Celan suffered intimate losses in his early adult life that were echoed across millions of families in and beyond Eastern Europe. His parents both died soon after their deportation to Transnistria; after spending the war years in work camps, he lived the rest of his life in both a physical and metaphysical exile in Paris.[43] Celan—an assumed name, a loose anagram of the name he was born into, Antschel[44]—wrote haunting, ambiguous poems of suffering in German, a language his mother insisted he learn in its most literary form and one he stretched to its edges and beyond.[45] He confronted darkness in his own work, and in the work of others—in the latter, perhaps most profoundly through translating the words of exiled Russian poet Osip Mandelstam, who died in a Soviet labour camp in 1938.[46] Celan looked straight into dispossession and damage—but then also beyond it, lifting his pen against the silence that could have been in response to that scale of loss.

We know so little in a world that contains so much. In a poem dedicated to the writer Nelly Sachs, with whom Celan exchanged a sustained if sporadic fifteen-year correspondence, he ends with lines that evoke our limitations within the larger mysteries: "We don't know, you know, / we / don't know, do we?, / what / counts."[47] When we pause from our extractive fury, an act both of rest and of respect for an order in which we are new arrivals,[48] we might open the possibility for other voices to survive. When we pause from our noisy flurry, we might open the possibilities for others to be heard, even if we, ourselves, might never hear them.

What do bears dream on clear, quiet winter nights, when the stars hold court with the sky? Of blueberries and salmon and dandelions. Of rushing water and tangled riverbanks and the rough bark of rub trees. Or maybe their dreams are troubled and interrupted, jumbled fragments of fear and loss. Perhaps those bears in their dens have left behind dreams altogether, their restlessness quelled. Over their thudding heartbeats, slow in the frozen season, they listen for the winds of spring to rouse them to the light. Listening, when all is hushed and calm around them, to the sound of the earth and to the falling snow.

IN HIS POEM *KEEPING QUIET*, THE ONCE-EXILED Chilean poet Pablo Neruda asks, urgently, for us, "for once on the face of the earth," to "stop for a second, / and not move our arms so much."[49] But in this stillness, where "those who prepare green wars, /

wars with gas, wars with fire" have paused from their vicious plans, he clarifies: "What I want should not be confused / with total inactivity."[50] I think of this as I write this passage, while Ukraine's capital city, Kyiv, is being shelled by Russia. I read of civilians enlisting—a 58-year-old history professor, a 33-year-old nightclub manager—and others lining up to give blood: a 24-year-old programmer, a 42-year-old psychologist.[51] Citizens picking up guns; forming militias; making Molotov cocktails; mopping floors; defiantly offering up sunflower seeds to invading soldiers.[52] "We are a huge amount of ants," said Alex Riabchyn, a former Ukrainian parliamentary deputy, describing the collective work of his underarmed, outgunned people.[53] Little rest is possible in a country under siege, filled with tanks and fire and the sounds of brutality.

There hasn't been a year without war in any human history of this planet I can find: whether contained within nation-states or spilling across borders, somewhere, always, there are families seeking refuge from violence, trying to live their lives amidst strife. Displacement, damage, destruction. The same sounds of war echoed in so many places, across continents and countries, drowning out the buzzing of possible pollinators, even if the fields hadn't been torn up and rendered treacherous by tanks and mines and the chemicals of those green wars.[54] It isn't inactivity that the families sheltering from conflict in these places so desperately desire, but the chance, as Neruda suggests, to "walk about with their brothers / in the shade, doing nothing,"[55] the possibility of catching sight, as Woolf's Jinny does, of that "speck of sun."[56]

In war, in suffering, in grief, in despair, it is sometimes the smallest of gestures that make us come undone. But these, too, can hold us together. During a particular period of darkness for each of them, in difficult lives shaped by persecution and loss, Celan offered to Sachs a piece of the earth: "I am sending you something here that will help against the little doubts that sometimes come to one"; he wrote in the summer of 1960, "it is a piece of sycamore bark. You take it between the thumb and the index finger, hold it very tight and think of something good."[57] The bark of a kind of maple tree, sent from France to Sweden to help mend a fractured soul. These poets are not alone in seeking solace in these tangible ways. When so little could be taken by Ukrainians fleeing their country, seeking refuge across borders in Poland and Romania and Moldova and elsewhere, it wasn't just passports and documents that made it onto trains and across borders. For one woman, tucked into her pocket were a pine cone and an oak leaf—something of the roots and soil of her homeland.[58]

Along with the bark that Celan sent by post was a fierce belief in words: "I can't keep it from you —" he continued, "poems, and yours especially, are even better pieces of sycamore bark. So please, start writing again."[59] Poetry requires a kind of silence; like the sycamore tree, it is a response to and a way through devastation. Silence and words, intertwined, inextricable. As in an earlier letter from Celan to Sachs: "When your letter came the day before yesterday, I wanted most of all to get into the train and travel to Stockholm to tell you—with what words, with what silence?—that you must not believe words like yours can remain unheard."[60] The whisper of poetry as the rest of the world roared; a fragment of bark in a trembling hand. A pinecone held tight while fleeing war.

Late one summer season, I visited the weir at the Nakina River for a few days. My time there was short, but those with me—fisheries and wildlife experts with and from the Taku River Tlingit First Nation—had longstanding relationships with the place: years, decades, even generations for some, back to time immemorial along the river. They had seen the banks in high and low water years, could navigate the currents with eyes closed, traced cubs back through their maternal lineages recognizing siblings and grandparents, felt the presence of ancestors. When even they were surprised at the ferocity of the winds one night, I knew the storm was serious. We stood on the high porch of the cabin, a building perched on stilts to separate our living space from the bears' river access, bundled up against the gusts, watching the trees sway and bend. I jumped at the sudden cracking and crashing sounds of branches breaking, and we watched a series of trees topple nearby. Nothing about

CHAPTER II

the surging world around us was still—winds, trees, water—yet even so I felt a quietude, the seven of us gathered close. The pace of life at the weir is set by forces outside ourselves, the bears and the river and the salmon and the wind. The next morning we watched branches and entire tree trunks carried away by the river, the aftermath of the storm. Celan's bark, along with those floating logs and the bears themselves, serve as a reminder of what Neruda wondered when he wrote, "Perhaps the earth can teach us / as when everything seems dead in winter / and later proves to be alive."[61] We drank coffee on the porch, warming like the metaltails in the morning sun, newly awakened to the world.

CHAPTER III

BEAVER BLOCKADES: ON RESISTANCE

Aspen shavings. Merwin. Sisyphus. Big Lonely Doug. Slash. Wetlands. Forest Service. Dam demolition. Alice and the Red Queen. Orthogenesis. High fashion. Imperialism. Refusal. Clapping. Blockades. Imagination. Hope. Refuge.

All that was left of the aspen, my friends told me, was a sharp stump and a scattering of small twigs and leaves. They hadn't even seen the beavers at work: one day, they found a young tree near their cabin had been felled; a few days later, it disappeared completely. Upon close inspection, they spotted a few piles of wood shavings here and there, but otherwise, the labour of the beavers left little trace.

A CLEAR CUT—THE PHRASE SUGGESTS A BLANK SLATE. But when we demolish forests, we leave so much behind. Language often obscures damage through euphemism, but in the case of forestry one term illuminates it: the debris left behind from razing a forest to the ground is known as *slash*, conjuring up vivid images of sharp destruction.[1] Walking through a new clear-cut is an experience of both frustration and desolation: this is no pine forest understory, low and open and strewn with needles. On the west coast of Canada, it is snarls of devil's club and salal and huckleberry, logs askew and crisscrossed at uncomfortable angles, broken stumps.[2] Tough footing for anyone moving through without wings.

Rarely, in such an area, is there a full tree left standing. It's striking, then, that there is a more than 60-metre-tall Douglas fir in an otherwise deforested tract on the west side of Vancouver Island, in Pacheedaht territory.[3] This tree, for still-unclear reasons, was excluded from the cutting by a forester tasked with demarcating buffer zones and road locations, brightly coloured flagging tape showing which trees to take down and which to leave. The now-iconic tree escaped the fate of his neighbours, in spite of a straight, tall trunk that signalled high-value wood.[4] The rest of the trees were consigned to mills and trucks and container ships, for floors and doors and beams and posts, bound for Vancouver, for Japan. It is unclear if evading the saw blades was lucky: "Big Lonely Doug," as the survivor is now known, towers alone over an expanse of low saplings and brush.

The old-growth forest itself in this part of the world never had an open understory, the writer Harley Rustad reminds us, in his book about Big Lonely Doug. Under the canopy has long held a botanical world intertwined: trunks rising and encircled with vines, thickets of prickly shrubs and tangles of groundcover, fallen trees turning slowly to soil with new saplings taking root in the shafts of light their canopies no longer block. But while both are hard to navigate on foot in a linear path, the understory of a flourishing old-growth grove looks markedly different from a clear-cut block. As Rustad reveals, west coast temperate rainforests are not places of uniformly tall trees, but vibrant demographic jumbles. Rustad writes, "These forests are not simply original; they are complete."[5] Ecologically complete, that is, until they are taken apart by chainsaws and other machines. What is taken away from those cut-blocks is organized, catalogued, referred to as roundwood and measured in cubic metres and board-feet.[6] What is left behind is in disarray, uncounted, the aftermath of a brutal storm. Cedar, spruce, hemlock, false hemlock: unclaimed shards and fragments haphazardly strewn where they fell. Yet even with all this vegetation on the ground, it is an empty place. Wounded. Then the bulldozers are deployed, pushing the slash into massive piles to be burned.[7]

"START WITH THE LEAVES," ADVISES THE POET W. S. Merwin, "the small twigs, and the nests that have been shaken, ripped, or broken off by the fall; these must be gathered and attached once again to their respective places." This is the start of an instruction manual for "Unchopping a Tree."[8] As Merwin offers strategies to undo the damage of a broken trunk and its myriad parts, he is specific, detailed, even encouraging at first. "It is not arduous work," he reassures us—until this caveat: "unless major limbs have been smashed or mutilated." And it's not just the felled tree that needs reconstituting, but all its adornments and attachments, the nests and caches made by birds and mammals and insects. "With spiders' webs," Merwin concedes, "you must simply do the best you can."

The best you can: against all logic, against all odds, against, even more, all hope. In Greek mythology, King Sisyphus—son of the minor god Aeolus, master of the winds[9]—is said to have once cheated death, thus earning the wrath of the gods.[10] According to myth, Sisyphus traps Thanatos, the embodied figure of death, using his legendary cunning against his fate. The absence of death, goes the story, caused much suffering in the world, as those grievously injured and racked by illness had no release from their pain until Thanatos was freed. Was it Sisyphus' deception and enchainment of death that earned the deities' anger? Perhaps a series of prior transgressions—the violation of his niece, Tyro; the betrayal of the confidences of the god Zeus; his vicious breaches of the laws of hospitality—already had him bound for punishment in the underworld. In any case, he is consigned, when death finally comes for him, to eternal punishment in Tartarus, the abyss below Hades.[11] Here, he must push a massive boulder up a mountainside; each time, as he nears the top, the rock escapes his grasp and rolls back down. He labours in vain through eternity. Any hopeless task, or endlessly frustrating undertaking, we now call a *Sisyphean* one. But here we are, amidst fallen trunks and broken branches.

Is it just a lament, this prose-poem, thinly veiled as a guide to undoing the damage we wreak through our work? Or is this call to restoration less ironic, less *defeated* than that? After all, we could read those lines as an exhortation to attempt the impossible. Does it help to know that Merwin himself spent forty years planting trees on damaged agricultural lands, tenderly placing seedlings in soil? So gather up the twigs and splinters, the silky strands of a broken web.

HERE WE ARE AT THE SURFACE: UNWOVEN SPIDERS' webs, Sisyphean punishments, desolate clear-cuts. Let's go back to that beaver-felled aspen, or, rather, its absence, to uncover a few more layers. The disappeared tree was one of many among stands of trembling aspen, balsam poplar, lodgepole pine, and white spruce along the shore of the glacial Atlin Lake on unceded Taku River Tlingit lands. Everyone was constructing their homes from wood in the neighbourhood that summer. My friends, artists both—a painter and a poet—were planing pine boards to repair the roof on a small bunkhouse by their main log cabin, itself only one room with a sleeping loft, set back a hundred metres or so from shore. The beavers—artists, too, if we understand the term expansively—constructing their own house with sticks and branches closer to the water's edge, partly submerged. A few escaped aspen leaves could be seen nearby.

They worked alongside each other that summer, the painter, the poet, and their bucktoothed neighbours. Their labours had visible results: a solid roof on the bunkhouse, a beaver lodge gaining form.

In the evenings, as the winds calmed and the noise of saws and dogs and bustling life subsided on land, sometimes a splash was heard in the water, a flat tail slapping the surface. A warning signal of some disturbance to its family, or perhaps the start of a playful exchange. But mostly, it was steady work for humans and *Castor canadensis* alike.

The beavers were not new arrivals to this place; on a kayak paddle around the marshy bay, I saw many angled stumps, some fresh and others weather-worn over years. Beaver lodges and dams range from a makeshift pile of sticks, loosely held together, to empires of closely woven grids placed at strategic points along a waterway.[12] The ones in this bay landed somewhere in between: a new tidy lodge under construction, and several other domed structures along the bank, either a growing family complex or remnants of previous years' efforts. Beavers hold together such ecosystems, which sequester carbon, control stream gradients, regulate runoff, and offer habitat and protection to a wide range of avian, amphibian, mammalian, and invertebrate companions.[13] Their dams still flowing waters and create quiet eddies, making fish nurseries and frog hideaways and calm surfaces on which insects can breed.[14] And where our clear-cuts leave slash to be set aflame, what the beavers don't build with, they snack on. They fill their lodges with food for the winter, young twigs and leaves, the outer layers of bark.

Beavers are paragons of productivity in our usual storytelling; the eager beaver, the ever-busy chewer, the dam constructor holding back rivers. The tireless labour of these large rodents staunches the flow of water, thwarts gravity, takes down trees—like that aspen—with small persistent bites. And we follow suit: ever busy, ever active, ever looking to the next tree, the next river bend, the next place we can assert control. Still, are we truly like the beavers in our endless labours? We are certainly less committed to selective cutting, Big Lonely Doug notwithstanding. But it is more than that that holds us apart.

CHAPTER III

FOR MY FRIENDS, THE BEAVERS WERE BUT SELDOM-SPOTted neighbours in the bay, occasionally taking a tree here and there; an easy coexistence. But often the tireless efforts of beavers undo our own work: plugging culverts, slowing river flow with sediment, challenging our attempts to drain and manage our farms and dams and roads. Beavers, alternately, are described as pests, "detrimental species," and even "predatory animals" by those trying to wrestle lands and waters into agricultural production and roadways.[15] In national forests in the United States, their dam construction has flooded enough adjacent cropland to provoke deep resentment. One senator in a subcommittee hearing with the Forest Service noted—apparently ruefully—that "of course, private landowners cannot legally go onto the public lands and tear down a beaver dam or blow up a beaver dam."[16] He stopped shy of asking for the laws to change, but given the tenor of the exchange, I suspect he wished they would.

Sisyphean indeed—but for whom? Beavers are certainly resisters of human labour. They work against us—but then, let's flip the view: we work against them. We straighten winding rivers with our canals; speed up waters with our channelizing efforts; erode banks with that faster water flow, then pile up rock and rubble—known as rip-rap—to try to slow that erosion. We might say that we each are running to stand still, as with Alice and the Red Queen in Lewis Carroll's famed *Through the Looking Glass* story.[17] "Well, in our country," says young Alice to the redoubtable Red Queen, "you'd generally get to somewhere else—if you ran very fast for a long time, as we've been doing." The Red Queen scoffs, "A slow sort of country!" Here, the Queen tells her, "it takes all the running you can do, to keep in the same place."[18] Carroll's tale has sparked generations of biologists to use the story as a metaphor for evolutionary processes. Some describe these as an escalating arms race[19] and others as "non-progressive" evolution,[20] wherein the adaptations of predators and prey, or of the sexes, or of parasites and hosts, continually ratchet up in response to those of the other, leaving both—in relation to each other—roughly where they started.

BEAVER BLOCKADES: ON RESISTANCE

Progress stymied. Energy wasted. Is this just a story of a deadlocked impasse, with the same outcomes as if we and the beavers stayed still, without all the building and tearing down of dams? We call it *idling* when a car engine runs out of gear, turning and turning. We establish ordinances against this, restrictions and bylaws, as much, it sometimes seems, to guard against the absence of productivity as to reduce emissions or local noise. Energy expended must not be in vain—from the Latin *vanus*: empty, without substance, producing no result. We could speed up, shift into a higher gear: as the Queen proffers, "If you want to get somewhere else, you must run at least twice as fast as that!"

But speeding up is what we've already done: we trap beavers, dislocate them, destroy lodges, dismantle dams. This seems the wrong lesson to take from Alice. It is unfair to compare the work practices of the beavers to our own rapacious ones, or to suggest some kind of equitable arms race. They may threaten our productivity, our domestic and industrial efforts, but the labour of the beavers is not for them alone. They are the creators of space for others, the enablers of others' work. Their dams and lodges slow currents, fill ponds, create pools and channels. While they might not unchop the aspens or repair bird nests and spiderwebs as per Merwin's advice, their painstaking work offers up new abodes and sustenance beyond themselves, lives and livelihoods for other species. To the Queen, Alice counters: "I'm quite content to stay here."[21] A static "here" is never quite a place to stay, of course, and the industrious beavers know this. For the sake of overwintering fish, breeding insects, and feeding moose, we might hope the beavers continue their measured forestry practices and their rearrangements of river currents; to enable this, though, we humans might do well to follow Alice's lead and stay a little more still.

STILLNESS IS ANTITHETICAL TO PROGRESS, AT LEAST in colonial approaches to modern life. Prior to European settlement, estimates of beaver populations put their numbers in the hundreds of millions.[22] A measured—and in many accounts, reciprocal and respectful—human relationship with beavers existed on the continent.[23] Scholar Heidi Kiiwetinepinesiik Stark writes of Anishinaabe governance systems and treaty making, highlighting the offerings made by beavers of their bodies for food and clothing and, in return, the gifts given to them by the Anishinaabe of tobacco and household goods, along with the return of beaver bones to the water.[24] But the arrival of colonial powers shifted the terms of coexistence into a relentless plunder, feeding a growing demand from transatlantic trade.[25] For settler colonists in North America, beavers were not named as predators—as they are in Oregon's expansive definition in its current trapping and hunting regulations[26]—but as prey. By that time, European beavers (*Castor fiber*) had nearly disappeared from Great Britain and northern Europe, along with ermine, sable, and other small furred species, their pelts destined for high fashion and luxury attire.[27] Rather than confront their ecological limits, mercantile interests expanded further afield, in this case westward to the riparian landscapes that were home to *Castor canadensis*.[28]

Such expansionist commercial hungers were not restricted to beavers; at the same time, whales, walrus, fox, cod, and other terrestrial and aquatic species were being exchanged along transatlantic and transpacific trade routes, swallowed by mechanized processing in a relentless acceleration of industrialization.[29] The fur trade ramped up around the same time as logging on the BC coast; the mid-1800s saw the establishment of commercial logging and sawmills on Vancouver Island and up the Burrard Inlet.[30] Where the abundance of old-growth has plummeted, logging efforts have intensified. In some places, loggers use the literally named "feller-bunchers"—machines that take down trees, strip their unwanted limbs, and gather them together in neat stacks.[31] These are not deployed on Vancouver Island, as the uneven terrain is too challenging,[32] but the idea of logging tools, as with all the industrial machinery for processing living beings into tradable commodities, remains the same: add power to dismantle centuries of growth in hours or minutes.

The surge by colonial arrivals in hunting and trapping—with snares and nets and cages and eventually steel traps[33]—propelled what historian Thomas Wien describes as "fur-trade imperialism"[34] shaping the political economy of North America and radically reorienting its terrestrial and aquatic ecosystems. Political economist Harold Innis traces the trade back to the 1400s,[35] but it is in the nineteenth century that his account offers particular insight into the intertwined rise of commerce and empire.[36] Innis' assessment of the political dynamics of the fur trade among French, English, and Indigenous leaders and traders, and whether economic relations were determined more by North American or European forces, has been contested by other economic historians.[37] But regardless of these power relations, by whose authority prices were set and in whose political favour these controls tipped, the rise of this trade from the 1600s onwards—in the pelts and furs and skins of beavers, otters, foxes, marten, ermine, lynx, and more bound for British and European markets[38]—paid no attention to the autonomy and agency of the animals themselves. It certainly did not consider their roles in their wider communities and landscapes. As with Douglas fir in the timber trade, in the fur trade beavers were not individuals but bulk commodities: in the 1700s, beaver shipments to France were measured in bales, 120 pounds each, classified by quality and type.[39] By the mid or late 1800s, beavers were "effectively extirpated" in many parts of the United States,[40] and by the arrival of the twentieth century, it is estimated there were only 100,000 beavers remaining on the continent.[41] The journalist Frances Backhouse reports the conclusion, in 1892, of a Canadian Fellow of the Zoological Society of London that, "As to the ultimate destruction of the beaver, no possible question can exist."[42] A sealed fate, it seemed. The collapse of *Castor* species on both sides of the Atlantic appeared the only way to quell the insatiable hungers of this commodity trade.

And yet, by the 1980s, there were some 6 million beavers—or perhaps even double that—in North America, and there may be as many as

CHAPTER III

20 million or so now.⁴³ Collapse of a species, it turns out, is not the only way to reorient relationships between humans and others. Protection efforts might not have fully restored their pre-colonial numbers, but the seemingly inevitable loss of the beaver was narrowly avoided in the twentieth century. A falling demand for furs was accompanied by concerted trapping limits and moratoria, habitat conservation measures, and reintroduction programs.⁴⁴ Skirting the fate of so many other abundant-turned-extinguished species—the passenger pigeon as a particularly iconic example, that "biological storm," in preservationist John Muir's words, silenced and stilled⁴⁵—the beaver refused its disappearance.

IN THE SPRING OF 2011, A SERIES OF NEARLY SILENT flash mobs erupted in Belarus. Since January of that year, when Alexander Lukashenko was sworn in for a fourth term as president in an election the BBC reported was "widely condemned as fraudulent,"⁴⁶ opposition leaders had been jailed and dissent violently stifled.⁴⁷ These new protests were different: no shouting, no slogans, no clear leaders⁴⁸—nothing, really, that could be directly identified as belligerent or disruptive. Just some clapping: collective, undirected applause. But the government knew these new crowds were not innocuous and tried to crack down. As one journalist wrote, "authorities responded with their usual farce—they banned applause unless directed at veterans. They arrested a one-armed man for clapping."⁴⁹ Clapping—so often a celebratory gesture—can be a form of building political community, not just an act of individuals decrying a brutal regime. After clapping was outlawed, protestors timed their cell phones for collective ringing; this, too, led to arrests, with a government official calling any such gathering "an activity of mass disorder."⁵⁰ As the flash mobs continued, more prohibitions followed; by late July, there was draft legislation that banned "standing around doing nothing in a group."⁵¹ Idling, as ever, posed a threat to social order. Although Lukashenko remains in power, Belarussian resisters have continued over the decade that has followed to devise new strategies to organize, protest, and agitate for a different future, ever creative in their refusal to comply with an authoritarian regime.[52]

Refusal is, in anthropologist Carole McGranahan's account, a concept akin to, but distinct from, resistance.[53] Resistance pushes back against disturbance, disruption, damage. Refusal offers something else—an unwillingness to accept the terms offered or conditions imposed, and the creation, instead, of a distinct and autonomous path. Abstention, rather than engagement; reimagining, rather than defying.[54] For McGranahan, this staking of a claim to independence and self-determination, this ability to deny consent, is generative and relational and, perhaps unexpectedly, *hopeful*.

Back to the bucktoothed rodents. Rather than just mounting opposition to the forces that threaten to snuff them out, beavers have and are living their own lives and shaping their environments in ways that foster the communities they need and want. They create contradictory orders and infrastructures to the ones thrust upon them. Damming a culvert is not just a response to human interventions, although it can seem that way to road-builders, but a necessity of living as a beaver—not resisting human impositions exactly, but refusing them entirely, responding instead to the sound of water moving. In recognizing and respecting these beaver ways, there are possibilities for different relationships with them, ones already imagined in some places, newly revived in others, and, in still others, long enacted and maintained. A range of vibrant traditions and teachings and practices that offer something generative: beyond the idleness of a stalemate created through competition and without the intensified race of industry that the Red Queen suggests.

So often we think of resistance as antagonistic: protesters are hostile, combative, pugnacious. As the writer Astra Taylor puts it, the term activist evokes less a set of political commitments or principles or values than "a certain temperament,"[55] which, in general, is belligerent.[56] But artist and scholar Leanne Betasamosake Simpson reminds us that resistance can be tender, compassionate, imaginative, even joyful. Recalling Anishinaabe, Dene, and Nêhiyawak accounts of giant beavers—along with Western scientific ones, which tell of beavers the size of bears in the Pleistocene[57]—Simpson tells her own version of a story of a beaver gone rogue, brought back to the community through diplomacy. She describes principles that guide both beaver dams and Indigenous blockades: consent, respect, and the recognition of shared worlds. The work of beavers, Simpson explains, benefits the wider world around them—their infrastructure offering drought protection, winter fish habitat, cool retreats in summer months for ungulates seeking refuge from biting insects. In parallel, she shares the vibrant life that happens within and alongside Indigenous blockades against extractive disruptions—the ceremonies, stories, community care, and sacred practices that thrive even in places where people put their bodies in the way of damage. These practices do more than sustain protest; they nurture a process to, as Simpson puts it, "imagine other worlds."[58] Other futures, other possibilities, other ways of being—pathways that, like the beavers, might enable the flourishing of not only ourselves but also others. Resistance can be generous.

In 2020, a new wave of protests erupted in Belarus in the wake of what many viewed as another rigged election,[59] with citizens taking to the streets in spite of riot police and water cannons.[60] The organizer Yotam Marom writes of how to live when it seems our worlds are ending: how to find beauty, belonging, meaning, and possibility by "taking agency"—joining together with others in creative, defiant, collective action, "the old fear and a new courage mingling together."[61] Creative rearrangements of protest at every turn, collective ingenuity taking material form in the streets; here are actions of brave dissent and belonging. But while direct action can be valuable and necessary, effective forms of resistance and refusal are not always fast-paced: along with the transformative "electric moments in the streets"[62] that Marom describes and Belarussian citizens enact, we also need sustained imagining, quieter moments of rebuilding, seeking out stillness.

As he withstands the winds, the storms, the empty space around his towering trunk, Big Lonely Doug must feel very alone indeed. And not only above the ground; under it, too. As forest ecologist Suzanne Simard's research reveals, mycorrhizal networks link tree roots, enabling them, across species and ages, to transfer water and nutrients.[63] Without this tangle of others in his roots, Big Lonely Doug must feel a particular kind of isolation, an invisible hunger that comes from the inability to both give and receive in community. Research has shown that when other species were removed—neighbouring birch and aspen and cottonwood trees—new Douglas fir seedlings proved less hardy than their more crowded counterparts.[64] But consider this: Doug is surrounded by recently planted trees. Not the diverse forest that formerly surrounded him, but still, a collection of living, breathing trees making their way up into the sunlight. Maybe his roots are reaching out towards those newly established saplings, sending out resources and sustenance and wisdom: a tough survivor holding up the future.

ON A COOL SPRING WEEKEND, I CAMPED BY A SMALL lake not far from the shoreline where my friends have their cabin with its recently missing aspen tree. Migration was in full swing: Arctic terns with their forked tails circled and swooped over still waters, mimicked by Bonaparte gulls with their black heads, and in the marshy edges, a festival of swallows—barn, bank, tree, violet-green—in aerial motion. Barrow's goldeneyes flew overhead, uttering rapid-fire cries. The lake was one of a series of lakes, each one slightly stepped down from the next. Pulling my canoe over the berms of mud and grasses between them led, at the third, to a large, messy beaver dam holding back water at the brink of overflow, just a few trickles moving through.

Here was a vivid illustration of both resistance and creation: the beavers pushing back against the water's downstream flow; the marshy lake offering a sanctuary for pike, moose, those migrating birds. The emergence of a place of calm, filled with both movement and stillness. In such placid pools brimming with life, we see the paradoxes that hold hope. Refusal as hope, restoration as hope, imagination as hope. Writer and environmental historian Rebecca Solnit calls hope an "embrace of the unknown and the unknowable,"[65] a call for action in the face of an uncertain future, where uncertainty provides space for possibility. Here, the not-knowing is what enables us to go on, even in the face of the seemingly impossible: hope as a stubborn, persistent feeling that propels us.

Is unchopping a tree a hopeless task? It seems impossible to restore to the world the trees we dismantle. We would do well to pay attention to the beavers—chop a tree here and there, but only when you need it, when you leave no trace, and when, through your labour, you nurture those around you. Although we might never rebuild that spider's web, we might not be doomed, with Sisyphus, to failure in reconstituting smashed limbs and torn nests. Instead, from those fallen branches, we can quietly rebuild something meaningful within a damaged world, offering up refuge to others. Listen closely to what else Merwin advises: "Practice, practice. Put your hope in that."

CHAPTER IV

FIR DEFERRALS: ON SLOWNESS

Resin. Camphor. Krummholz. Anthropomorphism. Inches. Quill pigs. Contradictions. Yeast. Pandemic. Online teaching. Off-grid cabins. Breath. Balance. Shortcuts. Progress. Wildness. Convenience. Evergreens. Luxury. Exposure. Sublime.

There are visual cues: flat, blunt-edged, blue-tinged needles; blisters of dark resin rising from smooth, grey bark; a tapered crown ready to shed snow[1]—but really, I know I'm among subalpine fir even with my eyes closed. I've been stomping my way up a narrow dirt trail surrounded by the sweet, woody smell of spruce and pine when a sudden astringency fills the air. Some describe the almost-citrus scent as camphor[2] and others, vaguely, as *"rich."*[3] Our words, as ever, metaphors for something else, an effort to gesture at the world around us. I stop and breathe deep.

Here on a rocky windblown slope, the late fall light comes in low-angled, shadows long even at midday. I look up at the uneven crowns of the trees, their grey-purple cones perched upright on branches. The firs are understated: the slender spires are not that tall, and some are wizened with age, their bark scaly. At higher altitudes, they tend to be stunted and crooked—known, among botanists, as *krummholz* in form.[4] Subalpine fir are slow-growing, both in roots and shoots—sometimes seedlings grow less than an inch each year.[5] But don't let these less-striking aesthetic features dissuade you from close attention to these impressive conifers.

CHAPTER IV

Look again at the angled pyramids of trees with their short needles, each one a bit more distinct now. They are frost-tolerant, they can withstand acidic soils and nutrient deficits, they persist through heavy snowfall and flooding. They are shade-tolerant, too, content to live in the shadows of others, but also are among the first trees to return in a disturbed area. Although they grow more slowly the higher up they are, they are also longer lived in these exposed places.[6] Like other conifers in the mountains, subalpine fir sometimes stop growing over winter; they pause photosynthesis as they endure ice crystals forming in their cells and guard against water loss through their waxy needles.[7] A stand of these trees is a quiet lesson in tenacity.

Botanical guides, though often terse and technical, seem to soften when describing this species, with entries suggesting a patient and adaptable and undemanding being. In reading of subalpine fir, I learn that it is "a hardy tree,"[8] which "is not exacting in its soil requirements."[9] They aren't the longest-lived trees, but these firs may "cling to life" for upwards of 200 years,[10] say the guides. We might try to guard against anthropomorphism in our science, but as these field guides reveal, it's so hard not to see the world in our own terms. It's hard for me, anyway, to imagine a relaxed life on this exposed slope in howling winter winds. Still, even if we are limited by our own understanding of what their internal lives might comprise, hewing to the imagined interiority of others is of central importance in a world so often seen as ours for the taking. In doing so, we admit to the possibility that we are not alone in possessing agency, desire, purpose. A recognition of complexity, and of distinctiveness, is crucial in a time where we are obsessed with speed and growth, in a culture where we equate expansion with value, where it is so easy to overlook the significance of an inch of a seedling on a mountainside.

THE CABIN IS NESTLED IN THE SPRUCE-WILLOW-BIRCH zone, a bit below the stands of subalpine fir, protected from the winds.

This is a landscape dense with poplars and aspen, shrub birch and willow, spruce and pine; seedlings are always moving into any cleared patch. To reduce the risks from wildfires, an ever-increasing threat in our hotter, drier summers, each year I cut back the grasses and shrubs that take hold beside and under the elevated floor, raking out dried leaves and thorny stems. My partner takes down saplings that take root too close to the building. The idea that we could stave off fire seems absurd, though, when we take a few steps back. The cabin itself is made of spruce logs that were never stripped of their bark, the rough exterior flaking off in pieces. The uneven walls provide traction for the claws of red squirrels that sometimes scrabble along the outside. The building blends into the nearby stands of live spruce; a fallen tree nearby is covered with mosses and mushrooms, a mix of dry branches and damp soil. One year, we had a consultation with wildfire experts, who gave us all their best advice—remove the bark and sand and stain the logs; install metal guards and spark-resistant screen around the pressure-treated wooden posts that hold the cabin off the ground; cut back all the trees, branches, brush. When my partner protested that this would make our home unrecognizable, they shrugged and agreed that all the options involved trade-offs. The bark is protection from the elements, as much as it is propellant for flame. Trees nearby provide shade, block the wind, filter air, store carbon. We try to strike a balance between maintaining habitat for the birds and reducing the buildup of fuels that could amplify flames, recognizing that our domestic choices have consequences beyond ourselves.

Our home is part of a world that "does not belong to us alone," as the writer Helen Macdonald puts it[11]—we brush up often against our nonhuman neighbours. One summer night, an unfamiliar scraping sound on the porch woke us up. This wasn't the sound of squirrels, who usually gave away their presence with noisy chatter—and were mostly active in daytime hours—and it sounded bigger than a mouse. Cautiously opening the heavy wooden door of the cabin, I ventured onto the porch with a headlamp, and a rotund, spiky silhouette reluctantly shuffled down the stairs. A *"quill pig,"* as the translation goes: a porcupine. It had been gnawing on one of the wooden chairs we'd left on the porch. Over the next few nights, it returned, leaving smooth gouges in the wood of the upright bark-clad posts holding up the porch roof beams. Not wanting to risk an encounter between our soft-snouted, curious dog and this quill-covered visitor, we took steps to deter these nightly visits, spraying water from a squirt bottle and making loud noises. It's not clear whether the porcupine was scared or just bothered, but it went elsewhere.

Porcupines are slow-moving, near-sighted, nocturnal animals. They're a bit clumsy, and though they're good climbers, they're also known for falling out of trees.[12] Taciturn? It's hard to say, but they live mostly solitary lives. Like beavers, they're drawn to the culverts in roadways, but porcupines tend not to be the cause of floods and washouts; they're more known for hiding in than dismantling those overflow diversions. Their most dangerous quality—launching their quills at those they perceive as threats—is a myth. Invented. The quills do come loose upon contact, and the barbed tips make them hard to dislodge from skin, but porcupines hold their ground through defense, not offense. Their main predators are of the feline and mustelid varieties—lynx, bobcats, fishers, wolverine—and sometimes also canine, as wolves and coyotes occasionally take the risk to secure a fatty meal.[13] With speeds of only three or four kilometres an hour[14]—a human's casual walking pace—porcupines don't stand a chance of outpacing one of these animals on the hunt, so they instead rely on warding off most attacks by bristling tens of thousands of quills.[15]

The boreal forest is a place replete with contradictions and extremes: between seasons, light, nutrients, speed. Slowly staking out a hold on shallow soils on windblown slopes or holding firm against the claws and teeth of an attacker might not, at first glance, seem like flourishing. But what do these strategies enable? Dozens or even hundreds of summers the fir spends soaking up the sun in alpine regions, or, for porcupettes (the endearing name for baby porcupines), the calm of a nap in a hollowed-out log following a session of shadowboxing each other with their tails.[16] It's clear from these narrow conifers and prickly herbivores that speed is not the only pace of resistance. Possibilities arise from slowing down.

I ONCE TRIED MY HAND AT MAKING SOURDOUGH FROM scratch. With some attention and a warm undisturbed corner, a jar of flour and water becomes frothier by the day as colonies of yeast and bacteria establish themselves.[17] That summer, I tended and nurtured my developing starter, marvelling at the activity burbling up in the jar. After a week or two, it was ready. Whether wild or cultivated, yeast—referring to a range of fungi in the genus Saccharomyces—bubble up and produce heat, providing through fermentation the energy needed to lift dough. We corral this turbulence into productivity in the kitchen, a directed kind of movement in service of culinary outcomes. With sourdough, the yeast agitate for hours, with a pre-fermentation stage followed by periodic folding of dough, hours of waiting in between. I've long been drawn to slower paces of life, though I've never quite been able to maintain them. Over time, I lapsed in my efforts amidst the other pulls of life, more frequently turning to the quick rewards of instant yeast, if I made bread at all.

But early in 2020, coronavirus lockdowns prompted panic buying in North America, leading to supply chain disruptions for, among other commodities, baker's yeast. When those hitches in supply chains in 2020 led to bare shelves in the baking aisles, and my partner and I found ourselves in total isolation for a few weeks, a friend dropped off a batch of her starter for us.[18] This time, it wasn't the same playful experiment as that first summer of sourdough, laden as it was with a sense of necessity, but it did feel more communal—a rare feeling in a time of so little direct connection with others. And with both of us working from home, we had the patience, at least in the early days of lockdowns, for the many rounds of rising and folding and waiting.[19]

As the pandemic's reality settled in and lockdowns continued, and strategies and technologies emerged to enable some semblance of regular online teaching, my time for sourdough baking disappeared. My hours weren't just consumed by screens. Through much of the first full winter of the pandemic, my mornings would go like this: a soft alarm at an absurdly early hour; exchange pyjamas for layers of wool and fleece; pull on a tuque and a headlamp; pile kindling into the cold cast-iron woodstove. All this within a few footsteps in this one-room cabin—desk in one corner, kitchen in another, stove just past the foot of the bed, trying not to awaken my still-sleeping partner. Coffee into a thermos, a little more wood into the fire, ski boots on, and out the door. Most mornings, there was heavy cloud and a fresh layer of powder on the sometimes-plowed road. I would ski a kilometre or so, then tug open a heavy wooden door of another little cabin. No one was sleeping there as I padded around the frosty space, lighting the wood stove, coaxing the warmth. Before my neighbours built a bigger house, this was where they lived; it became a guest cabin and, for a year of the pandemic, a university lecture hall.

In the morning on skis, my breath was visible in the thin beam of my headlamp, scarf tugged up high. I thought about breath often during those early, slowed-down pandemic days, the tenuousness of that involuntary reflex. Each inhalation creates a vacuum in the chest: breathe in, the diaphragm contracts, negative pressure draws air into the lungs; breathe out, positive pressure is restored. We breathe somewhere between twelve and twenty times each minute—at least when our systems are working well. Too many rapid inhalations leave us breathless, panicked. When this happens, it isn't the lack of oxygen, but not quite enough carbon dioxide in our blood that is the trouble. In a time of accelerated climate change, we so often think of carbon as waste, as pollution, as damage; but it, too, is part of our bodies, essential to our lives. Carbon—like work, like speed, like growth—isn't exactly the problem, the thing itself. The trouble, instead, is one of balance.

FIR DEFERRALS: ON SLOWNESS

The regularized flows of heat and light and power needed for highly scheduled industrialized life are ill-suited to the materials on which we depend outside of grid-connected space. At both cabins, I had to pay attention to the short days of light, since they rely on small off-grid systems run by solar panels, with batteries and back-up gasoline-powered generators. After days upon days of snow and cloudy skies, the flow of electricity was noticeable at all times, with the generator thrumming, loud in the -20-something weather. On sunny crisp days, a distinct quietness set in as the energy poured into those tilted panels, refilling the battery bank. I carried water into the cabin in five-gallon blue plastic buckets, although no indoor plumbing made the water limitations easier. Heat, too, had to be managed. With the stove blazing, it was tricky to find equilibrium between steady warmth and sweltering heat. In the mornings, it took an hour or so for the space to warm up; I wore gloves without fingertips to be able to type without freezing. Only once did a colleague notice this detail on one of our online calls; otherwise, my button-down shirt, like everyone else's in those online days, was enough to offer the illusion of shared regularity in the workday.

WHILE MOST OF MY COLLEAGUES HAD INDOOR PLUMBing and the option for electric kettles, I wasn't alone in my sleight of hand over screens. Through rotating lockdowns, others were hiding the signs of their children and pets, of pyjama pants and shared kitchen-tables-turned-desks, reinforcing through omission the myth that we can neatly divide and manage our lives. What the pandemic revealed beyond stark inequalities and uneven vulnerabilities[20] is the incongruity of our home lives—that is, the undervalued and deeply gendered domestic tasks of cleaning and family care and collective life—and our work lives, even for those who are usually economically and socially buffered from these conditions. The inequalities have long been present, but they become evident even to the wealthy when the usual cost-displacing shortcuts are suddenly absent. What so many people have long known has become more broadly visible and harder to obscure.

I think of the advice I've heard in recent years for early-stage professionals, especially women, on how the mythical "work-life balance" might be reached with just the right number of life hacks. Free yourself from domestic chores, it seems, so you can dedicate yourself to your waged work. These strategies are targeted on the wealthy and focused on individual achievement. The key to speed and productivity, in most accounts, is to outsource anything that can be outsourced. The goal is to optimize each hour of the day, with this efficiency made possible through consuming more electricity, more materials, and more labour from others. Online sources suggest that mobile applications can take over tasks such as paying bills and tracking transactions, delivery services can be used for grocery orders, and virtual assistants can be hired for data entry and booking appointments.[21] Plugging in a cord, pressing a button, texting an order: these seem to make both work and time disappear.

Technological solutions are often portrayed as liberating: domestic technologies, for instance, have long been held up as a way to release women from the drudgery of basic household tasks, to upend the uneven gender roles in domestic life. Electricity could power laundry done in machines, washing up in dishwashers, the making of soup and stews in pressure cookers. For some, these innovations promised a revolution against tailored roles in a family that left little room for women's more varied ambitions. But these tools are not themselves the agents of liberation, and they are not necessarily accompanied by equality. In fact, the advertising for these products has focused less on the emancipation of women from housework and more on the increased quality and precision that can be achieved in the domestic realm.[22] Sociologist Bonnie Fox tracked decades of advertising in a women's magazine through the 1900s, documenting the claims they made. With some new appliances, it was suggested that women would gain freedom and time. "You can even leave the house and enjoy a refreshing afternoon with your friends," announced one such ad. But mostly, Fox found, these ads lauded the possibility not for a housewife's leisure, but for her *excellence*. As the marketers of one stove gushed, the neighbours would wonder "why do all her cakes succeed?"[23] These products would ensure consistent, exemplary outcomes in the kitchen and other domestic realms, a constellation of cleanliness, purity, and mastery. Technology might not lead to less work, but to *better* work: the fundamental premise of progress.

But progress as a goal is suspect. These demands remove us from our physical places in unsettling and damaging ways. As historian Bathsheba Demuth writes in her compelling account of industrial incursions into Beringia over centuries, traditional life paths in the Bering Strait region involved shifting dependence on whales, walrus, caribou, seal, fox, and more, and were supplemented and mediated by trade and travel.[24] Ever-expanding production, whether structured through American capitalism or Soviet communism, has tried to overwrite these variable patterns through technology and more intensive harvesting, leaving a trail of devastation in its wake. My own experience of a roaring generator on an overcast winter day in the subarctic is just a scaled-down version of these approaches.

The political scientist Paul Wapner writes of the search that humans, especially and most effectively those who are affluent, have long undertaken for security and for convenience, to avoid the unknown and the uncomfortable.[25] It is not just saving time that people are after, he suggests, but an attempt to escape wildness itself. Wildness: the world as "self-willed," outside of our control and intervention, with its own agency.[26] This involves unpredictability and chaos and uncertainty and complexity.[27] Wildness, Wapner offers, can also be understood not as a specific state, but as an *effect*. This is "the capriciousness of living in a world of others,"[28] he tells us. The problem, Wapner explains, is that wildness, like energy, can't be created or destroyed.[29] Instead, through our efforts to control and avoid it, it is displaced—those who gain predictability and comfort and control and ease push it away from themselves, onto those who are less privileged, and outward to the planet itself. Each of our time-saving strategies comes with costs, and often, these are indirect, dispersed, or dislocated elsewhere and onto others. Daily lives fed by on-demand deliveries carried on the bicycles and backs of underpaid workers; temperature-controlled rooms powered by fossil fuel energy that undoes the thermostat of the planet. The result is wildfires, tropical storms, mass extinctions, increasing social inequality: calm and control within ever-smaller confines for ever-fewer people, and wildness unleashed everywhere else.

A reckoning with the costs of so-called modern conveniences is sometimes taken as an attack on technology and a deliberate retreat from contemporary life—some kind of imaginary construction of a past of widespread social and ecological harmony and equality.[30] But if ever I held such romantic notions, they were dashed by cabin life. Yoking diets to wild yeast—so-called slow food, and the slow making or fixing of anything, really—is decidedly not leisure. It takes so much work to make and clean and repair and tend and grow what we need in our lives; the "from-scratch" versions are not particularly compatible with the push for productivity in the kinds of employment so many are enmeshed in, whether poorly or highly paid, whether gig-based or salaried, whether with benefits and stability or without.

In our quest for efficiency, we swap human labour for the power of stored sunshine held in creatures buried for millennia. We collapse time and space in our moves towards convenience. I can understand why, since when we don't, it is difficult to keep up with modern life. My strict schedule of classes and meetings aligned poorly with the woodstove's demands for more fuel, and I would mute my Zoom microphone to stuff logs into it. That year, my partner and I bought our firewood from an acquaintance in town, cut to length, instead of harvesting it ourselves; we still had to split and stack it, though. A virtual assistant isn't much help chopping kindling, it turns out.

FIR DEFERRALS: ON SLOWNESS

IN WINTER, SUBALPINE FIR REMAIN GREEN, STAY ALIVE, but stop growing. Not only are the trees themselves surviving, but they enable mountain caribou to nibble lichen from their branches through the dark winter months, and grouse to munch their needles.[31] These conifers support a thriving community, even without—or with only very slow—growth. Perhaps this is what we need: not a greening of the economy, exactly, a dubious proposition where somehow perpetual expansion comes without ecological costs, but, instead, an *evergreening* of it. The cycles of fir reject dichotomies, allowing for speed and slowness, for work and idleness.

We must not construct an idealized version of artisanal, low-technology living. But rethinking the pace and distribution of work is not a naive longing for an invented, utopic, slow-moving society. And so that brings us back to the question of pace: *whose* speed is needed—and racing towards *where* and *what*, exactly? Whose labours, and which labours, are barreling ahead, and which ones move—or could move—at a different tempo? The challenges of work can also be the rewards, but only if, in the distribution of those tasks, there is fairness, autonomy, recognition, and respite.

The displaced costs of convenience need serious attention, but there's more to wildness than the distribution of burdens and discomfort. As the philosopher Arne Naess once observed from Tvergastein, his remote and rustic cabin in Norway, "What does a gallon of boiling water mean in the cities? Nothing. At Tvergastein, it is a formidable luxury."[32] I nodded when I read this. There can be great pleasure involved in returning to the basics. But beyond that, brushing up against wildness offers a form of encounter with others and ourselves that can bring us more alive. Instead of Wapner's effect, the writer Gretel Ehrlich describes wildness as a *process*: the "source and fruition at once, as if every river circled round, the mouth eating the tail—and the tail, the source."[33] The origin and the outcome, all at once. Exposure to the elements, a loss of comfort, offers something in return. Seeking wildness brings us into contact with the sublime, something that provokes terror and awe. It leaves us astonished, in the root sense of the word as recounted by the poet Don McKay in his *Strike / Slip* collection: a geologic state, a feeling of being "astounded, astonied, astunned, stopped short / and turned toward stone."[34]

The sublime is a concept or a state or a response that provokes our most intense emotions and, as a result, transforms. Rebecca Solnit writes of the changing understanding of large-scale natural phenomena through the Romantic era, the turn in postmodernity to the sublime as "the aesthetic of vastness, magnificence, power, and fear."[35] The artist Simon Morley offers a parallel historical account of the sublime, our attraction to forces that "cannot be commanded or controlled," that reveal our limits in a world that is beyond us.[36] Seeking encounters with the sublime, or allowing wildness in—"inviting *more* unpredictability, inconvenience, and even danger into our lives,"[37] as Wapner urges—is risky and vulnerable. Living in wildness is slow and difficult and uncomfortable. But it is also, so often, magnificent. Green and white northern lights wavering above the horizon while skiing to work in bone-deep cold. A woodpile foray on a frosty fall afternoon interrupted by a barrage of spruce cones from above, followed by the rapid-fire chattering of a red squirrel. The sound of the creek through the open door of the cabin in spring, as the returning loons call overhead in an edgeless sky.

CHAPTER V

SALMON MIGRATIONS: ON DETOURS

Against the current. Fish scales. Pilgrims. Getting lost. Prospect Park. Painted bunting. Vagrancy laws. Checkers. River piracy. Hydrologic whims. Bedrock. Aeolian and fluvial forces. Woody Guthrie. Columbia River. Mushrooms. In-stream flow. Staying home. Returning home.

Your whole body a muscle pointed upstream. Your whole body, or what is left of it, shedding pieces in the river along the way. Thrashing against the current, those fragments of skin and scales held together by determination or necessity or whatever it is that urges you onward, pulls you home. Out in the Pacific, you could be silver or red or pink, the regal King, the staple chum— your hooked-nose family revered on the coast since, as it is said, time immemorial. Up any of the watersheds of the western coast of North America, of Turtle Island, you make your way to the one place you know among all possible places in a land laced with streams, bevelled with lakes. Past beaver dams and rockfall, up chutes and cascades, through rapids and around whirlpools; pausing in eddies, but never for long, avoiding bear paws and eagle strikes. If you were on the east coast, from the Atlantic, you might take leaping journeys between ocean and freshwater several times in your life; here, though, you make your pilgrimage a single time only, following magnetism or memory or the specific taste of water.[1] As poet Anne Carson once

CHAPTER V

wrote, "Pilgrims were people to whom things happened that happen only once."[2]

WE DON'T KNOW, I SUPPOSE, WHETHER SALMON EVER lose their way. We know of blockages and barriers, the rockfall and stick-and-mud beaver dams and concrete human ones that prevent access to upstream waters, and of fishing boats and nets that intervene along their routes. But do they ever come to a fork in the river and not know which branch to take? I wonder this, too, about birds in migration. In 2015, a painted bunting showed up in New York City's Prospect Park, far from his fellow buntings' usual flyway between their wintering grounds in the southeastern and central United States and their summer habitat on the Gulf Coast and in the northern Caribbean.[3] Was he blown off course by a storm? Did he mix up north and south, taking off confidently and erroneously in exactly the wrong direction? Scientists have not yet settled on an explanation for these stray individuals who turn up far from their usual routes and habitats, and it may be there is no single reason.[4] Perhaps he chose to let go of duty and destination, allowed himself "a voluptuous surrender," as writer Rebecca Solnit describes the process of losing oneself, "utterly immersed in what is present so that its surroundings fade away."[5] That bunting, so fully alive in the act of flight that he forgot where he was, where he was going, until he landed among red maples and eastern white oaks,[6] realizing his error only when he saw the iconic white terra-cotta Beaux Arts Boathouse, now home to the Audubon Center[7]—a fitting, perhaps, if unintended, arrival near the site of a nature initiative run by a society named after famed ornithologist John James Audubon. Solnit considers this state of self-erasure, of being lost in a moment, as open, transformative, filled with both "uncertainty and mystery."[8] It might be that the bunting was seeking this kind of experiential possibility; we don't really know. What we do know is that the term for a bird found far from its expected range is "vagrant."

SALMON MIGRATIONS: ON DETOURS

Vagrants are, varyingly, wanderers, vagabonds, homeless, irregularly employed, inconstant, outlawed. In the 1300s, according to the scholar of English James Kearney, laws against vagrancy were tools of the English state to ensure the availability of workers to the moneyed class. These were a response to the shortage of labour—a "scarcity of servants," according to statutes of the time—resulting from so many deaths during the bubonic plague epidemic,[9] a shortage that the powerful feared would embolden workers to demand higher wages, better conditions. To protect the prevailing economic order, mobility itself— the lack of a fixed address, for instance—became the target of legislation. These laws continued in the centuries to follow. Another English scholar, Andrew Knighton, lists the punishments meted out to those accused of vagrancy in the 1400s and 1500s under King Henry III, from whippings to the loss of part of an ear to being forcibly exiled "to the place where he was born, or last dwelt for three years, and there put himself to labor."[10] The unwillingness of potential workers to labour for others for meagre wages could be mitigated, the logic went, by limiting mobility. Against the law, too, was the unmeasured provision of help and supplies to those asking for it, with restrictions on almsgiving starting in the 1300s.[11] Work was effectively mandated for those who had not inherited land and wealth of their own, and where it could happen was restricted.

Strictures against the movements of the poorer members of society spilled over into colonial interpretations of places beyond the borders of England. As the writer J. M. Coetzee finds in the accounts of British travellers and authorities, the perceived shortcomings of the Khoikhoi people of the southern Cape of Good Hope region—their reluctance to engage in waged labour, their communal ownership structures, and their nomadic pastoralism—mapped on to the sins and offenses of laziness and sloth, thievery and trespass, and vagrancy that were prohibited in the heart of the empire.[12] Coetzee tracks down a series of British travellers' writings about the Cape from the 1600s and 1700s, finding echoed lines about the idleness, laziness, and indolence of the people there—at least of the men, in a rare recognition of the gendered nature of many household labours.[13] These racist accounts are painful to read, even with Coetzee's commentary and critique, and I wouldn't direct anyone to the text. The people of other places are reluctant to be enslaved, these travellers' accounts lament. And not just in Southern Africa. The historian Shino Konishi documents similar perspectives expressed about Indigenous peoples in Australia, particularly when they refused to act as servants, unwilling to carry the gear of European arrivals.[14] The colonists could not imagine that Aboriginal people on the northwest coast of Australia would not be drawn into service by the allure of European fashions, with clothing offered up to persuade them—unsuccessfully—to haul six-gallon water barrels back to their ships.[15] It was easier for these colonists to imagine laziness and sloth than autonomy in the people they met, and ignorance rather than resistance in their refusal to acquiesce to servitude.

British elites and aristocrats saw the mobility and recreation of those assumed to be lower in class and stature than themselves as a problem to be managed, yet they viewed their own explorations and pleasures, it seems, as the mark of their superiority. When voyage was paired with plunder, and leisure with prestige, the wealthy and powerful viewed the pursuits in high regard; when undertaken absent visible reward, though, they were renamed vagrancy and indolence. The distinctions were drawn by their support of or threat to the prevailing social order. The problem for these upper-class observers, whether at home or abroad, was not that hours were spent away from work, filled with travel or entertainment, but rather that those with less privilege seemed to lack the ambition for acquisition that accompanied their own endeavours. This willful misreading of the refusal of subservience was used as a justification for the further enclosure of land and exclusion of people from the places and practices that had sustained them, and—in parallel—for limits on dispossessed peoples' ability to move away in response. Idleness was to be regulated and restricted and punished.

Then, and now. In New York City, tens of thousands of people are unhoused,[16] and the city has long developed and adopted restrictive measures on the actions of those who live on the streets. In 2001, for instance, the New York Civil Liberties Union opposed a bill under consideration by the State Assembly that included provisions against "aggressive begging."[17] The bill did not just specify restrictions against menace and harassment but also against "loitering for the purpose of aggressive begging."[18] As the Civil Liberties Union explains, such laws leave open to interpretation the intent of those idling about in public places—what makes for malicious loitering versus benign forms of hanging around? Work, it seems, can enable a distinction. One example from their memo is illustrative. They write, "the prohibition against sitting or lying down does not apply to persons who sit while engaged in an artistic activity on sidewalks,"[19] and go on to note that no reason is offered "for why that activity is less an inconvenience or safety hazard than sitting for non-artistic activities (such as hearing discussions on topics of public interest or playing sedentary games such as checkers) or for no purpose at all." For no purpose at all. The unproductive diversions of checkers; the languor of inactivity. These were threats to those in power in the 1300s and remain so in the 2000s.

It seems fitting that the vagrant painted bunting landed in Prospect Park. The park was designed as a place for all, regardless of status and means. The landscape architect Frederick Law Olmsted, upon visiting the grounds of a Welsh castle, had lamented the inaccessibility of natural spaces to those without privilege, wondering "Is it right and best that this should be for the few, the very few of us?"[20] Until his mid-thirties, when he started work on Central Park, Olmsted had been—in his own words—"a loitering, self-indulgent, dilettante sort of man."[21] His own loitering may have been just a sidenote to a distinguished career, planning Prospect Park, Central Park, and dozens of other green spaces around the United States in the late 1800s;[22] but we might imagine, as per Slouka's suggestion that idleness provides space to imagine the world otherwise, that Olmsted's period of dabbling and dallying was instead a necessary precursor to the concrete expression of his political convictions through public parks. He wrote against slavery,[23] against the "nervous tension" and "over-anxiety" that accompanied city life,[24] in favour of a national park system,[25] and for widespread access to nature and art as a source of balm[26]—and indeed, of democratization, of possibility beyond and across class lines.[27] As with so many grand historical figures[28]—including Audubon, whose legacy includes both owning slaves and cataloguing the birds of North America[29]—Olmsted's social ambitions were laced with contradictions, including a checkered history with collaborators and actions of his own.[30] His famed and now-beloved Central Park—accessible to all, regardless of wealth and stature, at least in theory[31]—was only built through the use of eminent domain laws,[32] dislocating the residents of Seneca Village and disrupting a site of Black political activism and empowerment in the process.[33]

Whether purposefully or unintentionally unmoored and out of place, the bunting might be seen, at least in some readings, as a drifter, a tramp, a dangerous idler—upending the disciplined and predictable rhythms of seasonal migrations. But in a world gone awry, in a time of rapid climate change, I doubt that lone bunting is shirking its duties, though am unsure if he is confused and adrift or purposefully trying out different habitats for the future. Perhaps he is a pilgrim, making a singular journey; perhaps there is something sacred in the East River, dividing Long Island from Manhattan, worthy of a once-in-a-lifetime odyssey. We will never know the motivations of that multicoloured songbird, but on a walk through that park in Brooklyn, we can readily imagine him lifted by thermal updrafts, drifting past the familiar and out over unknown terrain, surrendering to that wider mystery.

IN 2016, THE CBC ANNOUNCED THAT A RIVER IN THE southwest of the Yukon territory had disappeared, nearly overnight.[34] The *Yukon News* called it the "vanishing river."[35] Between April and

May of that year, the Kaskawulsh Glacier that fed the Slim's River—or Ä'äy Chù, as it has been known for longer, its Southern Tutchone name—had finally retreated far enough that its meltwater opened a new channel through ice. The water tumbled through the new gap, draining eastwards to the Kaskawulsh River then south to the Pacific Ocean, rather than into Kluane Lake and out through the Yukon River to the Bering Sea.[36]

With the rivers, it is not just water that rewrites the landscape; the ground underneath, too, participates in these revisions. As the writer Ellen Meloy observes, "Unless it scuffs up your shoes, few people take serious note of the bedrock that underlies their lives." As she describes the desert landscapes of the US Southwest, home of side-blotched lizards and juniper trees and claret cups, she attends to what is underfoot: "Around here bedrock—inert as well as friable and movable—is the main event. This seemingly immutable landscape spends much of its time coming apart."[37] And so, too, the land moves in Ä'äy Chù's subarctic surrounds, a part of the earth that, like the red sand mesa of Meloy's home,[38] bears the signature of water, the tracks of wind. To understand the river, we must look to the mountain. Ä'äy Chù translates as "By Itself Water," and is fed from the nearby "By Itself" mountain, in the St. Elias range.[39] What happens to the mountain is echoed in the flow.

The CBC article suggested, "It's possible the Slims River was only ever just a temporary variance in the landscape — a 300-odd year hydrological whim."[40] The whims of water: streams wind sinuously across the landscape, with riffles or steps and pools, interspersed with runs and glides. Speed and angle shift the oxygenation, turbidity, temperature, and sediment loads of rivers, with water degrading or aggrading the stream bed. Rivers silt up, are scoured out, loop around, overflow, braid. They are, as the writer David James Duncan writes, "meandering and free-flowing."[41] The so-called "river piracy"[42]—the Kaskawulsh's thieving of the Slim's water—brings us back to the mobility we so often have constrained with enclosures, whether rip-rap and concrete for water or penalties and ordinances for people.[43] A vagabond river, we might say, the vagrant waters.

Yet the water's rerouting was unsurprising for those paying attention to climate change, even those to whom the Athapaskan language was unknown. In this case, it seems more hopeful than truthful that this was a river asserting its independence, flowing where it wants. That is, for observers tracking the retreat of this and other glaciers, this was clearly not just a moment of changing "hydrological whim" but a visible response to the often obscured and dispersed consequences of unrelenting carbon emissions. With human intervention as a driver of these changes, the rerouted water reminds us that Newton's classical laws of motion still have traction. Actions have reactions. But that only takes us so far when it comes to integrated and complex systems: while the Kaskawulsh Glacier was retreating, others in the St. Elias range are surge glaciers—that is, they advance in quick bursts.[44] Overloading carbon in the atmosphere alters circulation, shakes up regimes of moisture. On average, compared with the pre-industrial period, the Earth's surface temperatures in 2020 were more than 1 degree Celsius warmer, and in our record of planet temperatures, the ten hottest years have all occurred since 2005.[45] But in places like the southern Yukon where winter days usually dip into the minus 20s and often colder,[46] warmer—when it's wet—still looks like snowfall, not snowmelt. Meltwater and redirected flows are not the only response to a warmer world, then; it is the extremes that find their expression in this new system. *That* things will change is predictable; *how* things will change at any given moment or in each specific place remains mysterious to us, at least until the waters are already flowing elsewhere, or not flowing at all.

> Uncle Sam took up the challenge in the year of 'thrity-three,
> For the farmer and the factory and all of you and me,

He said, "Roll along, Columbia, you can ramble to the sea,
But river, while you're rambling, you can do some work for me."[47]

The American musician Woody Guthrie might be best known for his politics, his songs of protest, his advocacy for civil rights and unions and social reform and against war and fascism.[48] He was surveilled by the FBI, deemed an activist and communist, declared seditious.[49] But he was not, it must be clear, against government or public works. In fact, in 1941, while still in his 20s—having fled Oklahoma's Dust Bowl and weathered the hungry and threadbare Great Depression—he was hired in Oregon by the Bonneville Power Administration to write the music for a film they were making about public power and dams.[50] A series of odes, it turned out, to the possibilities of harnessing these rushing rivers to serve social welfare, to provide work for the unemployed, to enable democracy to prevail. The Bonneville Power Administration, a federal agency formed only a few years earlier, had been tasked with expanding electricity provision through dams along the Columbia River, organizing transmission and sales, in a bid to challenge the control of the then-dominant private power utility in the region.[51] Guthrie's songs captured the enthusiasm of America, and beyond, for the transformative possibilities embodied in dams.

Dams really do seem to capture our collective imagination. Other than disasters—floods, droughts, cyclones, mudslides—dams are what we envision when we think about power and water. Not the stick-and-mud constructions of beavers, of course, piling up in ponds and blocking culverts, but behemoth structures of concrete, steel, and iron drilled into and blasted from bedrock. Massive reservoirs countering gravity, creating the illusion of placid lakes out of the force and fury of rivers, corralling unruly water through turbines and spillways. Producing roughly 20 percent of the world's electricity,[52] hydropower dams wrestle the movement of water into energetic, containable, and transferrable *work*. With output measured in gigawatts, the largest dams in the world—among the top, Brazil and Paraguay's Itaipu on the Paraná

CHAPTER V

River; China's Three Gorges on the Yangtze River; Venezuela's Guri complex on the Caroni River; the US's Grand Coulee on the Columbia River[53]—generate enormous quantities of power. In the process, they also generate enormous displacement. The Three Gorges Dam, for example, accounts for about a tenth of China's electricity needs,[54] and, with a reservoir spanning just over 100,000 hectares, displaced well over a million people.[55] Estimates suggest the number of people displaced by dams worldwide may be over 80 million.[56] I have not found estimates of the number of other species displaced or damaged by dams, but indirect measures suggest it is worrying indeed. Some 20 percent of the entire global population of tigers has been dislocated for hydropower;[57] the best dam turbines still have fish kill rates of five to ten percent.[58]

But although dams have a heft and weight that seems immovable, and cause such immense damage, they are not invulnerable to the unpredictability of water. Those extreme events that come to mind when thinking of water and power pose threats to dams, and to the communities downstream. When the Kaskawulsh Glacier's retreat changed the course of Ä'äy Chù, it was news but not disaster. This is not always the case when shifts take place in geologic and cryogenic systems. In February 2021, part of the Nanda Devi Glacier in India, near its borders with China and Nepal, broke off. The event triggered a mud and rockslide that washed away the Rishiganga dam, killing at least eighteen people and leaving hundreds more missing.[59] Waters flowing out of place and those not flowing at all both pose threats to our industrial orders: built to produce; built from production. Rivers, like beavers, follow their own laws, resisting human efforts to regularize and control their movements. The rivers' unsteadying of human ambitions is aided by their underlying bedrock, among other things. "[D]ams have a lot going against them," said writer and former political aide Jamie Workman, who once served on the Secretariat of the World Commission on Dams, outlining that "seismic shifts shake them from below; water pressures scour them from behind; silt fills them upstream; the sun evaporates faster than cities can drink; methane emissions accelerate a fast-changing climate that brings drought followed by deluge on scales for which dams were not built to cope."[60] Unruly water, indeed, with its rebellious companions of rock and sun and air.

UNRULY: TO BE DISRUPTIVE AND ROWDY; TO BE WILLful and lawless; to not be amenable to discipline. While unruliness may be filled with energy—it is restless, active, boisterous, rambunctious—this energy is not aimed towards a clear and specific end; nothing that can be measured, controlled, or exchanged. Such a state is at odds with organized, orderly labour. It is rarely a synonym for idleness, though, which is more likely to stir up thoughts of languid motion, sleepy yawns, and reclining bodies. And yet, both unruly and idle states refuse to operate along productive, directed lines—at least, not ones that add up to legibility, predictability, and accumulation.

Is the escape from directed outcomes the same as freedom? In her philosophical examination of laziness, theorist Zuzanna Ladyga considers the connection between doing nothing and freedom. She observes that "laziness, it seemed, was for [philosopher Theodor] Adorno the ultimate symbol of an unruly thought"[61] and so opened possibilities for individual autonomy. In contrast, though, she notes that other philosophers "singled out laziness as the exact opposite of contemplation"[62]—and such unconsidered existence was not, for them, any expression of a flourishing life. These debates rage on amongst philosophers, some pairing and defending the restless and the listless—the unruly and the lazy—against the exhortation of others for studiousness and focused intent. To avoid melancholy, advised the seventeenth century writer Robert Burton, "be not solitary, be not idle,"[63] suggesting "laborious studies" for men, and arts and crafts—"curious Needle-workes, Cut-workes, spinning, bone-lace, and many pretty devises of their owne making"—for women;[64] not so different from fourteenth century counsel to avoid "the synne of... slouthe."[65] The debate hinges, it seems from a distance, on whether the good life in its ideal form must be *productive*.

In an essay, anthropologist Anna Tsing announces her delight in the discovery of chanterelles and king boletes, as she reflects on the blurry, unruly edges between domesticated and wild, controlled and autonomous, individual and collective that are illuminated by the mushroom.[66] With mushrooms, there are symbioses and relationships, Tsing observes, and sometimes exploitation. Interspecies dependence can lead to mutual flourishing, as with Douglas fir seedlings and slippery jack (*Suillus*) fungi, resources exchanged across species lines. But interactions can also irritate or damage their hosts or neighbours, as with *Puccina graminis*, she tells us, that live on barberry while producing spores that kill wheat. Not all gifts are welcome.

Broadly, Tsing's writings remind us that we are not able to live in a world absent flora, fauna, mycorrhiza, and the labours of others that are, from our perspective, unruly—not focused on our aims, directives, contemplations, or concerns; sometimes, even, working against them. We often struggle to value the unruly work of others around us, and further, often fail to even see that work at all. Or we deliberately ignore it, since it doesn't fit our ambitions. Like water running through a stream, undisturbed. Guthrie sang of the Columbia River on its way to the ocean spinning a few turbines along the way—just a little work, as the river rolls on—but that's a misleading account of the downstream flow from large hydropower facilities, let alone from other uses of water.

Consider that in the American West, colonial water rights have been predicated on extraction. In 1922, the seven states along the Colorado River divided up its flow.[67] They thought they were leaving a sixth or so of the river to continue downstream to Mexico, where the Colorado pours into the Sea of Cortez.[68] In the compact they signed, of the five-sixths claimed by the US, four of the states (Colorado, Wyoming, Utah, New Mexico) were slated to share half the anticipated water, leaving half to the others (Arizona, California, Nevada).[69] But they had estimated the river's flow in an unusually wet year; in most years, it turned out, the compact's provisions allocated more water than actually existed.[70] Beyond the injustices that arise in a cross-border sense from the upstream overuse of shared waters, the arrangements entirely exclude any responsibility to the river itself, and the myriad water users who are not bipedal.

From a legal perspective, water rights had to be "exploited"—that is, until quite recently, water left in river beds was considered wasted and rights to it were forfeited. Along with arriving early enough to the waterway to secure some of its flow—the principle of "prior appropriation" central to determining allocations in times of shortages[71]—potential users had to prove they would put the water to "beneficial use." In states such as Colorado, if a water rights holder stops withdrawing the water, or as much of the water (by, perhaps, conserving water through more efficient irrigation), they risk having the government deem those rights as having been abandoned.[72] That water can then be reallocated to other users. If they expanded production in the future, that water would no longer be available to those original rights-holders. Use it or lose it, so the saying goes.[73]

Beneficial uses, in earlier iterations, are usually understood as consumptive uses: farming, ranching, mining, drinking. Anything that involves moving water elsewhere and making something else. Water plus work deserves recognition, in this account. This interpretation follows the Lockean tradition of how land becomes property, where ownership is the result of the application of labour, and enclosure the best protection for it. But labour, in such readings, is so narrowly defined. Water laws have tended not to consider the work of the water itself, and of the other creatures that live in and from it over, in the case of the Colorado River, its more than thousand-mile length—blue suckers and red shiners and largemouth bass swimming through; belted kingfishers and scissor-tailed flycatchers and barred owls overhead; blue- and green-winged teal paddling and willets wading; armadillos and coyote, rat snakes and rattlesnakes, eastern cottonwood, black willow, bald cypress, roughleaf dogwood.

CHAPTER V

This is hardly the start of a list. There are some pathways for defending these wider rights to water. Several decades of legislation defend the protection of "instream flow"—Oregon, the first state in the US west to implement such laws, did so in 1987[74]—where rights need not be demonstrated through withdrawal; these can, in some jurisdictions, be held by individuals, in others, only by the state.[75] In state laws, beneficial uses can be defined as non-consumptive ones: for pollution abatement, fish and wildlife, recreation, even aesthetic enjoyment.[76] But defenses of such uses—beyond serving the interests of humans alone—remain uneven across place and along waterways. In some places, additional efforts are underway: in Colorado, for instance, a program was started in 2013 to allow water users to join state-approved water conservation programs that would reduce their water withdrawals without risk of losing their rights.[77] Many of these strategies reinforce the private property regimes that have caused these troubling conditions of overuse—such as relying on water markets as the tools to control overconsumption, with the intent of more efficiently organizing use,[78] and perhaps, as a side benefit, enabling private investors to profit.[79] Still, laws and practices are changing, thanks to concerted efforts from advocates for the winged and feathered and scaled and hoofed and rooted lives along the river.[80] This is urgent, as drought and low snowpacks threaten water supplies even as populations along the river grow, and, in some years, even the mightiest of rivers no longer reach the ocean.

"THE MOST RADICAL THING YOU CAN DO IS STAY HOME." I first came across this reflection from the poet Gary Snyder in an essay by Rebecca Solnit.[81] In it, Solnit considers Snyder's claim in the context of climate change and finds some merit to the assertion. Of the busy flurry of movement, she writes:

> From outer space, the privileged of this world must look like ants in an anthill that's been stirred with a stick: everyone constantly rushing around in cars and planes for work and pleasure, for meetings, jobs, conferences, vacations, and more. This is bad for the planet, but it's not so good for us either.[82]

But Solnit does not offer a straightforward reinforcement of Snyder's claim. Instead, she turns her attention to the many people who, for reasons of conflict or extreme weather events or poverty or other forms of dispossession, are forcibly relocated. Those who must leave their homes, not by unfettered choice or desire and often under dangerous and precarious conditions, do not need lessons in restraint from travel; for them, as Solnit writes, "the situation looks quite different."[83] Peace, safety, climate stability, defense of livelihoods, subsistence possibilities, access to lands and waters and seeds: these are the conditions needed to live in place. Solnit asks what it might look like, then, to defend the *right* to stay home; not an urging of individual action, but instead the radical social and economic change that might enable families to remain in their communities, on their homelands.

Read in the early 2020s, Solnit's piece takes on new poignancy. During the Covid-19 pandemic, with widespread lockdowns affecting much of the world, we saw a shift in the patterns of movement of the privileged and wealthy: work, school, social, and family lives constrained in place and moved online, cross-border mobility limited and reduced. Part of the "staying home" exhortation fit the situation—more people spent more time right there in their kitchens and living rooms and bedrooms and, if lucky, their backyards. But this doesn't quite seem to be what Snyder in the 1970s or Solnit in 2008 was thinking about. For most, it certainly was not about "reclaiming home as a rhythmic, coherent kind of time," as Solnit hoped might be possible, or the digging into home that Snyder thought might cause us to take responsibility for the place.[84] Neither were, I'm sure, thinking of the shift as the result of a new infectious disease. Still, in spite of this different driver,

CHAPTER V

Solnit's observations offer insight into the contemporary moment: for those with precarious employment and limited options, the pandemic did not mean staying put. Grocery store clerks, delivery drivers, elder care workers, nurses, truck drivers, and others in what became known as "essential services" continued to go to work, take public transit, spend their days in close quarters with strangers, be exposed again and again to the virus. The right to stay home, indeed.

The salmon swimming upstream know in their disintegrating bodies the necessity of both: of vagrancy and of staying—or, more accurately, *returning*—home. And the connective pathways between the two that allow those freedoms, the conditions that make it possible for them to travel from spawning beds to the wide open oceans, to spend years out at sea, and at the end to find their way back through winding streams to those same gravel patches they came from. For each salmon, a journey taken only once; but, when taken together, adding up over years to well-worn routes, edging deeper those pilgrims' tracks not just for the next generations of fish, but also for the birds, the bears, the trees.

CHAPTER VI

WILLOW ROOTS: ON RESTRAINT

Field guides. Hybridization. Ptarmigan molts. Stunted growth. Genotypes. Suburban sprawl. Tulip trees. Birdsong. River names. Buckbrush. Categorization. Half-Earth. Overburden. Holding back. Holding up. Habitat. Unplugging. Frolicking. Sacrifice. Play. Wonder.

I still don't know which willows surround the cabin. The land around us is dense with shrubs, wet in spring, rivulets in new places each year as the water finds its way down the gently sloping banks to the creek. The budding leaves tell me whether it is shrub birch or willow—the former small circles of green, and the latter elongated lances, pointed at the ends—but that's where my classifying ends. In late May every year, with branches still bare and frost most mornings, it seems impossible to imagine that anything could hide in these thickets. But June comes, and with it the buds and then leaves and by mid-month, it's impossible to know where the dark-eyed juncos and song sparrows and orange-crowned warblers have their nests—all I see when I walk down to the rushing creek are flashes of wings as they flit through brush. I know from the guidebooks that the willows in this "spruce-willow-birch zone" could be grey-leaved or tea-leaved, woolly or Barratt's or Barclay's, or others, too. But the distinguishing features escape me. I am reassured, though, by the cautionary words of a man who was top of his field in the study of European willows, who came to catalogue North American willows during World War I. "In determining willows one is only too often entirely misled at first, and even by a slow and careful examination it is not always possible to determine the proper identity of the plant,"[1] wrote C. K. Schneider in 1919, referring to the bewildering array of characteristics of the many species of willow. I am not alone in having only a vague acquaintance with the willows around me in the subarctic, which often are summed up simply as "*Salix* spp."

Schneider's understated counsel on the difficulties of salicology was offered up by George W. Argus in 2004 to readers of his field guide to willows in "Alaska, the Yukon Territory and adjacent regions." Argus explains the difficulties more specifically—among the many challenges presented by the phenotypes of willows, which change according to environment and developmental stages: hairs appear and are lost; catkins elongate over time and may be attached at the branch or grow on a shoot; stipules, those small leaf-like appendages at the base of leaves, may disappear with age; flowers are of one sex only on a given plant; access to water and nutrients can change leaf shape, size, and position. Most confusingly of all, *Salix* species hybridize. Not only are species themselves inconsistent across specimens, but species blend and blur, foiling the hopeful taxonomist in their effort to categorize and requiring us all to restrain from quick judgements.

Such identification challenges are not limited to willows but spill out, too, to their avian compatriots. Willow ptarmigan, *Lagopus lagopus*, have up to nineteen subspecies, although the online crowd-sourced iNaturalist site notes, "the taxonomy is confused."[2] Mostly, the uncertainty results from the birds' multiple seasonal plumage changes. White in the long winters of the Arctic and subarctic, with a black fringe on the tail, and mottled through the rest of the year—mostly chestnut brown, but with a rusty mix of reds, blacks, whites, and golds—these feather-footed grouse are the largest of the ptarmigan species.[3] Complicating identification, in the British moors these grouse remain in reddish-brown plumage year-round, and subsist mainly on heather.[4] They sport vibrant orange-red eye crowns when breeding;

spend non-breeding months in flocks; prefer shrubby low areas above tree-line.[5] In their North American tundra habitats, willow ptarmigan live among the snowshoe hares, linked by ecosystem and linguistics, with the Greek-derived *Lagopus* meaning "hare-footed"—a nod to the parallels of furred and feathered feet.[6]

Do *L. lagopus* distinguish among the many shrub willow species that confound even the professional botanist? Are they seeking the soft hair-covered seeds of the shining willow (*Salix lucida*), or drawn to the reddish stems of MacCalla's willow (*S. maccalliana*), or pulled to stream margins to taste the tawny floral bracts of the long-beaked willow (*S. bebbiana*)? In the deep snow of winter, shrub willow and birch become crucial sources of food for the ptarmigan, so they must eat what they can, indiscriminate in their hungers. Able to browse only on the tallest willows that poke out of snowdrifts, their appetites stunt the growth of *Salix*.[7] In the spring, they shift their winter-white plumage to blend with lichen, rock, and—with those eye crowns—the bright berries of kinnikinnick (*Arctostaphylos uva-ursi*—the *ursus* for bear and *uva* for grape, known, from this, as red bearberry). As they change colour, perhaps they also shift their palate, searching for certain stages of willow on which to munch: the necessity of winter replaced by a dazzling array of options for buds, catkins, twigs, leaves, with species less important than texture, taste, variety. The species lines identified through Western science—first by phenotype with naturalists in the field, and now genotype, with plants pulled apart and parceled into test tubes and petri dishes, spun in thermal cyclers and examined under UV light—are constructs, of course.[8] The willow ptarmigan surely know far more of the distinctions among the plants that sustain them. But perhaps they hold back on judgement through categorization, with each bird preferring to encounter each willow as an individual: a source of comfort, a place of rest, a thin branch drawing the border between breath and stillness in the coldest nights.

CHAPTER VI

ONE SUMMER IN UNIVERSITY, I LANDED A JOB WITH A provincial Ministry of Natural Resources,[9] tasked with circumnavigating the remnant woodlots of southwestern Ontario to find nesting birds, putting out transects to count salamanders, enumerating shrubs and groundcover in small vegetation plots. I was by far the least experienced of the team, having made my way through my teenage years with distinctly non-avian obsessions: joining letter-writing campaigns with Amnesty International and paddling kayaks, rather than noticing eye rings and undertail coverts and committing to memory the mnemonics of birdsong. But I had awakened to the thrill of ecology during a first-year lecture course and was sure my future would be in field biology. My unbridled enthusiasm must have compensated for my missing knowledge during what could only be described as a complete disaster of an interview, and I found myself that summer discovering that a landscape I had known mainly as fields of corn and canola and tobacco, with rapidly encroaching suburban sprawl, was also home to tulip trees and hooded warblers, wood thrush and jewelweed. How had I missed this before? I was determined to make up for lost time.

Collecting individuals into groups is not always an erasure of the specific and the distinct, I soon learned. I traversed woodlots with Roger Tory Petersen and Audubon field guides tucked in my pockets, different versions of the same abundance of species that surrounded me, as indistinct calls and warbles and trills began to resolve themselves into identifiable species. I fell asleep most nights that summer to tapes of birdsong—a calm voice intoning the name, a brief melody or buzz or chip, the name repeated—trying desperately to learn these new languages, to know a landscape by its voices. I had to reorient my listening, in part to compensate for my still-beginner skills with binoculars, where I'd finally get the lenses into focus just as the bird flew away, nothing but a blur of motion in the dappled light of the canopy. What I wanted that summer, more than anything, was to blend myself with the forest, to be indistinct from the sugar maples and white oak. I tried not to make the ovenbird nervous in her journey to her woven domed nest in the understory, though I never did achieve this. Mine was a singular purpose: to become intimate with the land I grew up in. I had returned to Ontario from some high school years out west, a region I loved and still love fiercely, and one that would call me back in my adult years. But I needed that summer to learn the terrain of my childhood in a new way, to become less estranged from it, and so less resigned to its destruction by strip malls and highways and monocultures.

The river I grew up near was so beaten by industrial pollution that we were warned at the city rowing club not to trail our hands in the water over the side of the boat, and especially not to flip, at risk of skin rashes. What I only learned later was that the river's Anishinaabemowin name, Deshkan Ziibi,[10] translates to Antler River,[11] gesturing to the branched structure that forks near what is now the city centre. In these lands of the Anishinaabe, Haudenosaunee, Lūnaapéewak, Wendat, and Attawandaron,[12] the river sustained many nations before the Carolinian forests were replaced by subdivisions, before blight wiped out the sweet chestnut.[13] The river's colonial English name—the Thames—has no such connections, recalling instead the Cotswolds, foggy cobbled streets, the distant North Sea. What if I had always known the river's earlier name? If I had grown up recognizing velvety ungulate bones reflected in those waters, rather than a second-rate replica of a famous waterway from another continent, would I have seen it as distinct, seen it for itself? There, with the black willows and cottonwoods, might have been a sycamore tree that had been alive since before the colonial renaming of the river, a line connecting the past to the future, and the possibilities still held in those flowing waters.

As Kenyan writer Ngũgĩ wa Thiong'o recalled on another continent, "All those places had names before – names that pointed to other memories, older memories."[14] Names are being lost so quickly, and with them, ways of knowing—each representing what anthropologist and writer Wade Davis describes as "a flash of the human spirit."[15] Within recent human lifetimes, we have seen the disappearance of thousands of languages; over two decades ago, Davis warned, "Linguists tell us that within another century, this diversity may be condensed to only a few hundred languages."[16] Even without entire lexicons disappearing, we can still lose a world of words within widely spoken tongues. This impoverishes us, the writer Robert Macfarlane tells us, as he documents the wide-ranging "place words" across the British Isles, hoping to stave off this diminishment and rekindle a more varied vocabulary for the living world around us.[17] Terms specific to Devon, Shetland, Exmoor, Yorkshire; expressions emerging out of the East Anglian coast, the Norfolk fens, the Outer Hebridean islands. When we lose the descriptors for the specifics of a place, Macfarlane tells us, "so our competence for understanding and imagining possible relationships with nonhuman nature is correspondingly depleted."[18] Remembering the names that came before colonial and homogenizing orders swept through— like Ä'äy Chù, pointing to its source, before that water was diverted to the Kaskawulsh; like the echoes of Eastern elk, now extirpated from southern Ontario, in the furcating waters of Deshkan Ziibi —might remind us that these lands and waters and the lives they sustain are not newly emerged, not just there for the taking.

THE LOCAL NICKNAME IN NORTHERN BC AND THE southern Yukon for a low-lying mix of willow, shrub birch (*Betula glandulosa*), shrubby cinquefoil (*Potentilla fruticosa*), soapberry (*Shepherdia canadensis*), and other tangled branches is "buckbrush." In this name, there is an indeterminacy, a willingness to collect a wide-ranging set of leaves and blossoms into a shared identity. I wonder sometimes if with this imprecise nomenclature I am evading the responsibility to recognize these distinct lives. But maybe, instead, the term is a helpful abdication of an eagerness to compartmentalize the world. I suppose it depends on my response: troubling if I take indistinctness as permission to raze the brush, ignoring the diverse beings wound among the branches; useful if I pay closer attention to the specifics, and to who else wanders the subalpine thickets—the possibility, in every step, that the next will reveal a moose and calf, grazing; or a black bear, coat shining, mouth stuffed with dandelion petals; or the sudden eruption of wings, a pair of white-crowned sparrows flushed up from below. In a world of fuzzy edges between this type and the next, holding back on certainty—and thus on exploitation—seems a measured and rational response, though not one widely adopted in this accelerating world, a dominant culture that defines value through productivity. Suspending judgement; waiting to see.

Holding back, some ecologists propose, requires radical land use changes across the planet. One strategy, embraced by some in the conservation community, can be summed up by a slogan: "nature needs half."[19] In international negotiations over conservation, states have long bickered over targets for protected areas as ecological systems continue to crumble. Under the Convention on Biological Diversity, an international treaty launched in 1992, many states agreed to the "Aichi Biodiversity Targets," setting out commitments to conserve "through effectively and equitably managed, ecologically representative and well connected systems of protected areas and other effective area-based conservation measures" at least 17 percent of the land and 10 percent of the oceans by 2020.[20] These targets have not been met.[21] But even if they had been, argue some, it wouldn't be enough—even doubled, they're too low.[22] Fifty percent. That's the amount of the Earth, at minimum, that needs to be left alone by humans, say those critics. Half for people, half for the rest of the species.[23] A "Half-Earth," as a project launched by biologist E. O. Wilson proposes, to protect the richness of nonhuman life.[24] The phrase has been echoed by conservation groups and scientists, including through a network coordinated by the WILD Foundation that calls itself by its goal: Nature Needs Half.[25]

Restraint and retreat: these are so often connected. Among the synonyms of restraint is "abstemiousness," understood as a self-denying and puritanical ascetic stance. We pull away from the world as isolated individuals. But language, again, offers different ways of seeing the same phenomena, pulls us into different interpretations. In mining, everything at the surface—soil, trees, lichens and mosses and fungi, buckbrush—is called *overburden*: something to be pushed aside to reach the metals and minerals and oil and gas underneath.[26] Seen otherwise, this surface material consists of living organisms, ecosystems, habitats, *homes*. It holds meandering rivers together: the migrations of winding rivers—how much their paths change over time—are slowed by stream-side vegetation, which reduces erosion and stabilizes banks.[27] A change in language, a change in perspective. And so too with restraint: what if it is not a matter of holding *back*, but holding *up*? Amplification through community, rather than reduction through isolation.

"Half-Earth or Whole Earth?" ask political ecologist Bram Büscher and his colleagues, challenging the easy separation between part of the Earth for people and part for everything else.[28] Their critique is not just that it's hard to imagine protected areas reaching half the planet when states have struggled to even set aside less than one-fifth[29]—it's also that the half-Earth model follows a long history of exclusionary conservation, a model that so often leads to displacement and dispossession.[30] And beyond the social injustices this creates, the "fortress conservation" model is not clearly a path to ecological well-being. Such "polarization between people and nature" won't lead to a flourishing planet for anyone.[31] In her teaching, Robin Wall Kimmerer writes of her students that, when asked, most could not offer up even a single positive relationship between people and the environment. Every interaction they could name was one of damage. She questions, "How can we begin to move toward ecological and cultural sustainability if we cannot even imagine what the path feels like?"[32] But biodiversity can thrive alongside people: although hard to quantify at the global level,[33] evidence suggests that much of the remaining diversity of life on Earth flourishes in Indigenous peoples' territories, under their management and care.[34] Many have forgotten—or in most cases, violently overwritten—these alternate models of life. But they have survived nonetheless, they can be remembered and revitalized, these other ways of being where human societies and economies are organized to recognize and support ecological integrity. Different ways forward in coexistence can be imagined, since in some places, they have long been enacted.

Naming can be a way of staking claim to something: a place, a being, a whole planet. We name to own, creating relations of control. In an essay on history and discovery and exploration, the writer Jamaica Kincaid considers that in the colonization of the Americas, naming was an act of conquest. She writes that Christopher Columbus "named places, he named people, he named things" in what he saw as the New World.[35] This could become "a tyranny of the nominal," in the words of Robert Macfarlane, imposing dominance through taxonomy.[36] A name can help us notice a new angle on the world: as Kincaid quotes from Isidorus, "If one does not know the names, one's knowledge of things is useless." But a name alone does not allow us to fully apprehend the world—Kincaid clarifies that the quote could be from the Greek or the Spanish Isidorus. Names are tricky, she suggests obliquely, their objects elusive.[37] In front of a willow shrub, puzzling over the scales of the buds (are the margins overlapping?), lobes of the leaves (at the distal end?), and position of the catkins (do these count as pendulous?), the restraint of the imagined ptarmigan willow—unwilling to too quickly categorize in its encounter with "*Salix* spp."—seems wise. We arrive quickly at the limits of our knowledge, but much more slowly at the limits of our curiosity, our affective responses. I think of how much more I notice of the willows, from the texture of the leaves to the patterns of the branches, when I don't yet know what it is. I keep looking.

As someone who has pursued a scholarly path—at a university, in a life of teaching and reading and research—I seek out knowledge. But I remember this, too: "it is not half so important to *know* as to *feel*," as Rachel Carson exhorted in a magazine article on how to cultivate love for the world around us.[38] In writing about Carson, the historian Daegan Miller observes that her emotive life was central to her "ethical, ecological, life-affirming science."[39] Feeling, for Carson, "was the path to wonder. Care was the way to cultivate it. And with wonder came a reverence for life."[40] We can name to see another being as fully itself, distinct and specific, worthy of recognition. Naming can be done without hubris, to come back to Macfarlane, who emphasizes that there need be no conflict "between precision and mystery, or between naming and not knowing."[41] This appeals to me as a way of encountering the world, with language revealing a multiplicity, not a singularity.

Returning to Schneider's considered advice against being too confident in assessment: what happens when we think we know the essence of the things around us? Observing the intensity of extraction in the Arctic, Barry Lopez asks, "What is it that is missing, or tentative, in us, I would wonder, to make me so uncomfortable walking out here in a region of chirping birds, distant caribou, and redoubtable lemmings?" He answers himself: "It is restraint" and the need to "derive some other, wiser way of behaving toward the land."[42] And this is not just relevant to our extractive hungers, but also to conservation. We are dangerous when we become too certain of what needs saving and what can be exploited, what is connected and what can be separated out—when we are sure we already understand what is happening around us.

THEY TOLD ME THEY FELT CAGED, ALONE, POWERLESS, and antsy. Some observed the world passing by as though at a distance, with no access to it; others experienced their independence suddenly wrested from them. They felt time more acutely, each lengthened and empty minute. Cut off from connection, communication, information. All this from only a single day without screens. These were reflections offered up by my students in response to a challenge to "unplug": an assignment to disconnect from screens for 24 hours, eschewing all pixels and electrical cords and tuning in, instead, to the analog world.

Some counted down the endless minutes of their assigned purgatory; others dove into pen-and-paper note-taking on readings assiduously printed prior to the offline day; a few distracted themselves with walks in the park, meditation practices, pre-planned social gatherings with classmates enduring the same assignment. A small handful felt relief, they told me, a moment's pause from relentless connectivity to the enormous online world. The chance to take a deep breath and notice the birds. But most experienced some form of loss. For some, this was mundane and quotidian: the sudden absence of their alarm clocks, for which they had long used their phones, and their transit access, since many stations required scanning access cards on small screens. For others, it was creative and aesthetic, with the disappearance of their photos and music, all stored on their phones. Deeper still was the social and collective, for those cut off from calling and texting friends and loved ones, left out of last-minute plans. Late. Unreachable. Bereft.

You might think these feelings of anxious and unhappy disconnection were justified two years into a global pandemic, where, for many, phones and computers and tablets served as lifelines to others in a time of profound isolation. But this was from the years before lockdowns and social distancing, when we met regularly in classrooms and gathered together in libraries and coffee shops, crowded into close quarters for concerts and dinner parties, crammed ourselves into subway cars and buses and elevators. My students—undergraduates studying politics in a major urban centre in Canada—had no shortage of face-to-face encounters with others in those years; solitude, in fact, was hard to come by for many, with days consisting of commutes on public transit, back-to-back lectures and seminars and tutorial sessions, endless activities and club meetings, busy family homes or shared apartments and dorm rooms. Nevertheless, through it all, technology had become an appendage.

A typical diagnosis of this condition is one of individual blame: students waste time, the story goes, providing too much detail of their personal lives on social media sites; they are narcissistic, turned away from the important matters of the world. They had no chance, we might admit, steeped in a world of technological abundance since their birth, but even so, why can't they just summon the discipline to put their phones down?

CHAPTER VI

But most of my students did not lament the pause from social media and silly distractions—in fact, many embraced the enforced hiatus from schedules overflowing with work commitments and essays to write. Instead, they pointed to the participation in urban life that was made possible only through technology: on that unplugged day, they could not access their university course webpages where syllabi and readings were posted; could not pay their utility bills, which came via email and were dispensed with through online banking; could not even let friends into their apartments, as the buzzers for the locked doors were accessed only through their mobile devices. Being connected was not just an individual choice but a collective necessity. Refraining from time on screens was not, then, a matter of discipline or its lack, but of withdrawing from the social world. A modern-day Thoreauvian escape to Walden Pond—only he could wander back to town as needed, and could host, at least once, the Concord Female Anti-Slavery Society,[43] while my students could not even unlock their apartment doors for their friends. Education, employment, mobility, community: these were the determinants of and the motivations for their connectivity. The TikTok videos and Snapchat exchanges were just a sideline perk.

During the pandemic, I assigned a revised version of the task to my students, recognizing the near impossibility (and potential harm) of demanding a full 24 hours off screens during a time where online life was required for school, work, and nearly everything. An hour was all I asked: go offline and off screens for an hour. Any time other than your night-time sleeping hours would count, I said (and while I didn't, in fact, specify that no naps could be taken, none of them slumbered the assignment away). I also requested that, if possible, they spend that hour outdoors, though with the recognition that it was winter and during a pandemic; they might have caretaking responsibilities or immune vulnerabilities or mobility challenges or safety concerns. But they all tried, even if they were constrained on an apartment balcony, or had to repeat a few circuits around the same neighbourhood block.

Although it was a required course assignment, meaning their offline hour still counted as part of their studies, some expressed a sense of unease during the time they spent away from their computers. A sense that they were not being productive; a disconcerting feeling that they were, in fact, being idle. Many, though, lost track of time without their watches and phones to draw them back indoors; they noticed the aural and visual details of their urban or rural surrounds; they contemplated the value of silence. Perhaps it shouldn't have been a surprise, but this time, students mostly were relieved by the assignment. Was it that the time—an hour, not a day—was short enough to be a break, rather than long enough to be a burden? Was it that—unlike my previous collective of political scientists—these students had chosen a class in environmental studies, and were, for the most part, quite interested in the out-of-doors, eager to enjoy a moment of fresh air? Was it that so much of their lives now took place on screens, with work and home and social realms blurred and indistinct? In any case, in the midst of the pandemic, most of my students seemed to find the assignment a break from the relentless demands of on-screen life. Based on their reflections, many seemed as taken aback by this as I was.

IMAGINE THIS: LATE MORNING, SUN BREAKING through cloud in the drawn-out late winter of the subarctic. A flock of white feathered bodies milling about in the snow among the willows, wings tucked back. A cold, shining day, following some warmer ones that augur spring; the low-angled light casting long shadows. Bright reflections everywhere you look; *ammil*, as they might say in Devon— as Macfarlane explains, that "thin film of ice that lacquers all leaves, twigs and grass blades when a freeze follows a partial thaw, and that in sunlight can cause a whole landscape to glitter."[44] Only not catching leaves and grass yet, here where spring has yet to arrive in earnest, the light snagging just the bare twigs of the willow and conifer needles encased in ice. A word from another continent, brought alive with the ptarmigan.

And then one bird, somewhere in the crowd, suddenly extends her head and bobs. She crouches low, then starts jumping, erratic movements matched by flapping her wings, one and then the other. Around her, other birds join in, and then the whole flock is in motion: tails, heads, orange-red eye combs flashing amidst feathers and wings. Although some have tried to explain this phenomenon in sober, practical terms—honing motor skills, strengthening social bonds[45]—others have acknowledged that this group commotion is best described as "frolicking."[46]

Play and restraint are rarely linked in our conversations and philosophical musings. The former is an activity for its own sake, for pure enjoyment; the latter, a matter of keeping things under control, within limits, restricting freedom of movement and expression. Letting go versus holding back. Pleasure against asceticism; hedonism against responsibility. Yet both play and restraint can be radical and upending responses to the consumption-focused hungers of our industrialized time. Each resists the siren call of ever-increasing production, of ever-expanding growth. And perhaps a more provocative claim: these are compatible states, maybe even necessary for one another—restraint in material and consumptive terms can, under some conditions, create the space for play, connection, and well-being. This isn't just about limiting oneself to base necessities—at least, not unless we think of those fluid ptarmigan movements, those joyful leaps and flaps, as *necessary*.

Hedonism, understood colloquially as the pursuit of pleasure, seems a self-indulgent kind of aim, fleeting and superficial and crude. But in philosophical terms, it holds more weight and complexity: an ethical theory about the satisfaction of desires as the highest good, though what those desires *are* remains open to debate. Sheer positive physical stimulation or "*ease, contentment, repose*";[47] self-oriented concern or reciprocal care; gustatory and experiential novelty or meaningful sustained engagement; constant bacchanalian excess or titrated moderation;

power and glory or friendship and connection—these are not settled matters. To meet the ecological and social challenges of our time, philosopher Kate Soper suggests that we need to embrace an "alternate hedonism,"[48] where limiting consumption and accumulation is experienced not as self-sacrifice but as pleasure. An enriched life can arise from certain forms of restraint. If we reject a quick consume-and-discard idea of acquisition, we might deepen our relations with our tactile surroundings. Maybe, then, this is the ultimate materialism, the deepest form of it in the world: not moving past care and desire for tangible things, but rather a true valuing of them. Our embodied selves, thriving in the physical world, fully expressed.

We often have an idea of sacrifice that is onerous and heavy, involving self-denial for some greater purpose. Consider any practice steeped in restriction and, often, abstraction—accepting limits is so often presented as a diminishment of life, a gnawing hunger and attenuation of possibility. Posed as difficult and depressing, these acts tend to be seen as something for those who view rewards as occurring only in an afterlife, another realm, or a different order. But sacrifice is rarely so straightforward a form of loss; giving up one thing often involves gaining another. We can follow more expansive ideas about sacrifice, those that upend a simple account of denial, hardship, and penury. We are always sacrificing something, explain environmental politics scholars Michael Maniates and John Mayer: our time, energy, or attention; our space, environment, or freedom.[49] But in the process, they continue, we are always gaining something else, whether money and material goods, or prestige, relationships, and experiences. The question, then, is what to give up, and for what, although a conceptual distinction is important: we must delineate *sacrifice* from *being sacrificed*, says the scholar Cheryl Hall. The former is a voluntary, consensual move, while the latter is involuntary, a forced imposition.[50] Chosen sacrifice can be fulfilling, providing a source of purpose and meaning. It allows us to make an offering, of sorts, to something beyond ourselves and, in return, feel not loss but gain. My students experienced the full range of these possibilities. For some, the unplugging task seemed a form of deprivation—not entirely coerced, but not entirely optional, either. But for others, sacrificing onscreen time, whether an hour or a day, provided something in return—a pause from the pressures of their oversubscribed schedules, a reminder of their place in the world, a signal of what they give up by being constantly plugged in. A disruption of their entanglement in uninterrupted technological connection; a moment of exposure to other ways of living.

It seems a stretch to move from sacrifice to play, perhaps, but that shift in perspective might be helpful. The writer Paul Gallant recalls that ideas of "degrowth"—the opposite of expansion—are also described as "'post-growth,' 'frugal abundance,' and voluntary simplicity.'" All of these are terms that focus on volition, not coercion. And also pleasure—he adds: "Sometimes, it's called 'convivial degrowth' to add a sense of joy and affirmation."[51] Convivial—derived from words for festive, feasting, and meaning, most directly, *"with life."* The potential is in the contradictions and trade-offs. Contrasts are important in the assessment of pleasure, it seems to me; fulfillment and stimulation, too. I think back to my early university days, and the exhilarating vertigo I felt as banal woodlots in southwestern Ontario suddenly resolved into a flood of diverse forms of life, once I learned to see them: the yellow cheeks of a hooded warbler here; in the air, the black border on the wings of a Karner blue butterfly; at eye-level, the mitten-shaped leaves of sassafras. Was this hedonism? It certainly wasn't penance, as I collapsed each night into bed, bug-bitten and exhausted and delighted, all senses replete.

That summer, I was connected to place in a way I'd never before known, learning plumage and the songs of birds, and, in their names, an old world revealed itself. Perhaps alongside the alternate hedonism posited by Soper, we should think more about relationships and interdependence when we consider restraint. Quietly, holding back our noisy selves—holding up our deepest attention—we could watch frolicking ptarmigan in a world shining with ice: is this not pleasure, ours and theirs? Instead of a cordoned-off planet, I suspect so many of us desire a whole Earth, a global community of respectful, reciprocal relations. But how to get there? Kimmerer points to an integrated path for mutual flourishing: "Action on behalf of life transforms" she writes, and, "As we work to heal the earth, the earth heals us."[52] We so often resist the idea of accepting less;[53] we see reducing as a process of *being* reduced—sacrifice *as* deprivation.[54] But consider the exchanges that are being proposed not as reductions but as trade-offs: more consumer goods, unrestricted electricity, food untethered from seasons—these involve less clean water, unstable climates, reduced diversity of nonhuman life. The bobbing heads of the ptarmigan—reverence and restraint, sacrifice and frolicking. I look out the window of the cabin to the catkins on the willows: *Salix spp.*, I think, and classify it only as wondrous.

CHAPTER VII

OWL OBSERVATIONS: ON ATTENTION

Hunter. Hunted. A quarter-inch. Wings at dawn. Mesopotamia. Laments. Anthropocene. River Lethe. Shifting baselines. Shifting ranges. Dutch painters. Lemons. Shimmer. Loneliness. Monastic doubts. Loons. Lungs. Wolfhounds. Sorrow. Unseen nests. Open space.

Dawn slips out from a featureless sky, an empty canvas raked clear of moonlight. A call released from shadowed branches pierces the still, dry air, shatters the refuge of this liminal hour. Four feet of wings stretch wide over the shrubby opening, hover over unseen prey, then: a bullet of feathered concentration. A snowshoe hare's last breath.[1] Or, maybe, a moment's indecision from above makes space for another day's survival, evoking poet Wislawa Szymborska's lines on close calls, "You were in luck — a rake, a hook, a beam, a brake, / A jamb, a turn, a quarter-inch, an instant."[2] Whose luck this time, and whose loss, this hunter and hunted?

I have never seen this moment of attack, only imagined it in the early morning light. All I've ever caught is a brief blur of movement through the trees; a muted baritone *whoo-hoo-hoo-oo* in the distance; hare tracks ending abruptly in feathers imprinted in fresh snow. Dream-like and shadowy, with tufted ears and yellow eyes,[3] the great horned owl is more often heard than seen. *Bubo virginianus* and its relatives possess the night, alert in the dusky hours of others' rest. It is fitting, or perhaps ironic, then, that owls are so associated with sleep and with dreams—for Mesopotamians, a portent of trouble, accompanying the underworld deity Ea; in Hebrew psalms and Aramaic texts, a mournful sign, suggesting despair and desolation; for the Roman Pliny, a "grave omen" and "terror of the night."[4] The bird's nocturnal restlessness has long evoked ideas of knowledge, as in Hindu traditions where the goddess Lakshmi has an owl guide, seeking knowledge in the night.[5] But knowledge is linked with death, as the Greeks attached Athena and the Romans Minerva—goddesses of both wisdom and warfare—with owls, while for the English, in folklore dating back to the 1200s, the birds prophesy death.[6] Owls have flown alongside sorrow across centuries and continents: for the Mesopotamians, nestled between the Tigris and Euphrates Rivers, these were birds of "heart-sadness," crying out "lament, lament" from the sky.[7]

Owls might be well-suited to our times, then, a reasonable companion as our world comes apart under us. A sorrowful age—epoch even, to the scholars who call this industrialized time "the Anthropocene"—with its nearly incomprehensible loss. We are deeply implicated in these losses, at least some of us: we tear up and pull out and plow over. And the world responds with fires and floods and storms and plagues. The disappearance of countless species we've not yet encountered, along with myriads of ones we have; rivers that no longer reach the oceans, even as the coasts move inland with rising tides; islands of plastic gathering in the seas.

Our actions leave marks: we have altered carbon cycles, forcing changes in atmospheric and oceanic circulation; we have amplified the rate of biodiversity loss, wiping out species at a rate that has led to the declaration of a sixth mass extinction; we have exploded nuclear weapons, with radioisotopes detected in soil layers.[8] When did human activity begin to mimic geologic forces? Maybe it was the mid-twentieth century with its "Great Acceleration," of population growth, plastic production, industrialized agriculture, or a few years earlier than that, when atomic bombs were dropped on the Japanese cities of Hiroshima and Nagasaki, followed by nuclear testing on Bikini Atoll in the Marshall Islands spanning over a decade. Or was it in the late eighteenth and early nineteenth centuries, with the start of the Industrial Revolution and its onslaught of steam power and coal burning; or somewhere between the 1400s and 1600s, with the violent colonization of the Americas, marked by genocide and enslavement and the alteration of a continent's forests; or back as far, even, as the rise of agriculture some ten thousand years ago?[9] Some scholars turn to the term Capitalocene, but—with different emphasis on uneven power and devastating colonial expansion, of the inequalities and exploitation of certain peoples by others, of growth and accumulation for some at the expense of others—I've also heard our present time called the Eurocene, Technocene, and, tongue in cheek, the Manthropocene.[10] These terms remind us that the boundary point of geologic change matters for who we now understand to be responsible for these tremendous planetary losses: the generic "we" of humanity at large, with our thousands-of-years-old agricultural innovations or the industrialized "we" with our legacy of steam engines and flagrant burning of fossil fuels; the specific "we" of colonizing empires, descended from those who stormed over the humanity of those already at home in those so-called frontiers, or the expanding set of "we" of capitalist economies and our seemingly fungible commodities.

The naming of an epoch centred on humans is both contrition and conceit. It is an acknowledgement of the damage (some) people have inflicted on the many lives of this planet, and maybe a collective taking of responsibility for our radical disruption of Earth systems in a short stretch of time. But, troublingly, it may also give humans undeserved significance, and reflect too much optimism about our ability as a species to last the millions of years that comprise such a stretch of deep geological time.[11] "The arrogance of the Anthropocene," according to Atlantic writer Peter Brannan.[12] While our impact is planetary in scale, we may not be the defining force of this epoch but instead its boundary event, as poets Jan Zwicky and Robert Bringhurst suggest.[13] For them, our human significance is overblown in our account of the epoch: it is substantial but not temporally lasting, and will not be the determinant of what comes next on this planet. We are more akin to the meteor that catalyzed the extinction of the dinosaurs, ending the Cretaceous Period and Mesozoic Era, rather than an ongoing dominant force of the Cenozoic—the rise of flowering plants, say, or modern birds—in the millions of years that have followed.

But even if we are just the disturbance, rather than the continuing force, the expanses of human empires and their many legacies have left marks on the planet. We must confront the damage we unleash on the systems of the planet that sustain us, even when the we, as always, remains fraught. Especially since those culpable for the damages, or those who benefit from the legacies of those disruptions, are not the only ones—and often not the primary ones—who bear the burden of loss. There is so much damage underway that psychologists are diagnosing ecological grief, sociologists are cataloguing the dimensions of loss from climate change, and philosophers have coined a new term, solastalgia, to describe a form of melancholy that arises in a beloved spot that is being harmed—a "homesickness you have when you are still at home."[14] Is the owl's call, in the early morning quiet, a lament for a lost meal or for the Earth itself being undone?

"On love, on grief, on every human thing,
Time sprinkles Lethe's water with his wing."[15]

So wrote the English poet Walter Savage Landor, sometime during the Industrial Revolution. In Greek mythology, the River Lethe flows through the fields of Elysium in the underworld of Hades. The souls of the dead travel first across the River Styx, with the ferryman Charon paid by coins from their mouths, buried with them,[16] and pass the many-headed canine Cerberus guarding the shores. Those who committed no crimes against the gods skirt the torments of Tartarus and turn instead towards the peaceful Elysium. To drink from the River Lethe, it is said, allows those souls to forget their earthly lives and surrender all longing for what they left behind.

I first heard Landor's brief couplet read aloud by poet and translator Robert Hass, in a public radio broadcast he recorded with the lyric experimentalist poet Brenda Hillman[17] on environmental activism and poetry.[18] His low and gentle voice still echoes when I recall those lines. Later, I encountered the poet Robert Pinsky's reflections on the "paradoxical joy in the slowing down of time achieved by swiftness" that the brevity of the poem offers.[19] Landor's rhythms, his assonance and consonance, provide a sort of comfort of scale to human endeavours, a reminder that time—sped up and slowed down—can mute the intensity of both the daily sorrows and the joys of human existence. It only struck me later, with owls on my mind, that in Landor's poem, time itself has wings. Perhaps owls, those birds of heart-sorrow and night terrors, are not the harbingers of loss, but the bearers of distance and comfort, bringing on their wings the relief of oblivion. Following grief, rather than preceding it. In the midst of searing loss, it is easy to desire the waters of forgetfulness, to choose blankness over unrelenting pain. But is it really *forgetting*, those placid waters of the Lethe, that soothes heartbreak? Are the owls the wings of time or something else entirely, carrying with them something other than amnesia?

Knowledge, perhaps, as the Greeks might suggest, these winged bodies coming to rest on Athena's shoulder. We come to know, and perhaps then to feel, that we are part of a bigger order, that our losses are held within something larger than ourselves. Or maybe it isn't the knowledge of our belonging in a world of loss, but instead of the knowledge that those we loved—other beings, treasured places—existed at all. On the banks of erasure, in a sky filled with space, we hold on to the awareness of a time, too brief though it was, when our beloveds shone with specificity and radiance. Grief is not something to forget, something to move through and past, but instead something that accompanies us throughout our lives. What time enables, then, is the muting of the moment of rupture; the chance for the love that came before to return to us. We learn to live with absence without being entirely undone. Owls fly nearly silently, I've learned, their massive wings carrying them aloft so slowly they need rarely flap.[20] Their feathers dampen turbulence—on the leading edge of the wing, they are serrated combs; on the trailing side, fringed—allowing them quiet passage through the air.[21] Better for hunting, goes the scientific theory; better for carrying the grief of others, I think, for quieting the pain to make space for memory, and for the wonder of anything having been alive at all.

This remembering of both love and loss is maybe our greatest need in the present moment. We can manage without the waters of the Lethe: we already lose track of the world around us so easily. What we know from the present becomes our benchmark for normalcy. Fisheries ecologist Daniel Pauly labelled this the "shifting baseline syndrome," where we take as our starting point the system when we first encountered it, and measure change against those initial observations. As more is lost, each generation finds their own impoverished world as the basis against which further loss is evaluated.[22] We accommodate ourselves to our surroundings: a diminished world as our foundation. The writer J. B. MacKinnon offers an anecdote of this syndrome in action, recounting memories of a field near the house where he grew up in the US Northeast. There were red foxes in the field, he recalls, the epitome, for his younger self, of wild nature. But in his adult years he learned that red foxes were introduced to that region; the fields, too, hosted introduced grasses, not the native species that had been overrun in just a few decades by urban expansion and human disturbance. He calls these misreadings of our surroundings "illusions of nature," where our early encounters with the world shape how—and whether—we later see change and damage unfolding.[23] Our timescales of experience matter when we set out to identify the boundaries of a system, its intactness or resilience, its very essence.

Population estimates for the great horned owl are, according to British Columbia's Bird Atlas, unreliable.[24] There are decades of data from the Canadian Breeding Bird Survey that suggest populations may be relatively stable. But these owls have long lives, sometimes skip breeding years when prey are scarce, and are often hard to detect, making accurate estimates of reproduction rates and future owlets difficult. If our baselines of the populations of this tufted-eared species of the Strigidae family are fuzzy, our projections moving forward are even less clear. Perhaps these are resilient birds and their wing beats will continue to fill forest nights for centuries to come. It may be that the great horned owls of the subarctic will adopt the sooty colours of their Pacific Northwestern kin,[25] their near-white plumage giving way to colours more suited to a melting region. They already adopt the nests of other birds from other years, occupying the abandoned and sometimes ramshackle creations of hawks, crows, magpies;[26] they are creative and resourceful, at home in what some describe as "rough terrain."[27] But if we have misjudged their adaptability to a constantly changing landscape, will we notice their missing calls, their haunting voices failing to echo in the twilight? Will we, drunk on the Lethe's waters, forget they existed at all? We may never know what knowledge these birds would carry away if they were to disappear; we already know so little of the mysteries entangled in the branches above us.

THE STILL-DARK MORNING WITH ITS CRESCENT MOON stretches thin shadows of branches on the ground. This could be a still life painting, an owl offset at the edge. It might remind us of the perishability of life, the fleeting state of being, the decay that awaits us—or of the wonder that is this singular moment. In a tender essay, the writer Mark Doty considers still life paintings as he wrestles with the tensions between individuation and connection, "between staying moored and drifting away, between holding on and letting go."[28] He turns to Dutch paintings of lemons from the 1500s to confront the contradictions of both craving and fearing intimacy. Lemons: so often painted, so familiar.

CHAPTER VII

Not long ago, a friend of mine lost someone close to her. No matter when I've written this, that statement is true—always we are losing, always someone dear to us is reckoning with absence. For this specific friend, as the raw shock turned to sorrow and weeks passed, she described the world as having been drained of colour—life having become muted, veiled. Deflated. As a writer she spends her days striving to articulate the ineffable, but I suspect her words of colour and vision, and of the collapse of atmospheric space, were not just metaphors. She said her body was pressed inwards, her senses dulled. This one grief, entirely hers to bear, in a world teeming with absence. How many of us are grieving right now, adding new losses to all the ones we already endure? So many sorrows are collected, so many forms of heartbreak; ever so common, quotidian, a shared human experience—and yet each one singular. In mourning her father, the writer Helen Macdonald notes that bereavement comes "from the Old English *bereafian*, meaning 'to deprive of, take away, seize, rob.'" The etymology leads her on: "Robbed. Seized. It happens to everyone," she acknowledges, but even so, it always feels unparalleled, unprecedented, immeasurable—"you feel it alone. Shocking loss isn't to be shared, no matter how hard you try."[29]

It seems we ought to become inured to absence after so many generations of experience with it, but our capacity to grieve keeps pace with our capacity to love, and so is never exhausted. The still life scenes described by Doty might offer some balm, and some company in the gaping loneliness that comes with loss: in one painting, the artist tends to the translucency of a strip of lemon peel, a slight edge of white pith below, the distinctiveness of a single seed. Here, the contradictions blur: we see the "lovely perishable, ordinary thing" of a lemon, and its seed "held to scrutiny's light, fixed in a moment of fierce attention."[30] An extraordinary lemon, from a basket filled with many like fruit. Through careful brushstrokes, this one imbued with singularity, elevated through attention.

Attention: this is a form of reverence, even worship, at least if we follow the philosopher Simone Weil, who tells us, "Absolutely unmixed attention is prayer."[31] Paying such close attention to citrus, or to the owl in the night, requires a kind of stillness ourselves, a quieting of the distractions that surround us. It is not just a feeling or an expression, but a practice, and one that requires some kind of letting go. "Summer / and sunset, the peace / of the writing desk / and the habitual peace / of writing, these things / form an order I only / belong to in the idleness / of attention," writes Robert Hass in his poem "Measure."[32] This "idleness of attention" of which Hass writes allows him to take in the "coppery light" in the plum trees, the other light that "rims the blue mountain," the very pulse of the world around him. To hear that pulse and to see that light requires not constant effort but, unexpectedly, *release*. An idleness, rather than a striving.

Stillness need not be static—is that a contradictory claim? Perhaps what I mean is idleness need not be stillness; stillness is not the only way to pay attention. Then again, I am tempted to embrace this paradoxical condition. Meditation, across spiritual and secular traditions, is a form of both focusing and releasing our hold on the world. Expressed through seated practices that eschew movement or walking practices that embrace it, involving both a taking-in and a letting-go, allowing pauses and continuations: these are all strategies to quell the ever-present voice of the self, to loosen our usual teleological attachments. Waiting, without planning; watching, without judging; attending, without acting. A still life painting can be read as an imprisoned moment in a moving world, a butterfly with wings pinned; alternately, it can hold and radiate light, reflected across centuries, carrying impermanence and eternity in its layers of thick glaze. We can move and be still, we can hold and release, we can feel grief and loss and damage to their heaviest extent and, in the same moment, let them go.

The Dutch painters offer one path to perceiving the light that emanates from the world; environmental humanities scholar Deborah Bird Rose's work explores another.[33] She relays how the Yolngu, a people indigenous to northern Australia, have a term that translates as "brilliant" or "shimmering" in English. For the Yolngu, in Bird Rose's account, "bir'yun" is a form of movement, an "experience of being part of a vibrant and vibrating world." Such luminous qualities can arise in paintings, although Bird Rose writes of her closest encounters with this brilliance in the context of music and dance. But not just human actions can capture this connection to unfolding life and ancestral power, says Bird Rose—so, too, is shimmering part of the "pulse between wet and dry seasons," the vibrancy that arises not from one caught moment, but in transitions between the waxing and waning of colours, movement, light. These are cycles of light and dark, juvenescence and senescence, rainy and arid, arrival and loss. "The ephemeral dance of it all," as Bird Rose puts it. If we expand with love, do we then constrict with loss? It may seem so, in the deflated and veiled days of sorrow, our worlds turned inward; but then again, we also expand with loss—even after we are buffeted by so much absence, a new loss can unmoor us yet again. No matter how many losses there are in the world, in our own small lives, each one occupies a distinct space.

We cannot prepare ourselves for grief or inure ourselves to it without turning to the cold remove of irony, without losing something of the love that led to loss. In an elegy to her beloved dog, to an orphaned elk calf, and to the damaged world, writer and scholar Pam Houston observes, "It is hard to be ironic about a dying dog. It is hard to be ironic about an elk calf when her nose is touching your face.... It is hard to be ironic when your pasture erupts after an unexpected May blizzard into a blanket of wild iris."[34] Later, she continues, "a broken heart—God knows, I have found—doesn't actually kill you. And irony and disinterest are false protections, ones that won't serve us, or the earth, in the end." Every time I've read this essay from Houston, I've wept. Better pain than denying the world, than forgetting it: though we might desire to drink of the Lethe's waters and succumb to the comforts of those shifted baselines, we do so only if we accept an impoverished world, missing the wild iris and the great horned owl. We are held within sorrow, and also within love. We reach out for edges that do not exist—each lemon from a basket, each loss from our life.

ANOTHER NAME PROPOSED FOR THE CURRENT EPOCH—this time by biologist E. O. Wilson—is the Eremozoic: the age, not of humans or men or industrialization or capitalism, but, profoundly, of *loneliness*.[35] I suspect that deep down, Wilson wants a whole Earth, not just a battered half. Our current epoch is laced with absence. Still, loss and sorrow for the world is by no means new: grappling with the abundance of absence, the fifth century bishop of Emesa, a city in ancient Syria, categorized sorrows, trying to find a way to make sense of myriad forms of suffering—oppressive sorrow, a sorrow arising from envy, one that causes speechlessness, and, the last, *eleos*, a form of compassion or sympathy.[36] The bishop's categories followed a history of concern in monastic orders about *acedia*, a term whose interpretations range from laziness to religious despair, capturing everything from carelessness and indifference to a soul-heavy weariness and exhaustion.[37] Petrarch's "malady of the monks" takes *acedia* as a form of melancholy,[38] as do the fourth century writings of Evagrius, where it "dissolves the psychic stamina" and undoes the discipline of the monk.[39]

By the late Middle Ages, a complex ordering of *acedia* had emerged, handed down and revised by monks and abbots navigating the power of religious authorities alongside monarchic rulers. At the turn of the millennium, as the 900s came to a close, the Anglo-Saxon monk Aelfric wrote of *acedia*—transcribed as *accidia*—that it was one of the eight main sins, involving what translates as languor and sloth, with the latter—*slaewthe*—a form of slowness.[40] By the 1400s, *acedia* was understood as a suite of sins that could, alternately, "hinder the beginning of a good life"; "prevent the amendment of a bad life"; or "bring man to a bad end."[41] For the first, *"slugnesse"* and *"ydelnesse"* were among the threats to even beginning a good life, as they represented "laziness in the performance of religious duties" and "engagement in idle activities," and were associated with laxness in the responsibilities of a pious life. If one travelled down a path of sin, one could usually repent, but not, in the second category of *acedia*, if one engaged in *"forgetyng"*—omitting, even inadvertently, one's sins in confession—or *"tarying,"* with a delay in both repentance and the performance of compensatory "good works."[42] And both daily grumpiness as well as more profound despair could lead, in the final category, to eternal trouble, as when one spent time grumbling and *"grucchying"* or, bleakly, lived in a state of *"wanhope,"* having lost faith in the mercy of the divine.[43]

A re-devotion to work—to monastic study, to regular confession—was often the prescribed antidote to many of these lapses in character and soul, but a sober and grim duteousness was not the only response offered to those suffering from *acedia*. Back in the fourth century, Evagrius had offered strategies to restore the stamina of, and to re-centre reason for, monks so afflicted, advising "endurance and patience, aided by tears, prayer / recitation, and work with the hands."[44] Moreover, those stricken by a loss of purpose and meaning might not always need renewed discipline, but instead, in some Benedictine responses, the "cultivation of spiritual joy."[45] Work with the hands, whether on its own or while weeping and praying, is still valuable advice for those facing the deluge of despair of these times. Work with the hands, stillness with the mind. *Chop wood, carry water*: so goes the Buddhist exhortation, at least as translated for the uninitiated, to those seeking enlightenment and also to those who have already achieved it. A path to living in those contradictions of movement and pause that allow us to apprehend the shimmer that arises in between—if I understand, just a little, Bird Rose's account of the Yolngu concept.

Work, and labour, and also, just breathing. Until something goes wrong, it's so easy to forget the pause of breath, even as it dictates every moment of our lives; we often turn to meditative practice, yogic training, mindfulness exercises to remember the power of that autonomic system. Sometimes on a still evening, in the long light of subarctic summer, I take my kayak out on a nearby lake. The lake is a wide-open and moody place: winds turn so quickly, and the waters are glacial. This is a place to pay attention; brief errors in judgement can be unforgiving. But this vulnerability allows, paradoxically, the chance to stretch past the edges of the body. Breathing, while paddling, is something rhythmic and pulsing. Lungs, shoulders, hands, water: all connected. Once, I saw ten loons, never quite sure if I had the count right, as they took turns disappearing under the ripples, surfacing and calling softly, before dipping under again. I wondered, and wonder still, at their aquatic and aerial lives, how they inhabit both worlds with grace, surrendering themselves to each medium in turn. A marvel that they stay themselves, suspended; but then, perhaps they become air, or water, forgetting to differentiate their bodies from their surroundings. It may not be the lift of wings on breeze that carries them, but instead that they become the wind. It seems less physics than metaphysics, imagination and its limits, this thin line between being and becoming. And the ten loons, individual and collective in the same breath. In such moments, Juliana Spahr's poem rises—"How lovely and how doomed this connection of everyone with lungs," she writes[46]—and it strikes me again that the *everyone* she invokes is not just humans, and the *lungs* are the lungs of the Earth. The loons and the lake and the bedrock and me, all breathing.

When Houston penned those lines about surviving a broken heart, she was writing of spending one last weekend with her beloved Irish wolfhound before his death. She was writing, too, of the struggle to make sense of a world in pieces, being stripped of its species, heated to breaking points, fractured and poisoned.[47] Tending other beings—whether canine companions in their last days or the forests of the great horned owls—requires attending to them: that is, caring for those others involves a stretching of ourselves, an extension held in the Latin roots of the verb "attend." Not just the physical labour of caretaking, the feeding and cleaning and soothing, but the presence it takes, the breathing together, perhaps right to the last breath of the other, and beyond. Barry Lopez offers that "it is not possible for human beings to outgrow loneliness," and so we search for connection. He suggests that the "effort to know a place deeply is, ultimately, an expression of the human desire to belong, to fit somewhere," and in this, "the first rule of everything we endeavor to do is to pay attention."[48] When we attend to the world, we stretch the boundaries of our isolated selves to be part of a larger community, no longer alone in our sorrows or our joys. We stretch the capacity of our hearts to hold in tandem both love and loss. This requires a release of the strivings of the self, Hass' idleness of attention, that allows us to be fully present, and restores us from the throes of *acedia* to a belonging in the holiness of the world.

DECOYS OF OWLS SIT ATOP FLOAT PLANES AT THE DOCK on a little lake near the cabin, keeping other birds at bay. Thinking back to Athena and Minerva accompanied by owls, I recall that wisdom and warfare are closely linked for the Greeks and the Romans—is it because of the ferocity of owls and their feuds with other avian beings? Accounts of the enmity of owls and other birds date back to Aristotle, with ravens as a particular foe.[49] But these goddesses, too, are deities of handicrafts and domesticity—fitting, given the detailed painted features of these decorated figures at the dock. A pilot I know, who is also a painter, has no such avian ornamentation; the fabric wings of her two-seater plane have been pecked by ravens. Ravens, too, are birds associated with death. In a plane with holes in the wings, such folklore takes new life. She patched the wings, of course, before lifting off, but perhaps it's no wonder that her paintings frequently feature corvids, a sort of tribute to those defending the sky from other wings—even hers.

Seeing those imitation owls reminds me of a story recounted by anthropologist Anna Tsing, about a decoy of a spotted owl being attached to a logging truck in Oregon in the late 1980s, amidst furor over unsustainable forestry practices.[50] "In effigy," she writes of the mounted model owls, though we might also read this as "in elegy": a visual lament for the nearly-dead—the trees and the owls both. Do owls hold damage at bay, keeping small birds away from airplanes and, as German lore has it, their outstretched wings protecting homes and barns against lightning and magic?[51] Or do owls just carry the Lethe waters to wash clear our sorrows? The wisdom of owls might not be in their enabling of amnesia, but in the reminder, as writer Rebecca Solnit offers, that "sorrow and beauty are tied up together."[52] The owls on the logging trucks might not serve as an abstraction that "redeems the losses time brings, and finds beauty in the faraway,"[53] but they are certainly a poignant symbol of loss, and of the beauty and wonder being hauled from the forests, leaving only diesel fumes and slash.

Whatever the season, there is a cacophony at the lake at dawn—the multiple, intersecting voices of birds. As owls keep watch over float planes, depending on the season, I can hear black-capped and mountain chickadees, song sparrows and American robins, dark-eyed juncos and varied thrush, Wilson's and yellow-rumped warblers, northern flickers and Bohemian waxwings and pine siskins and the glottal waterdrop sounds of the ravens. I usually think of these songs as welcoming the morning light, celebrating the sun and light and day. But perhaps I've misread the attention of the birds; maybe the avian voices are singing the stars to sleep. A lament and a longing, with beauty and loss intertwined.

SILENCES AND ABSENCES OFTEN IMPLY LOSS—BUT ALSO possibility. The poet Tess Gallagher writes of saplings. It seems so straightforward, her plan to take down some trees that block her view of the mountains. But in a tender poem she recounts finding a nest in the branches she is about to take down. She points us to what she hadn't before noticed, and to what has not yet emerged, her hand stilled—"I don't cut that one. / I don't cut the others either" since "in every tree

CHAPTER VII

/ an unseen nest / where a mountain / would be."[54] What could be there, if we leave open both our attention and the space for others' becoming? An unseen nest. An uncut tree. The possibility of a tiny home—now, or perhaps yet unbuilt and still to come—tucked high in a sapling, against the distant mountains. To tend to the individual tree that could nurture the future of birdsong. For us, too, the quiet morning in which we do not hear the great horned owl, but, if we hold ourselves still and listen long enough, we might. It could arrive in this morning, or in some new morning, if we leave open that space. If we hold back from our own noises and distractions.

The Dutch painter Jan Vermeer came later than the still life masters of Doty's essayist tribute, but his artistic attentions in the 1600s similarly came into focus in domestic realms. In intimate scenes of the close and fleeting moments of daily life, he reveals glimpses of eternity in what is otherwise brief and temporal. In a poem entitled simply "Vermeer," the Swedish poet Tomas Tranströmer, translated by Robert Bly, considers these "seconds that have got permission to live for centuries."[55] But powerful as it is, it is not that line that stays with me. After considering, in an airy studio with paintings from Vermeer, the stillness and the pressure, the brushstrokes and the walls, Tranströmer takes us further:

> The airy sky has taken its place leaning against the wall.
> It is like a prayer to what is empty.
> And what is empty turns its face to us
> and whispers:
> "I am not empty, I am open."

Let us listen to that open space. The absences in the snow, no feathers of the owl, no footprints of the hare: we do not really know what we are losing by the tracks they do not leave. In light of this unknowing, we must attend to those that are still here, and to those that are gone. And not just in the collective. Let us see each one as a Dutch painter would: individually, tenderly. Let us take in each layer of light, each feather, each empty branch, freighted as they are with absence and possibility.

ROCKY CONCLUSIONS

ON PARADOX

Sun-drenched. Dissolution. Petrichor. Telephone lines. Eiders. Walking. Bee hives. Animal tracks. Patience. Contradictions. Lucretius. Sabbatical. Diesel fumes. Scuba diving. No reserve. Responsibility. Disillusionment. A single second of pigment. Meltwater.

At times I lie on a favourite outcrop near home, unsure whether to pay attention to the shape of the clouds, the smell of wild roses, or the hum of the drowsy bumblebee circling the pink petals. The brambles and grass tips poke against skin, and I feel the warmth of rock in the afternoon sun, ragged and uneven under my back. In those moments in the long days of the short summers of northern light, everything soaks up what it can, everything turned to the incoming rays. I shift between senses, unable to do more to capture the light than be fully present in it. Still, even sun-drenched and lit up, I sense that the season is already coming to an end and am filled instantly with regret. And I am flooded with longing. I imagine the dark, quiet nights of winter, with the sky filled with aurora, the promise of stars. In my tangled response, pulled between hanging on and letting go, I sense something released by the darkness as it hits the light, palpable and fleeting.

There are some things we only know in their dissolution; for these things, the moment of disappearance is the most vivid to us. One is the meeting of plant and stone and water—we apprehend this only briefly, as *petrichor*, that rich, earthy smell as rain begins after a dry spell.[1] It is the oils of decaying plants left behind on rock along with geosmin, the compounds left behind in the soil by bacteria, mixed with molecules of ozone brought down to the ground by rain:[2] the sky meets earth, and we know this for a moment through water. "We can only smell it as it is washed away," the writer Anne Michaels observes.[3] The vagabond petrichor arrives and disappears in but a few breaths, but long after the storm, we remember.

I've been trying to let go of my need to define and pin down, as I suspect the willow ptarmigan do. Is everything work? Composing a song, cultivating a garden, unchopping a tree, restoring the words of landscapes in English or Tlingit or Anishinaabemowin—these are energy-intensive activities, and need skills and effort. But they are also restorative and generative practices, and ones that require more than concerted labour: they need time, patience, inspiration, memory, luck, and perhaps especially a willingness for it all to elude us. Their origins and their outcomes are a collaborative effort, whether with the sun and earth and rain, with generations past, or with the unknown muses. Creativity and imagination and tenderness make these endeavours possible, meaningful. What we see when we look with our existing ideas, when we classify according to what we think we know, is a partial version of a world more alive than we imagine. "We lived in the city," writes the poet Conchitina Cruz, "and I thought you drew lampposts, telephone lines, the long rusty rods scattered in construction sites." In a haunting series from a collection entitled *Dark Hours*, which evokes the shadows of her urban Filipino landscape, her narrator's voice tells of certainty in seeing a familiar cityscape. But those "wide vertical lines" on the page were not the stuff of urban industrialism, she is told: "Your voice insisting, no, no, these are trees."[4] From my own academic and seasonal migrations from this rocky outcrop, I know it's hard to remember what a skyscraper looks like, but in the city, it's hard to remember the unconstrained lives of trees.

Through language and fable, we often position idleness alongside laziness and lethargy and contrast it with work and diligence. But not all mythologies reinforce this stark divide. The Greek god of sleep, Hypnos, slumbers in the underworld, guarded by an assemblage of figures: the hushed Quies and Silentia, the easeful Otia, forgetful Oblivio, and, with them, the goddesses of effort, Horme, and of sloth, Aergia.[5] The latter, known also by the Latin names Socordia and Ignavia, is the daughter, so the mythology goes, of Aether (Air) and Gaia (Earth), alongside the Titans, the Furies, and other affective siblings from grief to wrath to fear.[6] Idleness sits not in opposition, exactly, with work, but alongside her. Poetry can remind us of these blurred lines. It is a form of evocation and metaphor, of gesturing at things that cannot quite be pinned down. In a flashing poem that brings us to "a cliff / along the coast,"[7] the writer Don McKay shares with us the quick and easy movements of eiders. As we watch, through his words, the birds flash in choppy waters until, "each, one after the other, / dove, like this: as if, as if, as / if that surface were the border—" and he holds us along with the sea ducks at that liquid boundary, "suddenly porous— / between yes and no, so / and not so."[8] An indistinct line between atmospheric and aquatic. Allowing for the indefinite and undetermined is needed to enable the others around us—moths and molds and thistles and sunbeams in Woolf's writings, firs and beavers and porcupines and salmon in the boreal subarctic—to do their own work, claim their own lives. When our language fails to encompass what needs to be held in our minds all at once, art serves as a place to dwell, a thin edge where the border blurs between pause and movement, torpor and speed, *acedia* and hope, Aergia and Horme.

THESE DAYS, I'VE BEEN WALKING. MY PACE IS BEST described as meandering, my routes rambling and circuitous. From the cabin, the gravel road in one direction heads towards the main road— the only way into and out of town—which was paved a few years after I first moved here, the gravel replaced by chipseal. The other direction, up valley, follows the creek upstream in this land carved by ice. The maintained gravel road ends in a little pull-out, and from there, a smaller rough road—more a wide trail than a road—leads to a campground at a midsized lake, then continues dozens of kilometres further along eskers and over creek crossings to another massive lake. Sometimes I strike out on the gravel road, the familiar surroundings still catching my attention each time. In summer, at any moment there could be a porcupine or a bear up ahead—most years, a family of grizzlies, and another of black bears, spends time in the area. Our neighbours, the same ones who hosted my virtual teaching through those online pandemic semesters, kept bees one summer. Despite the electric fence, they came home one day to one of their hives destroyed, having been scooped out by large paws, and decided to forego honey in future years.

In winter, I can tell who has been spending time in the neighbourhood by the tracks in the snow. I follow them on snowshoes, trampling down trails along the creek's edge. The deep holes punched through the crust by moose or caribou hooves, the ungulates distinguished by the specific shape of the arch in the prints left where they crossed the plowed road. Wolf tracks: like my dog's, only much larger. Soft steps of the lynx, claws pulled in leaving no trace, their lithe bodies suspended on snow banks. Four-part tracks of snowshoe hares, lightly spread across the snow's surface; closely spaced pairs of ermine prints, suggesting speed; small spread pads of red squirrels, and the even smaller zipper tracks of voles and mice across the snow. Slide marks from river otters disappear into the brief sections where the dark rushing water is visible, lively under the ice. Last winter, the snow was so heavy that it bent the aspen and poplar trees to the ground, snapped branches from spruce, flattened the willows and shrub birch. What is usually a spiky landscape of bare branches just above eye level became spare and empty, deceptively clear, all the buckbrush pressed flat under a blanket of white. Climate change has settled into this region in earnest, with warmer wetter winters, more unpredictable precipitation. Here, warmer still means cold of course, just not six straight weeks of -40 weather, where Celsius and Fahrenheit meet. When the melt finally arrived in May, most of the willows and birches rebounded, resilient in ways that seemed impossible given what they endured for so many months. This year, the snow—though still deep, more than twice the annual average—wasn't quite as wet, or quite as early, or quite as concentrated in a few heavy falls. Flocks of redpolls and pine grosbeaks loitered through winter in the branches that poked up through the top of the drifts.

I am struck each time I walk into the woods and frozen-over marshy areas by how alive it all is, even on days when everything seems hushed. The creek's rush muted by piled-up ice over boulders, the winds still, the birds elsewhere, my own pulse the loudest sound I can apprehend. All our tracks—the lynx, the hare, my own, the long-decayed leaves—are transient and fleeting. But walking in the tracks of others brings me close to them in space if not in time, in feeling if not in voice. I think again of lines from one of Barry Lopez's essays, "Perhaps the first rule of everything we endeavor to do is to pay attention. Perhaps the second is to be patient. And perhaps a third is to be attentive to what the body knows."[9] It is that second one that is especially hard these days, in a time where everything seems so urgent, where nothing seems far away: runaway climate change, with these northern regions warming twice as fast as elsewhere; war and pandemic and industrial extraction and so many kinds of pain. Practicing patience, I am learning, is an active endeavour. Sometimes I walk very quickly in no particular direction—with a mix of speed and purposelessness, the pace of possibility—trying to capture what my body knows about how these contradictions of damage and beauty, hope and despair, rest and recovery, restraint and ebullience can coexist.

During these treks, while escaping updates of the wider world and responsibilities to anything but my immediate surroundings, I think of the writer Annie Dillard's reckonings with our specific moments in the long history of the world. "Dire things are happening," she observes, elaborating: "New diseases, sways in power, floods!" But, she asks, "Can the news from dynastic Egypt have been any different?"[10] Floods, fires, storms; plagues, pests; coups, wars, corruption—it's all the same, it seems, the old, tired news of the world. Except Dillard warns against complacency, cautioning that, "To generalize, as Cynthia Ozick points out, is to 'befog' evil's specificity."[11] Here again are these tensions: the world spins and stutters. As I watch chickadees engaged in acrobatic feats on the tips of branches, I turn back to the Roman philosopher Lucretius who, in the first century BC, wrote of the senescence of the Earth. In what historian Cara New Daggett described as a "brusque" or even "gleefully blunt style,"[12] Lucretius declared that "The doors of death are always open wide: / For sky, for sun, for Earth, for ocean's deeps / The vast and gaping emptiness lies in wait."[13] How to respond to the ever-dying universe and our consignment to that great emptiness? By "living modestly, / Serene, content with little,"[14] suggests the philosopher, not labouring for the material wealth that offers such fleeting gratification. "Do you not see," Lucretius asks, "That our nature requires only this: / A body free from pain, and a mind, released from worry and fear, / Free to enjoy feelings of delight?"[15] So little is needed for contentment if we pause from striving in these short lives of ours. In a tumultuous world, a pain-free body and worry-free mind seem impossible to so many. But we can at least imagine an alternative hedonism of sorts and strive for it in a world returning to dust. I live in hope that the philosopher Søren Kierkegaard was right when he wrote, in a letter to his niece, "if one just keeps on walking, everything will be alright."[16] And so I walk on.

REFLECTING ON IDLENESS IN ITS VARIOUS FORMS MIGHT seem the purview of a scholar on sabbatical, as I am. A sabbatical, its origins in the Hebrew word for rest, recalls the Judeo-Christian sabbath and its seventh day or seventh year of pausing from labour.[17] More than just a privilege, this is a luxury: a release from certain time-bound obligations, a pause in teaching duties and administrative responsibilities, a chance to pursue a contemplative life. But these matters of undirected imagining and unharnessed activity, of slowness and meandering, rest and refusal—all the turning away from the focused, productive, efficient, accumulative endeavours that so often constitute our understanding of work—should not just be for those endowed with the time and space of a sabbatical. In fact, such opportunities are even more crucial for all those who are scrambling and slipping and cannot pause. Sisyphus would sympathize.

"War to the palace, peace to the cottage, and death to luxurious idleness!" This call to arms, printed in the anarchist publication *The Alarm* on April 24, 1886, preceded a nationwide strike in the United States that saw hundreds of thousands of workers taking coordinated action on May 1 against exploitative working conditions.[18] Although *The Alarm* sounded a challenge to "luxurious idleness," it wasn't exactly against time off from work. Instead, it was a rallying cry against leisure being reserved for wealthy capital-holders alone, made possible by the backbreaking work of those reliant on waged labour. The core demand of those on strike was an eight-hour work day.

The call reflected long-simmering resentment by workers that had been building for decades alongside rapid industrialization. Organizer Benjamin Fong describes the shift in the nineteenth century from task-based to timed labour, and with it, new bargains between workers and employers, and new incentives and discipline to control leisure and production. Fong recalls that in pre-industrial life, along with a day of rest for the Sabbath, it was standard for all workers to have another day without labour: "Saint Monday," it was called, a break from work that was, in Fong's wry account, "much to the chagrin of emergent entrepreneurs."[19] One strategy used by employers by the 1870s to control this leisure time, he recounts, was the introduction of a "half-holiday" on Saturdays. Early release from work on Saturday would enable workers to join in on organized sport and artistic activities. At the same time, the temperance movement made efforts to restrict alcohol and the leisure time needed to enjoy it. These enticements and moral reproofs were then combined with more punitive measures: Fong explains that the shortened Saturday workday was paired with the expectation by employers for workers to toil extra-long hours on Mondays, enforced by the threat of being fired for an absence.[20]

By the 1880s, resentment could no longer be contained; waves of it washed across the country, with increasing coordination. At the centre of the organizing activity in the US for the May strike was the city of Chicago—a hub of the anarchist movement.[21] At McCormick Harvester Works, which made reaper machines for farms, workers had begun organizing in earnest in 1884 when their pay was docked even as company profits soared.[22] Striking: one of the few tools of the exploited—to refuse work, to reject subservience, to hold ground.[23] This is a group strategy, not an individual one, working only when enough people band together against unfair conditions. Conflicts between strikebreakers—known colloquially as "scabs"—and those on strike were fierce and even violent. To quell the unrest, the company reinstated its previous compensation levels, but antagonism between the McCormick family and workers only intensified.[24] In 1886, as workers took to the streets in cities and towns throughout the country, they were fired up by rallying cries for better conditions, as sounded in *The Alarm*: "Make your demand for eight hours," that April article declared, and it went on to specify armed resistance would be needed to counteract the security apparatus of the state and corporate power.[25]

What exactly happened next remains unclear, in light of conflicting historical accounts, but on May 3 violence broke out in Haymarket Square in Chicago.[26] Did striking workers move first to attack scabs, as suggested by some, or did police, agitated by the increasingly impassioned speeches of organizers, initiate the brutality as they moved to break up the demonstrations with clubs?[27] I suspect, as with porcupines, that the striking workers simply held their ground against threat, and quill-throwing mythologies arose. In any case, events escalated: police clubs were met with thrown rocks that were countered with gunfire; two strikers were killed.[28] A meeting was called the next day, tensions rose again: police moved to disperse the crowd, and a bomb was thrown.[29] Culpability was unclear, but in the end—after martial law was declared, hundreds of workers were arrested, and homes were raided—eight labour organizers were tried and convicted for conspiracy and murder, with four of them sentenced to death.[30] The Haymarket Incident, as it became known, prompted a backlash against labour organizing, but only a few years later May 1—"May Day," or, in Mexico, "Day of the Chicago Martyrs"—became a rallying point for those mobilizing for workers' rights around the world.[31]

This book is, in part, about some people being flurried and others badly exploited, and through it all, the planet being undone around us. But it is also about how, at the same time, so many people are collectively imagining other ways of being, other modes of living, rejecting the story that they are powerless to enact change. When I think about making change in the most unlikely of circumstances, I am transported in memory to the site of Cruz's poetry, to a brief stretch when I lived in Manila. The largest mall in Asia, at the time, had just been finished and a state-of-the-art lightrail transit system was expanding, but I visited informal settlements that were holding encroaching floodwaters at bay with municipal waste, and travelled to them in brightly painted, crowded jeepneys, the diesel fumes rising. At the university, I ran circles in the middle of campus with other joggers, seeking time in the scant green space of a city paved over; at night, I went for drinks with journalists who were risking their careers and possibly their lives to follow trails of corruption. Some weekends, I joined the staff of a local NGO I was working with to learn how to scuba dive in a team-building exercise. They were fighting, through their work, for clean water access for all; what could be more fitting than nurturing trust in each other through being entirely submerged? Water is life, goes the slogan; still, we cannot breathe it. Some contradictions are uncomfortable, others enlivening.

IT SOMETIMES SEEMS IRRESPONSIBLE TO ADVOCATE FOR idleness in a world that needs so much energy and imagination and action—a total reorientation, and quickly! But responsibility, I've learned, derives from the Latin *respons*: "answered, offered in return." Perhaps the idleness of at least some of us sometimes—whether holding back, or slowing down, or pausing, or fiddling on a summer afternoon—constitutes an offering to each other and to the besieged world that still sustains us and our neighbours of many species. If we reconsider our furious action, slow down our production and consumption and extraction, perhaps others might regain the space for their own labours. We might orient ourselves differently within the world. As the writer Steven Heighton wrote in the fall of 2020—half a year into the pandemic, and only a year and a half before his death from cancer—it is counterintuitive to scale back and slow down in a society focused on accelerating, expanding, and enlarging.[32] But while it may be uncomfortable, even painful, he says, "[t]o kick the addictive illusion that a life in large font equals happiness" there is something to be said for disillusionment.[33]

Expanding from eiders, Don McKay writes that "All birds live close to the edge." He explains: "Typically, they draw air into sacs throughout their bodies, and even, in some cases, into their hollow bones. They also expel all the air from the lungs with each exhalation, without holding back, as we do, a reserve."[34] Full-bodied living, right to the bones. There is nothing restrained about this complete exchange of inner and outer worlds. Yet it isn't quite acquisitive either; nothing kept, nothing withheld. Another poet writing of birds observed the aerial displays of skylarks in the Irish countryside: "Falling-warbling, a chunked gob of pure kamikaze water music, unbelievably fluid and beyond any melody," recounted Coleman Barks.[35] Poets, he suggested, were seeking that same abandon, those same heights. Letting go of the false safety of accumulation in favour of being fully alive. Rumi, the Sufi poet, offered similar lessons from the sea: "Fish don't hold the sacred liquid in cups. / They swim the huge, fluid freedom."[36]

Perhaps that is part of finding one's place on this bounded world in a limitless universe—as fish and birds know, and poets aspire to learn, we can try to hold back nothing, and in this letting go be more fully at home, one breath at a time. The writer Tim Lilburn says that "Philosophy, according to the German poet Novalis, is really homesickness; it is the urge to be at home everywhere."[37] But not at *work* everywhere, not always making and producing. Shortening work weeks and building bike lanes and tending gardens and repairing our clothes and our tools and our technologies are, each one, a limited act in a specific workplace or community or home—but destruction also takes place one act and one place at a time. Extraction and demolition have mostly stopped seeming radical to many people, since they are so common, and so the cumulative impact of unrelenting quotidian damage all adds up. But even feller-bunchers can only raze one cutblock at a time, and sometimes, if rarely, they leave a lone Douglas fir standing. Each act of refusal, each moment of resisting the frenzy of producing and consuming, each time we notice a skylark's aerial abandon, we create new political spaces, new possibilities for our shared world.

Here, I turn back to Anne Michaels, and her novel on memory and sorrow that provided me with the language for the smell of those first drops of rain. In that book, she tells of the French painter Pierre Bonnard, who, "the day before he died, traveled hours to an exhibit of his works so that he could add a single drop of gold paint to the flowers in a painting."[38] One of her characters reflects that "even had Bonnard known that these were his last hours, he would still have taken that journey for the sake of a single second of pigment."[39] Sometimes it takes a painter, or fiddling grasshoppers, to remind us how each moment and action matters. As Annie Dillard put it, "How we spend our days is, of course, how we spend our lives."[40] Bonnard knew this, and chose that day, for those hours, to tend to his flowers. We have so many examples of other ways of being, of responsibility being both enlivening and joyful: Beston's other nations, Carson's wonder, Celan's silence, the Yolngu's shimmer. So even in these brief and fleeting days, in what might be our final hours, during these times of great urgency and damage, let us return to what is under us, to what sustains us: the breathing Earth itself. And our own breath, too. Sometimes the best we can offer to the world is a bit more meandering, a bit more idleness, a single brushstroke.

The outcrop by the cabin overlooks the creek that flows downstream into Atlin Lake, the one I snowshoed beside in winter, following the tracks of unseen animals. This land was once engulfed in ice. Everything here was shaped by water and scoured by rock over epochs of uplift. When I look up, I see layered horizons of buckbrush and aspen and poplar, then spruce and pine and fir, then worn ridges of old mountains, and then just sky. All the place names here are being reclaimed by the Taku River Tlingit, and this creek, I've learned, is called T'ooch' Héeni, which translates loosely to charcoal river or black river. The name carries memories of ancient buried life or of wood and fire, or maybe just describes the rich dark hue of the waters that stream by.

One morning, having just returned to the cabin after a teaching semester in the city, I walked down to the creek's edge. The nearby lakes were still frozen in parts, melting out in sharp sections, but T'ooch' Héeni was already racing with spring meltwater. My seasonal migration can be disorienting at times—the abrupt switch from urban to boreal environs—but I find solace in tracing the return of winged creatures whose lives span continents, even hemispheres. Earlier I had watched gulls perched on a thin ledge of lake ice, their hollow bones allowing them refuge on that fragile surface. I'd spotted flashes of yellow and black and chestnut feathers between still-bare branches of the buckbrush, chickadees and robins and warblers all aloft. And that May morning, in an eddy between riverbank and rock, I saw two ducks riding the charcoal edges of the water, turning spray into sky, feathers into flow. Stillness into motion into stillness as they turned and circled and paused; then the edges blurred, with reflected sun on the creek erasing all but the light itself.

ACKNOWLEDGEMENTS

I wrote this book mostly while living on the unceded territory of the Taku River Tlingit First Nation. In the essays, I draw from a life I have lived on many territories—including the lands of Anishinaabe, Haudenosaunee, Lūnaapéewak, Attawandaron, Sc'ianew, xʷməθkʷəy̓əm (Musqueam), Sḵwx̱wú7mesh (Squamish), and səlilwətaɬ (Tsleil-Waututh) nations—away from the places of my own distant family roots, generations removed from belonging in any ancestral lands. I hold a responsibility to those whose laws and languages and relations are interwoven with these places. This is not a burden, but a powerful opportunity: to learn and re-learn, to remember and undo, to recognize and respect, and to support so much more life, so many more ways of life.

I have so much gratitude to express for the ideas and experiences and exchanges over many years that informed this book, more than will fit here—but a few words, at least, of thanks:

To the Sowell Family Collection in Literature, Community and the Natural World, *Terrain.org*, and Texas Tech University Press, and especially my editors Elizabeth Dodd and Travis Snyder, who offered generous reading, perceptive questions, and enthusiastic encouragement, as well as compassion and understanding in difficult times;

To the team that dreamed up and established the galvanizing Sowell Emerging Writers Prize—some of whom I've had the honour to meet, others whom I admire from afar: Diane Warner, William Tydeman, the late and luminous Barry Lopez, Rick Bass, David Quammen, Travis

ACKNOWLEDGEMENTS

Snyder, Joanna Conrad, Katie Cortese, Simmons Buntin, Elizabeth Dodd, Pam Houston, Derek Sheffield, Kurt Caswell, and Kristin Loyd;

To the wonderful editing, design, and marketing team at TTUP, including Christie Perlmutter, Hannah Gaskamp, and John Brock; and

To the Port Renfrew Writers' Retreat for the exceptional gift of time in Snuggery Cove by those giant and wise old trees.

To those who have been astute, generous, and constructive thinkers, readers, editors, and interlocutors across many drafts of the book. I owe so much in particular to Kate Harris and Emily Nacol. Special thanks, too, to Fiona McGlynn, Lukas Neville, Dianne Chisholm, Kate Binhammer, Judy Currelly, Matt Hoffmann, Hana Boye, Oliver Barker, Stephan Torre, Sarah Martin, Amy Janzwood, the Environmental Governance Lab at the University of Toronto, and Ryan Katz-Rosene and colleagues at an International Studies Association panel on perspectives on growth.

To my students at the University of Toronto whose insights, enthusiasm, and curiosity have shaped my thinking on environmental politics and the future of our planet. In particular, my ENV197 students in the winter of 2021 discussed many of the ideas and themes that comprise this book—it was a difficult pandemic year to launch your university studies, and yet you brought such energy and imagination to all our classes. Thanks in particular to Emilie Nero for exchanges on Nature Needs Half. Thank you to students over the years in ENV413-2213 for delving into ideas of sacrifice and transformation, in POL205 for considering the Anthropocene and its many alternatives, and in ENV1001 and POL384 for thinking through shifting baselines, environmental movements, borders and migrations, and systems of political economy. For listening to draft versions of these essays, thanks to my classes in 2022 and 2023 on idleness and the environment, global environmental governance, and international relations, and to students in the Masters of Environment and Sustainability program at their spring retreat in 2023, especially Yichen Wu for our discussion of owls.

To colleagues at the School of the Environment and in the Department of Political Science for many reasons, including

ACKNOWLEDGEMENTS

allowing me to teach courses on idleness and the environment, on the Anthropocene, and on the politics of transformation;

To the School of the Environment for scholarly and material support (including financial support for indexing); and

A particular note of thanks to the administrative teams in both those units, especially Julie Guzzo, Sari Sherman, Michael Li, Meghan Sbrocchi, Emma Bernardo, and Stella Kyriakakis: without your tireless work, I wouldn't ever be able to contemplate idleness.

Some specific thanks to friends and loved ones who have contributed in so many ways:

Miche Genest for sourdough recipes and botanical walks, and for generative exchanges on writing, on grief, and on joy (and thank you for allowing me to share some of your words);

Hector Mackenzie for thoughts on anarchy and possibility, and for the names of birds and flowers and shrubs;

Erin Barnes for our igniting correspondence and the gift of Emma Goldman's autobiography;

Zack Donohew for debates on libertarianism and water markets, a shared love of water, and the introduction to the writings of David James Duncan;

Erin Barnes, Zack Donohew, Laura Jensen, Nadav Tanners, Kate Woodruff, and Kara DiFrancesco for that conference on big dams;

Philippe and Leandra Brient for helping me build a satellite university campus during the height of the pandemic and for rich friendship and adventure, and Justin for an astute literary critique of *Frederick*—the ending, indeed, could be stronger;

Fiona McGlynn and Robin Urquhart for wide-ranging conversations on the meanings of idleness, possibilities for utopias, and strategies for living flourishing lives;

Cathie Archbould and Jak Bedard for embodying the concept of community care, and Cathie for a sourdough starter at just the right moment;

Shauna Yeomans, Jerry Jack, Mark Connor, Angela Milani, and

ACKNOWLEDGEMENTS

Manu Keggenhoff for time at the weir with the salmon and the bears;

Judy Currelly for honouring ravens and for boldness in the sky, and Stephan Torre for tenderness and toughness in poetry and life, and to both for pointing out the absent aspen tree;

Manu Keggenhoff for warm friendship, the gift of a little greenhouse, and so often sharing garden abundance and tips as we learn how to negotiate the frosts and altitude;

Alex Moerschel for care for all beings, and especially for saving us from having to trap those mice by building beautiful and impenetrable watershed doors;

John and Linda Reed's grandchildren for their advocacy for beavers and their damming of the culverts, and John and Linda for neighbourly generosity;

Emily Nacol for insights into risk, rest, work, and wildness through sustained and galvanizing conversations over many months;

Matt Hoffmann for uplifting and challenging exchanges on beauty and damage and despair and hope, and for generous ongoing mentorship;

Scott Prudham for suggesting *The Mushroom at the End of the World*;

Libby Barlow for a shared love of this creek and valley and cabin;

the Decolonizing Water collective for resistance and imagination, to its many partners who so fearlessly contested the Site C dam even when all seemed lost, and to the late Karen Bakker for her vision;

Melissa Gniadek for questioning conversations on how to undertake scholarly work in meaningful ways;

Josh Berman and Kelly Levin for a shared love of owls;

Conchitina (Chingbee) Cruz for poetry and Robert Basilio for journalistic bravery, and both for their generosity in Manila;

Oliver Barker and Piia Kortsalo, and Aldo, for the way you bring your best attention to the world around you, wherever you are, and how that enriches my life, too;

Poppy and Willow and Gulliver and Archie for reminding me that even with shifting baselines the world is still astonishing and childhood

ACKNOWLEDGEMENTS

can be filled with wonder, and Mel Ashton whose artistic and creative vision makes possible that life;

Harley Rustad for his writing on Big Lonely Doug and the coastal forests of BC;

My colleagues and supervisors at the Ontario Ministry of Natural Resources for your patience and for teaching me so much that summer;

Paul Draghi for time in the Beinecke Library rare books collection with Rachel Carson's notes;

Adrienne Colby for shared hours on and by the Antler River;

Erika Mundel and Andrew Rushmere for years of conversations on the expansive nature of love, place-based connections, and walking;

Vance Martin for fierce dedication to people and to the whole Earth; and

Wayne Carlick, John Ward, James Williams, and Joan and Bryan Jack, for leadership, vision, and powerful kindness.

To many, many other friends along the way for enriching, nourishing, and wide-ranging conversations and reflections on work and meaning and fulfillment and resistance and joy and idleness. Your brave and boundary-crossing work and your commitments to community and care are inspiring. Among so many others, thanks to: Don Weir; Tanya Rosen; Cindy Merry and Maggie D'arcy, and also the much-missed Wayne Merry and Dick Fast, whose presences remain with us; Vince Esquiro and Marvin McDonald; Emily Darling; Zibba Leonardis; Cassie Flynn; Kim Rutherford and Kate Smolina; Amy Nihls and Ali Criscitiello; Rebecca Haspel; Nancy Williams; Anna Schmidt; Kate Walker; Ben Sanders and Meg Kizuik; Peter Steele; Laura and PJ Lee; JanaLee Cherneski; Lorelei Ormrod; Steve Johns; Paul and Mary Fennell; Mary and Peter Downs; Robert Osika and Norm Diewert; Erika Weinthal; Peter Dauvergne; Teresa Kramarz; Andrea Olive; and Nadège Compaoré.

And now to my family: the deepest gratitude to my Neville and Riley and Harris and Wells and Verrette and Jolink extended and chosen families for sustaining love and support, and for the many artists among them—writers and painters and photographers and musicians in abundance—who create so much beauty, and also to those we have lost, whose lives brought such richness to the world. And with my endless love and thanks to:

Lukas Neville and Indra Kalinovich for noticing and celebrating all the wonder and the absurdity of the world;

Jan and Pat Neville for valuing the gathering of summer colours along with the grain, for their ethics of reciprocity and deep community care, and for ever so much more;

Daniel, for endless enthusiasm for walking in the woods, and for reminding me that humans miss so much along the way;

And Kate Harris, for meandering, wandering, ambling, and rambling with me, in joy and in grief and in love and in wonder—and for always waiting for me, no matter how slowly I go.

NOTES

INTRODUCTION

1. Virginia Woolf, "Time Passes," in *To the Lighthouse* (London: Hogarth Press, 1927), Section IX.
2. Ibid., Section VIII.
3. Ibid., Section IX.
4. John Ayto, *Oxford Dictionary of English Idioms* (Oxford: Oxford University Press, 2010), 307.
5. Woolf, *To the Lighthouse*, Section IX.
6. Ibid.
7. Ibid.
8. Keynes' proposal is described by David Graeber in David Graeber, "On the Phenomenon of Bullshit Jobs: A Work Rant," *STRIKE! Magazine* 3, August 2013, https://www.strike.coop/bullshit-jobs/.
9. Paul Lafargue, *The Right to Be Lazy*, trans. Charles Kerr (Charles Kerr and Co., Co-operative, 1883, reprint 2000), accessed through The Anarchist Library, Anti-Copyright, online version from the Lafargue Internet Archive (marxists.org). Lafargue's proposal might have been understood as an eighteen-hour work week, as weekends were only just being reinstated into working life in the late 1800s. On this, also see Benjamin Fong, "Inventing the Weekend," *Jacobin Magazine*, 2018, https://www.jacobinmag.com/2018/07/leisure-time-holidays-religion-weekend.
10. Bertrand Russell, "In Praise of Idleness," *Harper's Magazine*, October 1932, https://harpers.org/archive/1932/10/in-praise-of-idleness/.
11. Some recent books on these themes that have informed my thinking in various ways include:

On questioning whether automation is the threat to workers: Aaron Benanav, *Automation and the Future of Work* (New York: Verso, 2020).

On care as the foundation of society: The Care Collective, *The Care Manifesto: The Politics of Interdependence* (New York: Verso, 2020).

On work week length and worker exploitation: Will Stronge and Kyle Lewis, *Overtime: Why We Need a Shorter Working Week* (New York: Verso, 2021).

On free time, spare time, and the conditions for individual freedom in a liberal democratic system: Julie L. Rose, *Free Time* (Princeton, NJ: Princeton University Press, 2016).

12. cf. Andrea Komlosy, *Work: The Last 1,000 Years* (New York: Verso, 2014, translation in 2018).

13. Quoted text from Hesiod in Hans van Wees, "The Economy," in *A Companion to Archaic Greece*, eds. Kurt A. Raaflaub and Hans van Wees (Hoboken, NJ: Blackwell Publishing Ltd., 2009), 446. See also Hesiod, *Works and Days, Theogony, and the Shield of Heracles*, trans. Hugh G. Evelyn-White (Mineola, NY: Dover Publications Inc., 2006), 11. In the Evelyn-White translations, those lines are: "Through work men grow rich in flocks and substance, and working they are much better loved by the immortals" or "working, you will be much better loved both by gods and men, for they greatly dislike the idle."

14. James Kearney, "Idleness," in *Cultural Reformations: Medieval and Renaissance in Literary History*, eds. James Simpson and Brian Cummings (Oxford: Oxford University Press, 2010), 572.

15. Yoshida Kenkō, "Essay 224," in *Essays in Idleness: The Tsurezuregusa of Kenkō*, trans. Donald Keene (New York, Columbia University Press, 1998), 185. This denigration of uncultivated lands was, at least in translation, quite aligned with the calls in the 1500s by essayist Michel de Montaigne, who advised that if fallow fields "continue to abound in a hundred thousand kinds of wild and useless plants," the response should be to "bring them under subjection." Here, Montaigne was using this familiar example of fields as a metaphor for what we ought to do with our minds, as he says: "if we do not keep them [our minds] occupied with a distinct subject, which curbs and restrains them, they run aimlessly to and fro, in the undefined field of imagination." While not quoted here, that passage also contains Montaigne's dismissive (and biologically

NOTES

suspect) view of women and conception. Michel de Montaigne, "Chapter VIII: Of Idleness," in *Volume I: The Essays of Montaigne*, trans. George B. Ives (Cambridge: Harvard University Press, 1925), 38–39.

16. Komlosy, *Work*, 7.
17. Ibid., 1.
18. Cara New Daggett, *The Birth of Energy: Fossil Fuels, Thermodynamics, and the Politics of Work* (Durham, NC: Duke University Press, 2019).
19. Mark Slouka, "Quitting the Paint Factory," *Harper's Magazine*, November 2004, 58.
20. Ibid., 61.
21. With thanks to Erin Barnes for the gift of Emma Goldman's biography, and even more for ongoing conversations on resisting tyranny and building just communities.
22. Notes on Emma Goldman's life are in part from PBS's "Anarchism and Emma Goldman," https://www.pbs.org/wgbh/americanexperience/features/goldman-anarchism-and-emma-goldman/.
23. Emma Goldman, "Anarchism: What It Really Stands For," in *Emma Goldman, Anarchism and Other Essays*, 3rd rev. ed. (New York: Mother Earth Publishing Association, 1917).
24. Ibid.
25. James Scott, *Two Cheers for Anarchism: Six Easy Pieces on Autonomy, Dignity, and Meaningful Work and Play* (Princeton, NJ: Princeton University Press, 2012).
26. Ibid., 17.
27. Ibid., 16.
28. Marina Sitrin, "The Anarchist Spirit," *Dissent* 62, no. 4 (2015): 84–86.
29. David Graeber, as quoted from his text *Fragments of an Anarchist Anthropology* in a tribute to him after his death: Molly Fischer, "David Graeber's Possible Worlds: *The Dawn of Everything* author left behind countless fans and a belief society could still change for the better," *NYMag Intelligencer*, November 9, 2021, https://nymag.com/intelligencer/2021/11/david-graeber-dawn-of-everything.html.
30. Kenkō, *Essays in Idleness*, 185.
31. Kenkō, *Essays in Idleness*. Kenkō writes of irises and wisteria in essay #19 (18–21) and of a series of trees and flowers, along with caterpillar infestations, in essay #139 (123–26); the *"spring weeds"* are mentioned but go

unspecified in terms of species, in essays #26 and #30 (27–28 and 30–31).
32. Kenkō, *Essays in Idleness*.
33. Ibid., 18–21. Kenkō does not write of his admiration of the birds; in essay #10 (10–11), he tells a story that criticizes a minister who keeps kites off his roof, but he follows it with a note of concern about crows hunting frogs. He does not specify the species, but golden kites were recognized as the national bird of Japan until after World War II, according to Manabu Waida, "Birds in the Mythology of Sacred Kingship," *East and West* 28, no. 1/4 (December 1978): 284.
34. Thomas Biggs, "Contesting *Cunctatio*: Livy 22.14, Fabius Maximus, and the Problem of Pastoral," *The Classical Journal* 111, no. 3 (2016): 281–301.
35. Ibid., 284.
36. Ibid., 285.
37. Piotr Schollenberger, "Idleness and Contemporary Art. On Taking One's Time," *Art Inquiry* 12 (2010): 72, 76–78.
38. Biggs, "Contesting *Cunctatio*," 283.
39. Ibid., 287.
40. Ibid., 286–87.
41. James C. Scott, *Seeing Like a State: How Certain Schemes to Improve the Human Condition Have Failed* (New Haven, CT: Yale University Press, 1998), 64. Along with this specific quote, my musings on legibility and classification are informed and inspired by this book more broadly.
42. These examples are drawn from multiple sources, including:

On biotechnology and conservation, Jesse L. Reynolds, "Governing New Biotechnologies for Biodiversity Conservation: Gene Drives, International Law, and Emerging Politics," *Global Environmental Politics* 20, no. 3 (2020): 28–48.

On assessing the outcomes of wetland mitigation banking in the US over thirty years, Shelley Burgin, "'Mitigation Banks' for Wetland Conservation: A Major Success or an Unmitigated Disaster?" *Wetlands Ecology and Management* 18 (2010): 49–55.

On the problems of measurement and governance associated with wetland mitigation banking, Morgan M. Robertson, "The Neoliberalization of Ecosystem Services: Wetland Mitigation Banking and Problems in Environmental Governance," *Geoforum* 35, no. 3 (2004): 361–73.

On "biobanking"—using habitat or ecosystem protection in one place to offset damage or loss elsewhere—Shelley Burgin, "BioBanking: An Environmental Scientist's View of the Role of Biodiversity Banking Offsets in Conservation," *Biodiversity and Conservation* 17 (2008): 807–16.

43. These forest management strategies and scientific findings by Suzanne Simard and colleagues are described by Ferris Jabr (with photographs by Brendan George Ko), "The Social Life of Forests," *New York Times*, December 2, 2020, https://www.nytimes.com/interactive/2020/12/02/magazine/tree-communication-mycorrhiza.html. Jabr's article includes an important point that while work by Simard and others revealed these mycorrhizal networks in terms legible to Western science, their findings aligned with long-standing Indigenous scientific knowledge of forest systems and their interconnections.

44. Jean-Luc Nancy and John Paul Ricco, "The Existence of the World Is Always Unexpected: Jean-Luc Nancy in Conversation with John Paul Ricco," trans. Jeffrey Malecki, in *Art in the Anthropocene: Encounters Among Aesthetics, Politics, Environments and Epistemologies*, eds. Heather Davis and Etienne Turpin (London: Open Humanities Press, 2015), 86. The search for equality demands the rejection of "catastrophic equivalence" in Nancy's account; for "common equality" we need to recognize "common incommensurability" instead of imagining an easy exchange, explains Nancy in that same conversation. Note that the description of Nancy's view on singularity in the introduction to the interview draws from Jean-Luc Nancy, *After Fukushima: The Equivalence of Catastrophes*, trans. Charlotte Mandell (New York: Fordham University Press, 2015).

45. Scott, *Seeing Like a* State, especially 63–64.

46. Woolf, *To the Lighthouse*, Section IX. In that section, she writes: "Slowly and painfully, with broom and pail, mopping, scouring, Mrs. McNab, Mrs. Bast, stayed the corruption and the rot; rescued from the pool of Time that was fast closing over them now a basin, now a cupboard; fetched up from oblivion all the Waverley novels and a tea-set one morning; in the afternoon restored to sun and air a brass fender and a set of steel fire-irons."

47. Woolf, *To the Lighthouse*, Section IX.

48. Ibid. This line is part of a longer passage, where Woolf writes: "And now as if the cleaning and the scrubbing and the scything and the mowing

had drowned it there rose that half-heard melody, that intermittent music which the ear half catches but lets fall; a bark, a bleat; irregular, intermittent, yet somehow related; the hum of an insect, the tremor of cut grass, disevered yet somehow belonging; the jar of a dorbeetle, the squeak of a wheel, loud, low, but mysteriously related; which the ear strains to bring together and is always on the verge of harmonising, but they are never quite heard, never fully harmonised, and at last, in the evening, one after another the sounds die out, and the harmony falters, and silence falls."

49. Hanif Kureishi, excerpt on the art of writing, *The Independent*, March 4, 2011, https://www.independent.co.uk/arts-entertainment/books/features/the-art-of-writing-hanif-kureishi-reveals-how-to-succeed-in-the-worlds-of-fiction-and-film-2231223.html.

50. Stacey D'Erasmo, "The Uses of Doubt," *Ploughshares* 28, no. 4 (2002/2003): 27.

51. On the displacement of labour, see Paul Wapner, *Is Wildness Over?* (Cambridge, UK: Polity Press, 2020). These themes will be further explored in "Fir deferrals" later in this collection.

52. Graeber, "On the Phenomenon of Bullshit Jobs." In the article, Graeber writes of the critiques often levelled at those whose work is meaningful to them: "It's as if they are being told 'but you get to teach children! Or make cars! You get to have real jobs! And on top of that you have the nerve to also expect middle-class pensions and health care?'"

53. With thanks to Matt Hoffmann for conversations on this idea, among many others.

54. Henry Beston, *The Outermost House* (Garden City, NY: Doubleday and Doran, 1928). In Beston's memoir, about a year spent mostly alone at a lighthouse on Cape Cod, he places humans in a broader, cosmic perspective, and laments the hubris of those who would see other species as lesser. "For the animal shall not be measured by man," he writes, and says humans err when they fail to recognize that we are new arrivals in an old world, with limited senses and knowledge. His claim is not one of kinship—"they are not brethren," as he says—but also not one of dominance or superiority: "they are not underlings." Shared citizenship on a planet, in which there are many nations. His perspectives—as a white settler American naturalist—are different from those of writings in other traditions, whether Metis or Anishinaabe or otherwise, but reflect one thread in the multiplicity

of nondominant Western traditions of thought. What his writings share with some of those writings from other traditions of understanding the relationships between humans and nonhumans, or other-than-humans, are challenges to human-centred hierarchies and domination, a sense of humans being only one among many nations. For some of those other perspectives, see, for instance (among so many):

Anja Kanngieser and Zoe Todd, "From Environmental Case Study to Environmental Kin Study," *History and Theory* 59, no. 3 (September 2020): 385–93.

Enrique Salmón, "Kincentric Ecology: Indigenous Perceptions of the Human-Nature Relationship," *Ecological Applications* 10, no. 5 (October 2000): 1327–32, https://www.fws.gov/nativeameri-can/pdf/tek-salmon-2000.pdf.

Vanessa Watts, "Indigenous Place-Thought and Agency Amongst Humans and Non-Humans: First Woman and Sky Woman Go on a European Tour!" *Decolonization: Indigeneity, Education & Society* 2, no. 1 (2013.): 20–34.

CHAPTER I

1. Austin R. Spence, Erin E. Wilson Rankin, and Morgan W. Tingley, "DNA Metabarcoding Reveals Broadly Overlapping Diets in Three Sympatric North American Hummingbirds," *Ornithology* 139, no. 1 (2022): ukab074, https://doi.org/10.1093/ornithology/ukab074.
2. V. S. Vernon Jones, *Æsop's Fables: A New Translation* (London: William Heinemann and New York: Doubleday, Page, and Company, 1912, reprint 1916), 125.
3. Avianus was a Latin fable writer from around AD 400. Roger L'Estrange attributes the fable "An Ant and a Grasshopper" (fable #217) to Avianus in Roger L'Estrange, *Fables of Æsop and Other Eminent Mythologists, with Morals and Reflections* (London: R. Sare et al., 1692), 189.

    J. H. Stickney includes the fable in a collection of Aesop's tales in J. H. Stickney, *Aesop's Fables: A Version for Young Readers* (1915), available from Project Gutenberg at https://www.gutenberg.org/ebooks/49010.
4. Thomas James, Fable 12 in *Æsop's Fables: A New Version, Chiefly from Original Sources* (London: John Murray, 1848), 12.

NOTES

5. Jones, *Æsop's Fables*, 125.
6. Leo Lionni, *Frederick* (New York: Pantheon, 1967).
7. Ibid.
8. Thanks to Justin Brient for this observant critique.
9. Corrine Segal and Ocean Vuong, "Ocean Vuong on Taking the Time You Need to Write," *Literary Hub*, April 8, 2022, https://lithub.com/ocean-vuong-on-taking-the-time-you-need-to-write/. In the interview, Vuong says: "Bashō talks often about the colors of poems. I think what he means by that is the moods and the tones, the sort of aesthetic principles of them. And I think that you can't just sit down and write that, you have to really embody it."
10. Ibid.
11. Piotr Schollenberger, "Idleness and Contemporary Art. On Taking One's Time," *Art Inquiry* 12 (2010): 82.
12. Ibid., 82.
13. For more on mandalas, see the Smithsonian Institution, "Mandalas," *Freer Gallery of Art and Arthur M. Sackler Gallery*, https://archive.asia.si.edu/exhibitions/online/mandala/mandala.htm.
14. Alex McNeil, "What's in a 'Nym'? Pseudonyms, Heteronyms, and the Remarkable Case of Fernando Pessoa," *Shakespeare Oxford Fellowship*, September 9, 2002, https://shakespeareoxfordfellowship.org/whats-in-a-nym/.
15. From a translation by Richard Zenith of Reis/Pessoa's 1933 poem *Odes*, in Fernando Pessoa, *A Little Larger Than the Entire Universe: Selected Poems*, ed. and trans. Richard Zenith (London: Penguin Classics, 2006). The Poetry Foundation, https://www.poetryfoundation.org/poetry-magazine/poems/26781/odes, has a translation by Edouard Roditi of that same passage that reads:
To be great, be whole: nothing that's you
Should you exaggerate or exclude.
In each thing, be all. Give all you are
In the least you ever do.
The whole moon, because it rides so high,
Is reflected in each pool.
16. On cicadas, see Montreal Space for Life, "Insects and Other Arthropods—Classification of Insects," https://espacepourlavie.ca/en/

chart-orders-insects, and the Amateur Entomologists' Society, "True Bugs (Order: Hemiptera)," https://www.amentsoc.org/insects/fact-files/orders/hemiptera.html.

On grasshoppers, see John P. Roche, "The Origin of Grasshoppers, Katydids, and Crickets: A New Study Resolves the Evolutionary Tree of the Orthoptera," *Entomology Today*, April 8, 2015, https://entomologytoday.org/2015/04/08/the-origin-of-grasshoppers-katydids-and-crickets-a-new-study-resolves-the-evolutionary-tree-of-the-orthoptera/.

Note that Orthoptera are closely related to Dermaptera (these latter are earwigs); on this, see John R. Meyer, "Orthoptera," in the *Index to the Compendium of Hexapod Classes and Orders*, 2020, https://projects.ncsu.edu/cals/course/ent425/library/compendium/orthoptera.html.

17. Plato, *Phaedrus*, trans. Benjamin Jowett, available from The Internet Classics Archive, http://classics.mit.edu/Plato/phaedrus.html.
18. Casey Cep, "Songs of the Cicada," *The New Yorker*, June 6, 2013, https://www.newyorker.com/books/page-turner/songs-of-the-cicada.
19. Annie Dillard, *The Writing Life* (New York: Harper & Row, 1989), chapter 3.
20. Ibid., chapter 1.
21. Brian O'Connor, *Idleness: A Philosophical Essay* (Princeton, NJ: Princeton University Press, 2018), 58.
22. On the latter, some employers have advocated for the removal of emergency response benefits to incentivize worker availability. For instance, see Mitchell Thompson, "Is the Canada Recovery Benefit a 'Workfare' Program in Disguise?" *Canadian Dimension*, June 8, 2021, https://canadiandimension.com/articles/view/is-the-canada-recovery-benefit-a-workfare-program-in-disguise.
23. UN Declaration of Human Rights, Article 23(1), 1948, https://www.un.org/en/about-us/universal-declaration-of-human-rights.
24. Guy Standing, "Why a Basic Income Is Necessary for a Right to Work," *Basic Income Studies* 7, no. 2 (2013): 19.
25. Ibid.
26. For more on unfree labour, see Genevieve LeBaron, *Combatting Modern Slavery: Why Labour Governance is Broken and What We Can Do About It* (Cambridge, UK: Polity Press, 2020). See also Genevieve LeBaron and Jane Lister, "The Hidden Costs of Global Supply Chain

NOTES

Solutions," *Review of International Political Economy* (2021), DOI: 10.1080/09692290.2021.1956993.
27. Standing, "Why a Basic Income," 21.
28. Ibid., 24.
29. Paul Lafargue, *The Right to Be Lazy*, trans. Charles Kerr (Charles Kerr and Co., Co-operative, 1883, reprint 2000), accessed through The Anarchist Library, Anti-Copyright, online version from the Lafargue Internet Archive, https://www.marxists.org/archive/lafargue/1883/lazy/. For those turning to this source directly, it's worth warning that Lafargue offers an account of Indigenous peoples that echoes patronizing colonial views, pointing to the "noble savage" as a model of the rejection of "servile labour." In his work, it seems he sees himself as admiring and respectful, but his language and portrayals deepen the myths that obscure the many economic systems, ways of life, forms of labour and cultivation, and complexities of numerous distinct nations and peoples around the world.
30. Lafargue, *The Right to Be Lazy*, 6.
31. Ibid. Lafargue's quotation of this line differs slightly from the version I have of that pamphlet from J. Cunningham, *An Essay on Trade and Commerce: Containing Observations on Taxes, as They Are Supposed to Affect the Price of Labour in our Manufactories: Together with Some Interesting Reflections on the Importance of Our Trade to America* (London: S. Hooper, No. 25, 1770), 56. There, the line is: "The laboring people should never think themselves independent of their superiors; for if a proper foundation is not kept up, riot and confusion will take the place of sobriety and order."
32. Lafargue, *The Right to Be Lazy*, 6. This, too, differs slightly from Cunningham, "An Essay on Trade and Commerce," 57, which reads: "It is extremely dangerous to encourage mobs in a commercial state like ours, where, perhaps, seven parts out of eight of the whole, are people of little or no property." Note that Lafargue quotes it as "such infatuations," while the pamphlet itself reads "mobs." Nonetheless, Lafargue's version seems true to the spirit of the text, as the next line in Cunningham reads: "Every idea of an accession to what the populace call liberty, tends to make them the more idle and debauched."
33. Ambrose Bierce, "The Ant and the Grasshopper," in *Fantastic Fables*

(New York and London: G. P. Putnam's Sons, 1899), 165.
34. Roger L'Estrange, "Fable 188: An Ant Formerly a Man," in *Fables of Æsop and Other Eminent Mythologists, with Morals and Reflections* (London: R. Sare et al., 1692), 166.
35. Bertrand Russell, "In Praise of Idleness," *Harper's Magazine*, October 1932, https://harpers.org/archive/1932/10/in-praise-of-idleness/.
36. Russell, "In Praise of Idleness."
37. Hans van Wees, "Chapter 23: The Economy," in *A Companion to Archaic Greece*, eds. Kurt A. Raaflaub and Hans van Wees (Hoboken, NJ: Blackwell Publishing Ltd., 2009), 445.
38. van Wees, "The Economy," 447.
39. Ibid., 448.
40. Ibid., 450.
41. Sian Lewis and Lloyd Llewellyn-Jones, *The Culture of Animals in Antiquity: A Sourcebook with Commentaries* (London: Routledge, 2018), 597.
42. Ibid., 597.
43. As discussed by an online F.I.R.E. advocate, "Mr. Money Mustache": https://www.mrmoneymustache.com/2011/04/13/what-does-early-retirement-mean-anyway/.
44. Lafargue, *The Right to Be Lazy*.
45. Trina Paul, "Interested in Retiring Early? 3 Lessons from People Who Retired in Their 30s," CNBC, December 8, 2021, https://www.cnbc.com/select/lessons-from-people-who-retired-in-their-30s/.
46. Affordable housing in Canada is often understood as a threshold, not a value—generally where households spend less than 30 percent of their income on housing. By 2018, according to an article in the *Georgia Straight*, about 40 percent of BC and Ontario renters spent more than 30 percent of their incomes on housing, and this situation only worsened following the pandemic. Based on 2019 data from Statistics Canada, roughly 10 percent of Canadians live under the poverty line. See BC Housing on thresholds for affordable housing, https://www2.gov.bc.ca/gov/content/housing-tenancy/affordable-and-social-housing/afffordable-housing/defining-affordable-housing, and Statistics Canada on Canadian poverty, https://www.statcan.gc.ca/en/topics-start/poverty). On BC and Ontario renters, see Carlito Pablo, "B.C. has Highest

NOTES

Proportion of Renters in Canada Spending over 50 Percent of Income on Housing," *Georgia Straight*, May 8, 2018, https://www.straight.com/news/1071531/bc-has-highest-proportion-renters-canada-spending-over-50-percent-income-housing.

47. I have not been able to track down the full original source, but a number of writers refer to a sequel to the ant and the grasshopper published in an 1851 book by Jacques-Melchior Villefranche, wherein the ants lose their winter supplies and turn to other insects for help. Part of the fable—with the bee, at the end, inviting the ant to "Live together in leisure:/all those whom I see suffer/deserve equal help" [my own translation]—is printed in Louis Medler, "Villefranche, Fabuliste Catholique (1829–1904)," *Le Sel de la Terre*, no. 70 (Autumn 2009): 165–83, https://isidore.co/misc/Res%20pro%20Deo/Sel%20de%20la%20Terre/Sdt%20N%C2%B0070/42%20PLM-Villefranche-(fini).pdf.

48. See details on 2021 road washouts in BC from the Government of BC, "2021 B.C. Highway Flood Recovery Projects," 2021, https://www2.gov.bc.ca/gov/content/transportation-projects/bc-highway-flood-recovery.

    On repeated extreme weather events in Sudan, and the consequences for local farmers and families, see Marwa Awad, "South Sudanese Struggle to Survive Climate Change Effects," *Newsweek*, February 10, 2022, https://www.newsweek.com/south-sudanese-struggle-survive-climate-change-effects-opinion-1677714.

    On flooding in Ecuador in 2022, see France24 News. "Quito Flooding Toll Raised to 27," February 4, 2022, https://www.france24.com/en/live-news/20220204-quito-flooding-toll-raised-to-27.

49. Leo Sands, "Pakistan Floods: One Third of Country Is Under Water – Minister," BBC, August 30, 2022, https://www.bbc.com/news/world-europe-62712301.

50. Rajesh Trichur Venkiteswaran, "Food Grains Rot in India While Millions Live with Empty Stomachs," *Lowy Institute*, November 16, 2018, https://www.lowyinstitute.org/the-interpreter/food-grains-rot-india-while-millions-live-empty-stomachs.

51. Sarah Martin, "The Political Economy of Distillers' Grains and the Frictions of Consumption," *Environmental Politics* 29, no. 2 (2019): 297–316, DOI: 10.1080/09644016.2019.1565461.

52. Ibid.

53. Venkiteswaran, "Food Grains Rot."
54. On these stories, see for instance Kyle Wanberg, "Echoes of the Ant People: Vocal Traces and Writing Practices in a Translation of 'O'odham Orature," *Canadian Review of Comparative Literature* 40, no. 3 (2013): 271–88. Also see Thomas Alexander, "The Fourth World of American Philosophy: The Philosophical Significance of Native American Culture," *Transactions of the Charles S. Peirce Society* 32, no. 3 (1996): 375–402. But on caution and restraint in taking stories out of context and without consent, see Paul V. Kroskrity, "Narrative Reproductions: Ideologies of Storytelling, Authoritative Words, and Generic Regimentation in the Village of Tewa," *Journal of Linguistic Anthropology* 19, no. 1 (2009): 40–56. As Kroskrity explains in work on Tewa language and storytelling, where he references the view of Ant People in the stories of the Tewa, it is often inappropriate and disrespectful for those from outside the community to share or interpret their narratives and texts. In that article (p. 46), Kroskrity writes of Tewa stories that centre the "family-oriented, team-player, work-ethic endowed, and otherwise socio-centric characters like the Ant People, the Deer, and the Birds."
55. Wanberg, "Echoes of the Ant People." In this article, Wanberg writes of the Akimel 'O'odham Ant Songs, and the stories and images of the language, songs, instruments, and dreams of ants.
56. Robin Wall Kimmerer, "The Serviceberry: An Economy of Abundance," *Emergence Magazine*, 2020, https://emergencemagazine.org/story/the-serviceberry/.
57. Ibid.
58. Cep, "Songs."

CHAPTER II

1. Common names in multiple languages listed in the Committee on the Status of Endangered Wildlife in Canada, "COSEWIC Assessment and Status Report on the Grizzly Bear *Ursus arctos* (Western population, Ungava population) in Canada" (Ottawa: Environment Canada, 2012), 5, https://www.sararegistry.gc.ca/virtual_sara/files/cosewic/sr_ours_grizz_bear_1012_e.pdf. See also Edōsdi, Judith Charlotte Thompson, "Hedekeyeh Hots'ih Kāhidi – "Our Ancestors Are in Us":

Strengthening our Voices Through Language Revitalization from a Tahltan Worldview" (PhD diss., University of Victoria, 2012), http://www.malsmb.ca/docs/thompson-judith-phd-2012.pdf.

2. These nutrient cycles and relationships are described in this article on salmon/forest interactions: Nancy Baron, "Salmon Trees," *Hakai Magazine*, April 22, 2015, https://hakaimagazine.com/features/salmon-trees/.

3. Charles C. Schwartz, Sterling D. Miller, and Mark A. Haroldson, "Grizzly Bear (*Ursus arctos*)," in *Wild Mammals of North America: Biology, Management, and Conservation*, 2nd edition, eds. G. A. Feldhamer, B. C. Thompson, and J. A. Chapman, chapter 26 (Baltimore: Johns Hopkins University Press, 2003), 562.

4. Jerey A. Keay, Charles T. Robbins, and Sean D. Farley, "Characteristics of a Naturally Regulated Grizzly Bear Population," *The Journal of Wildlife Management* 82, no. 4 (2018): 789–801, https://doi.org/10.1002/jwmg.21425.

5. Ibid.

6. On these factors influencing denning, see, for instance, Karine E. Pigeon, Gordon Stenhouse, and Steeve D. Côté, "Drivers of Hibernation: Linking Food and Weather to Denning Behaviour of Grizzly Bears," *Behavioral Ecology and Sociobiology* 70 (2016): 1745–54. On metabolic rates, see Enrique González-Bernardo, Luca Francesco Russo, Esther Valderrábano, Ángel Fernández, and Vincenzo Penteriani, "Denning in Brown Bears," *Ecology and Evolution* 10 (2020): 6851.

7. González-Bernardo et al., "Denning."

8. Ellen Meloy, *The Last Cheater's Waltz: Beauty and Violence in the Desert Southwest* (Tucson: University of Arizona Press, 1997), 41.

9. Ibid.

10. Brian Doyle, "Joyas Voladoras," *The American Scholar*, June 12, 2012, https://theamericanscholar.org/joyas-volardores/.

11. Lucy Hicks, "To Survive Frigid Nights, Hummingbirds Cool Themselves to Record-Low Temperatures," *Science*, September 8, 2020, https://www.science.org/content/article/survive-frigid-nights-hummingbirds-cool-themselves-record-low-temperatures.

12. Doyle, "Joyas Voladoras."

13. Blair O. Wolf, Andrew E. McKechnie, C. Jonathan Schmitt, Zenon

NOTES

J. Czenze, Andrew B. Johnson, and Christopher C. Witt, "Extreme and Variable Torpor Among High-Elevation Andean Hummingbird Species," *Biology Letters* 16 (2020): 20200428, http://dx.doi.org/10.1098/rsbl.2020.0428.

14. Ibid.
15. Jonathan Lambert, "This Hummingbird Survives Cold Nights by Nearly Freezing Itself Solid," *ScienceNews*, September 8, 2020, https://www.sciencenews.org/article/hummingbirds-black-metaltail-cold-torpor. See also A. Begazo, ed., "Peru Aves: Black Metaltail (*Metallura phoebe*)," Lima, Peru: CORBIDI, 2022, https://www.peruaves.org/trochilidae/black-metaltail-metallura-phoebe/.
16. Mark Slouka, "Quitting the Paint Factory," *Harper's Magazine*, November 2004, 59–60.
17. Suggestions for these strategies abound online; see, for instance: Entrepreneur Media, "101 Efficiency Hacks for Busy Entrepreneurs," *Entrepreneur*, November 10, 2016, https://www.entrepreneur.com/article/284768; Kristin Granero, "25 Time-Saving Hacks That Will Add Hours Back to Your Week," *NBC News*, August 12, 2019, https://www.nbcnews.com/better/lifestyle/25-time-saving-hacks-will-add-hours-back-your-week-ncna1041011; Jory MacKay, "10 Email Canned Responses That Will Save You Hours Each Week," *Rescue Time Blog*, August 2, 2018, https://blog.rescuetime.com/canned-responses-gmail/; and Aaron Brooks, "19 Productivity Hacks to Get More Done in 2022," *Venture Harbour Ltd.*, December 9, 2021, https://www.ventureharbour.com/productivity-hacks/.
18. Lambert, "This Hummingbird Survives."
19. Tim Kreider, "The 'Busy' Trap," *New York Times*, June 30, 2012.
20. Courtney Seiter, "The Science of Taking Breaks at Work," *Buffer*, August 21, 2014, https://buffer.com/resources/science-taking-breaks-at-work/.
21. Kreider, "The 'Busy' Trap."
22. Virginia Woolf, *The Waves* (London: Hogarth Press, 1931).
23. Ibid.
24. Michel de Montaigne, "Chapter XXXIX: Of Solitude," in *Volume I: The Essays of Montaigne*, trans. George B. Ives, 313–28 (Cambridge, MA: Harvard University Press, 1925).
25. Jess Housty ('Cúagilákv), "Winter Is for Regeneration. The Garden's

— and Yours, Too," *The Tyee*, December 14, 2021, https://thetyee.ca/Culture/2021/12/14/Winter-Regeneration-Garden-Yours-Too/.
26. Brown bears in Europe spend three to five months in reproductive activities (lactation alone can last this long): Claudia López-Alfaro, Charles T. Robbins, Andreas Zedrosser, and Scott E. Nielsen, "Energetics of Hibernation and Reproductive Trade-Offs in Brown Bears," *Ecological Modelling* 270 (December 2013): 1–10.
27. Charles T. Robbins, Claudia Lopez-Alfaro, Karyn D. Rode, Øivind Tøien, and O. Lynne Nelson, "Hibernation and Seasonal Fasting in Bears: The Energetic Costs and Consequences for Polar Bears," *Journal of Mammalogy* 93, no. 6 (2012): 1493–1503, https://doi.org/10.1644/11-MAMM-A-406.1. Schwartz et al., "Grizzly Bear," 567, also describe "walking hibernation" in brown bears in Alaska.
28. One to three cubs is usual, although Schwartz et al., "Grizzly Bear," 563, note that litters up to six cubs have been recorded. See also López-Alfaro et al., "Energetics of Hibernation."
29. Montaigne, "Of Solitude," 324.
30. Erling Kagge, *Silence in the Age of Noise* (New York: Pantheon, 2017), 13–14.
31. Ibid., 14.
32. Ibid., 12.
33. Ed Yong, "Plants Can Hear Animals," *The Atlantic*, January 10, 2019, https://www.theatlantic.com/science/archive/2019/01/plants-use-flowers-hear-buzz-animals/579964/.
34. Ibid.
35. Ibid. Research on the acoustics of the world beyond humans is also explored by Karen Bakker, *The Sounds of Life: How Digital Technology Is Bringing Us Closer to the Worlds of Animals and Plants* (Princeton, NJ: Princeton University Press, 2022).
36. Barry Lopez, *Arctic Dreams: Imagination and Desire in a Northern Landscape* (New York: Charles Scribner's Sons, 1986), 124–26.
37. Ibid., 126.
38. Sandra Steingraber, "The Fracking of Rachel Carson," *Orion*, September/October 2012, https://orionmagazine.org/article/the-fracking-of-rachel-carson/.
39. Rachel Carson, "Silent Spring–I," *The New Yorker*, 1962, https://www.

newyorker.com/magazine/1962/06/16/silent-spring-part-1.
40. Martin Straka, Ladislav Paule, Jozef Štofík, Ovidiu Ionescu, and Michal Adamec, "Genetic Differentiation of Carpathian Brown Bear (*Ursus arctos*) Populations Reflects the Human Caused Isolation," *Beiträge zur Jagd- und Wildforschung* 36 (2011): 77.
41. Ibid.
42. Although thousands now live in Romanian forests, with a ban against hunting them introduced in 2016, bear-human relationships remain fraught. On this, see Matt Davies, "Romania's Brown Bears," *Mossy Earth*, 2021, https://mossy.earth/rewilding-knowledge/romanias-brown-bears; and Luke Dale-Harris, "How the Brown Bear Became Public Enemy Number One in Rural Romania," *The Guardian*, November 22, 2017, https://www.theguardian.com/environment/2017/nov/22/how-the-brown-bear-became-public-enemy-number-one-in-rural-romania.
43. Robert Kelly, "A Love Affair with Silence," *New York Times*, November 9, 1986, https://www.nytimes.com/1986/11/09/books/a-love-affair-with-silence.html.
44. Ruth Franklin, "How Paul Celan Reconceived Language for a Post-Holocaust World," *The New Yorker*, November 16, 2020, https://www.newyorker.com/magazine/2020/11/23/how-paul-celan-reconceived-language-for-a-post-holocaust-world.
45. Chase Berggrun, "Mostly His Apocalyptic Star Glitters Wondrously," *Poetry* magazine, November 2, 2020, https://www.poetryfoundation.org/poetrymagazine/articles/154451/mostly-his-apocalyptic-star-glitters-wondrously.
46. Poetry Foundation, "Osip Mandelstam: 1891–1938," https://www.poetryfoundation.org/poets/osip-mandelstam. See also John Felstiner, "Paul Celan Translating Others," *World Literature Today*, November 11, 2014, https://www.worldliteraturetoday.org/blog/translation/paul-celan-translating-others.
47. This translation is quoted in Ilya Kaminsky and Katherine Towler, "Introduction," in *A God in the House: Poets Talk About Faith*, eds. Ilya Kaminsky and Katherine Towler, ix–xi (North Adams, MA: Tupelo Press, 2012), xi. An alternate translation of this passage reads: *"we / really don't know, you know, / we / really don't know / what / counts."*

NOTES

Paul Celan, "Zurich, At the Stork (for Nelly Sachs)," in *Selected Poems and Prose of Paul Celan*, trans. John Felstiner (New York: W. W. Norton, 2001). And another translation is:

"*We / just don't know, you see, / we / just don't know / what / counts...*" Paul Celan and Nelly Sachs, *Correspondence*, trans. Christopher Clark (Riverdale-on-Hudson, NY: The Sheep Meadow Press, 1998), 26–27.

48. We humans are new arrivals according to so many ways of knowing: Indigenous knowledges and Western science and so many more. However, these traditions come with different understandings and interpretations of what the timing of human arrival means for how we ought to live on this planet—whether in a position of learning from our elders, one of stewardship and responsibility, or one of superiority and domination. As one example, in Potawatomi traditions we are the "younger brothers of creation," as explained by Robin Wall Kimmerer, "Returning the Gift," *Minding Nature* 7, no. 2 (2014), republished by the Network for Grateful Living, https://gratefulness.org/resource/returning-the-gift/.

49. Pablo Neruda, "Keeping Quiet," in *Extravagaria: A Bilingual Edition*, trans. Alastair Reid (New York: Farrar, Straus and Giroux, 1972, reprint 2001).

50. Ibid.

51. Andrew E. Kramer, "'Everybody in Our Country Needs to Defend,'" *New York Times*, February 26, 2022, https://www.nytimes.com/2022/02/26/world/europe/ukraine-russia-civilian-military.html.

52. On these stories and actions, see, for instance, Isabelle Khurshudyan, Siobhán O'Grady, and Loveday Morris, "'Weapons to Anyone': Across Ukraine, Militias Form as Russian Forces Near," *Washington Post*, February 26, 2022, https://www.washingtonpost.com/world/2022/02/26/ukraine-russia-militias/; Pariesa Young, "'Hello from Ukraine': Volunteers Make Molotov Cocktails to Counter Russian Assault," *France24*, February 28, 2022, https://observers.france24.com/en/europe/20220228-citizen-volunteers-ukraine-russia-invasion-molotov-cocktails. For a video of the offering of seeds, see "Ukrainian Woman Offers Seeds to Russian Soldiers so 'Sunflowers Grow When They Die,'" *The Guardian*, February 25, 2022, https://www.theguardian.com/world/video/2022/feb/25/ukrainian-woman-sunflower-seeds-russian-soldiers-video.

NOTES

53. Luke Harding, "'We Are a Huge Amount of Ants': The United Front of Ukrainian Volunteers," *The Guardian*, March 2, 2022, https://www.theguardian.com/world/2022/mar/02/ukrainian-volunteers-united-front-against-russia-invasion.
54. Neruda, "Keeping Quiet."
55. Ibid.
56. Woolf, *The Waves*.
57. Celan and Sachs, *Correspondence*, 33.
58. Paul Waldie (photography by Anna Liminowicz), "Too Precious to Leave Behind," *The Globe and Mail*, March 4, 2022, https://www.theglobeandmail.com/world/article-ukrainians-fleeing-war-with-russia-share-the-items-they-couldnt-leave/.
59. Celan and Sachs, *Correspondence*, 33.
60. Ibid., 7.
61. Neruda, "Keeping Quiet."

CHAPTER III

1. Sierra Club, "About Clearcutting," 2022, https://www.sierraclub.org/grassroots-network/stop-clearcutting-ca/about-clearcutting.
2. Described from personal experience; for images of a west-coast clear cut, see Carol Linnitt, "In Photos: See Old-Growth Go from Stand to Stump on B.C.'s Vancouver Island," *The Narwhal*, December 10, 2020, https://thenarwhal.ca/bc-old-growth-forest-vancouver-island-caycuse/.
3. Harley Rustad, "Big Lonely Doug," *The Walrus*, September 19, 2016, https://thewalrus.ca/big-lonely-doug/.
4. Harley Rustad, *Big Lonely Doug: The Story of One of Canada's Last Great Trees* (Toronto: House of Anansi Press, 2018).
5. Rustad, "Big Lonely Doug."
6. Rustad, *Big Lonely Doug: The Story*. See also Statistics Canada, "Section 2—Forests and the Forest Sector in Canada," in *Human Activity and the Environment 2017: Forests in Canada*, 2018, https://www150.statcan.gc.ca/n1/pub/16-201-x/2018001/sec-2-eng.htm.
7. This is described by Sarah Cox, "Canada's Forgotten Rainforest," *The Narwhal*, July 27, 2019, https://thenarwhal.ca/canadas-forgotten-rainforest/. After burning the slash, herbicides are often used in the newly

cleared area, as reported by Melissa Denchak, "Want to Fight Climate Change? Stop Clearcutting our Carbon Sinks," NRDC, December 13, 2017, https://www.nrdc.org/stories/stop-clearcutting-carbon-sinks. Still, there are defenses of clearcutting, as in this North Carolina Forest Service brochure: https://www.ncforestservice.gov/publications/FM0313.pdf.

8. W. S. Merwin, "Unchopping a Tree," in *The Miner's Pale Children* (New York: Atheneum, 1970); reprinted in W. S. Merwin, *The Book of Fables* (Port Townsend, WA: Copper Canyon Press, 2007), 72–74.

9. Encyclopedia Britannica, "Aeolus (Homeric Character)," https://www.britannica.com/topic/Aeolus-Homeric-character.

10. Encyclopedia Britannica, "Sisyphus (Greek Mythology)," https://www.britannica.com/topic/Sisyphus. See also versions of the Sisyphus myth at: https://www.greekmyths-greekmythology.com/the-myth-of-sisyphus/ and https://www.ancient-origins.net/myths-legends-europe/sisyphus-king-cheats-death-annoys-zeus-and-receives-never-ending-punishment-021678.

11. On Tartarus, see https://www.greekmythology.com/Other_Gods/Tartarus/tartarus.html.

12. Ben Goldfarb and BioGraphic, "The Re-Beavering of the American West," *The Atlantic*, December 4, 2018, https://www.theatlantic.com/science/archive/2018/12/relocating-beavers-save-salmon-washington-state-tulalip-tribe/576916/.

13. Confederated Salish and Kootenai Tribes and Montana Fish, Wildlife & Parks, *Flathead Subbasin Plan: Part I: Flathead River Subbasin Assessment* (Portland, OR: Northwest Power and Conservation Council, 2004), 59 and 70–71.

14. Goldfarb and BioGraphic, "The Re-Beavering." Also see Ontario Parks, "The Beaver in Winter," Ontario Parks Blog, January 7, 2022, https://www.ontarioparks.com/parksblog/the-beaver-in-winter/.

15. Goldfarb and BioGraphic, "The Re-Beavering." Naming beavers as "predators" was done, Goldfarb writes, "logic and biology notwithstanding."

16. Committee of Appropriations, "The Department of the Interior and Related Agencies Appropriations for Fiscal Year 1998: Hearings before a Subcommittee of the Committee on Appropriations," United States Senate, Hearing 105-374 (1998): 204, https://www.govinfo.gov/content/pkg/CHRG-105shrg39858/pdf/CHRG-105shrg39858.pdf.

NOTES

17. Lewis Carroll, *Through the Looking Glass and What Alice Found There* (Los Angeles, CA: Enhanced Media Publishing, 1871, 2017 reprint).
18. Ibid., 20.
19. Joachim L. Dagg, "How Counterfactuals of Red-Queen Theory Shed Light on Science and its Historiography," *Studies in History and Philosophy of Biological and Biomedical Sciences* 64 (2017): 53–64.
20. C. Castrodeza, "Non-Progressive Evolution, the Red Queen Hypothesis, and the Balance of Nature," *Acta Biotheoretica* 28, no. 1 (1979): 11–18.
21. Carroll, *Through the Looking Glass*, 20.
22. Goldfarb and BioGraphic, "The Re-Beavering."
23. Leanne Betasamosake Simpson, "A Short History of the Blockade: Giant Beavers, Diplomacy, and Regeneration in Nishnaabewin," CLC Kriesel Lecture Series (Edmonton: University of Alberta Press, 2021). For further details on the lecture and for the book, see https://www.ualberta.ca/canadian-literature-centre/events-archive/kreisel-series.html and https://www.uap.ualberta.ca/titles/986-9781772125382-short-history-of-the-blockade.
24. Heidi Kiiwetinepinesiik Stark, "Respect, Responsibility, and Renewal: The Foundations of Anishinaabe Treaty Making with the United States and Canada," *American Indian Culture and Research Journal* 34, no. 2 (2010): 145–64. This respectful relationship is also described by Madeline Whetung in her writings of the colonial disruptions of interspecies international relations in Anishinaabe territory—see Madeline Whetung, "(En)gendering Shoreline Law: Nishnaabeg Relational Politics Along the Trent Severn Waterway," *Global Environmental Politics* 19, no. 3 (2019): 16–32, https://doi.org/10.1162/glep_a_00513.
25. Thomas Wien, "Selling Beaver Skins in North America and Europe, 1720–1760: The Uses of Fur-Trade Imperialism," *Journal of the Canadian Historical Association* 1, no. 1 (1990): 293–317, https://doi.org/10.7202/031021ar.
26. Oregon Department of Fish and Wildlife, "Oregon Furbearer Trapping and Hunting Regulations, July 1 2020 through June 30 2022," https://www.dfw.state.or.us/resources/hunting/small_game/regulations/docs/furbearer_regulations.pdf. The definitions specify that with regard to "furbearers" or "furbearing mammals": "For any person owning, leasing, occupying, possessing or having charge or dominion over any land (or

an agent of this person) who is taking or attempting to take beaver or muskrat on that property, these two species are considered to be predatory animals."
27. Strother E. Roberts, *Colonial Ecology, Atlantic Economy* (Philadelphia: University of Pennsylvania Press, 2019), 30–32.
28. Ibid.
29. Bathsheba Demuth, *Floating Coast: An Environmental History of the Bering Strait* (New York: Norton, 2019). As Demuth agues, this was not isolated to an emerging capitalist economic system, but an industrial logic of growth that spanned capitalist and communist political economies.
30. Geography Open Textbook Collective, "Chapter 6: Forestry in British Columbia—History of Commercial Logging," in *British Columbia in a Global Context*, BCcampus, 2014, https://opentextbc.ca/geography/chapter/7-3-history-of-commercial-logging/#:~:text=Commercial%20logging%20in%20British%20Columbia,Island%20and%20the%20Burrard%20Inlet.
31. Rustad, "Big Lonely Doug."
32. Rustad, *Big Lonely Doug: The Story.*
33. Thomas Elliot Norton, "The Fur Trade in Colonial New York, 1686–1776" (PhD diss., University of Tennessee, 1972), 45.
34. Wien, "Selling Beaver Skins."
35. H. A. Innis, *The Fur Trade in Canada: An Introduction to Canadian Economic History* (New Haven, CT: Yale University Press, 1930).
36. John A. Hawgood, "Review of *The Fur Trade in Canada: An Introduction to Canadian Economic History* by H. A. Innis," *The Economic History Review* 4, no. 3 (1933): 369–71, https://www.jstor.org/stable/2590659.
37. Wien, "Selling Beaver Skins," 294–95.
38. Neill DePaoli, "Beaver, Blankets, Liquor, and Politics: Pemaquid's Fur Trade, 1614–1760," *Maine History* 33, no. 3 (1994): 170–71.
39. Wien, "Selling Beaver Skins," 299.
40. Peter E. Busher and Paul J. Lyons, "Long-Term Population Dynamics of the North American Beaver, *Castor canadensis*, on Quabbin Reservation, Massachusetts, and Sagehen Creek, California," in *Beaver Protection, Management, and Utilization in Europe and North America*, eds. Busher and Dzieciolowski, 147–60 (New York: Kluwer Academic/Plenum Publishers, 1999), 148.

NOTES

41. On beaver declines, see Liz McKenzie (photos by Richard Nelson), "Beaver – Ecology," *Encounters North*, August 2, 2017, https://www.encountersnorth.org/beaver-summary/2017/8/2/beaver-ecology; Goldfarb and Biographic, "The Re-Beavering."
42. A quote from Horace T. Martin, as reported in Frances Backhouse, "Rethinking the Beaver," *Canadian Geographic*, December 1, 2013, https://www.canadiangeographic.ca/article/rethinking-beaver.
43. Busher and Lyons, "Long-Term Population Dynamics," 148. See also Backhouse, "Rethinking the Beaver."
44. Ibid.
45. William Cronon quotes John Muir on the passenger pigeon and its precipitous decline in William Cronon, "Landscape and Home: Environmental Traditions in Wisconsin," Madison Civics Club lecture, published in the *Wisconsin Magazine of History* 74 (Winter 1990–1991).
46. Oleg Boldyrev, "Belarus: Silent Protests Frighten Regime," BBC News, June 30, 2011, https://www.bbc.com/news/world-europe-13975788.
47. David Stern, "Belarus's Alexander Lukashenko Begins Fourth Term," BBC News, January 21, 2011, https://www.bbc.com/news/world-europe-12247664.
48. Boldyrev, "Belarus: Silent Protests."
49. Sarah A. Topol, "The Battle for the Mural — and the Future of Belarus," *New York Times*, March 30, 2022, https://www.nytimes.com/2022/03/30/magazine/belarus-mural.html.
50. Jason Motlagh, "In Belarus, Clapping Can Be Subversive," *The Atlantic*, July 21, 2011, https://www.theatlantic.com/international/archive/2011/07/in-belarus-clapping-can-be-subversive/242271/.
51. Topol, "The Battle for the Mural." See also Ilya Mouzykantskii, "In Belarus, Just Being Can Prompt an Arrest," *New York Times*, July 29, 2011, https://www.nytimes.com/2011/07/30/world/europe/30belarus.html.
52. Topol, "The Battle for the Mural."
53. Carole McGranahan, "Theorizing Refusal: An Introduction," *Cultural Anthropology* 31, no. 3 (2016): 319–325. There is also a wide and long history of writing about refusal from Indigenous and Black scholars, across multiple lines and approaches. Just a few examples include:

   On resurgence and the rejection of colonial compromise, Glen S.

Coulthard, *Red Skin, White Masks: Rejecting the Colonial Politics of Recognition* (Minneapolis: University of Minnesota Press, 2014).

On rest as a form of resistance to and liberation from systems of colonialism and white supremacy, Tricia Hersey, *Rest is Resistance: A Manifesto* (Boston: Little, Brown Spark, 2022).

On the creation and practice of art as "temporary spaces of joy and freedom," as proposed by Leanne Betasamosake Simpson in a conversation with Dionne Brand, Leanne Betasamosake Simpson and Dionne Brand, "'Temporary Spaces of Joy and Freedom': Leanne Betasamosake Simpson in Conversation with Dionne Brand," *Literary Review Canada—A Journal of Ideas*, June 2018, https://reviewcanada.ca/magazine/2018/06/temporary-spaces-of-joy-and-freedom/.

54. McGranahan, "Theorizing Refusal," 322–23.
55. Astra Taylor, "Against Activism," *The Baffler* 20 (March 2016), https://thebaffler.com/salvos/against-activism.
56. Although "activist" has been turned into a label to discredit opposition, argues the writer Astra Taylor, she says there are alternate terms that capture community-minded efforts, such as "organizer" or, more broadly, engaged citizen. See Taylor, "Against Activism."
57. Simpson, "A Short History of the Blockade." Other stories of giant beavers come from further down the eastern coast of North America; Strother Roberts writes of a Pocumtuck legend of "Ktsi Amiskw, the Great Beaver," whose dam-building shaped the Connecticut Valley—see Roberts, *Colonial Ecology*.
58. Simpson, "A Short History of the Blockade."
59. BBC News, "Belarus Election: Opposition Disputes Lukashenko Landslide Win," August 10, 2020, https://www.bbc.com/news/world-europe-53721410.
60. Ivan Nechepurenko and Andrew Higgins, "Belarus Says Longtime Leader Is Re-Elected in Vote Critics Call Rigged," *New York Times*, August 9, 2020, https://www.nytimes.com/2020/08/09/world/europe/belarus-election-lukashenko.html.
61. Yotam Marom, "What to Do When the World Is Ending," *Medium*, March 3, 2022, https://medium.com/@YotamMarom/what-to-do-when-the-world-is-ending-99eea2e1e2e7.
62. Ibid.

63. Ferris Jabr (photographs by Brendan George Ko), "The Social Life of Forests," *New York Times*, December 2, 2020, https://www.nytimes.com/interactive/2020/12/02/magazine/tree-communication-mycorrhiza.html.
64. Ibid.
65. Rebecca Solnit, "'Hope Is an Embrace of the Unknown': Rebecca Solnit on Living in Dark Times," *The Guardian*, July 15, 2016, https://www.theguardian.com/books/2016/jul/15/rebecca-solnit-hope-in-the-dark-new-essay-embrace-unknown. This article discusses the ideas she develops in her book: Rebecca Solnit, *Hope in the Dark: Untold Histories, Wild Possibilities* (Chicago: Haymarket Books, 2004, reprint 2016).

CHAPTER IV

1. For descriptions of the morphology of fir trees, see, among others: Northwest Conifers Connections, "Focus on Subalpine Fir," January 13, 2018, nwconifers.blogspot.com/2018/01/focus-on-subalpine-fir.html; Government of British Columbia, "Subalpine Fir," https://www2.gov.bc.ca/gov/content/industry/forestry/managing-our-forest-resources/silviculture/tree-species-selection/tree-species-compendium-index/subalpine-fir.
2. Chris Earle, "*Abies lasiocarpa* var. *bifolia*/Western Subalpine Fir," American Conifer Society, 2013, https://conifersociety.org/conifers/abies-lasiocarpa-bifolia/. See also Christopher J. Earle, "The Gymnosperm Database: *Abies lasiocarpa*," 2021, https://www.conifers.org/pi/Abies_lasiocarpa.php.
3. Central Yukon Species Inventory Project (CYSIP), "*Abies lasiocarpa*: Subalpine Fir," http://www.flora.dempstercountry.org/0.Site.Folder/Species.Program/Species.php?species_id=Abi.lasi.
4. Earle, "The Gymnosperm Database."
5. National Forest Service, "Subalpine Fir," US Department of Agriculture, https://www.srs.fs.usda.gov/pubs/misc/ag_654/volume_1/abies/lasiocarpa.htm.
6. Government of British Columbia, "Subalpine Fir."
7. On winter dormancy in subalpine fir, see, for instance, California Native Plant Society, "Species: *Abies lasiocarpa*

(Hook.) Nutt. var. *lasiocarpa*, Subalpine Fir," CNPS Rare Plant Inventory, October 5, 2021, https://rareplantfiles.cnps.org/scc/AbiesLasiocarpaVarLasiocarpaSpAcctSCC20211005.pdf. On downregulation of photosynthesis in winter by conifers, see, for instance, C. Ryan Zarter, Barbara Demmig-Adams, Volker Ebbert, Iwona Adamska, and William W. Adams III, "Photosynthetic Capacity and Light Harvesting Efficiency During the Winter-to-Spring Transition in Subalpine Conifers," *New Phytologist* 172, no. 2 (2006): 283–92, https://doi.org/10.1111/j.1469-8137.2006.01816.x.

8. Dana Kelley Bressette, "Subalpine Fir," Native Plants PNW, March 19, 2014, http://nativeplantspnw.com/subalpine-fir-abies-lasiocarpa/.
9. National Forest Service, "Subalpine Fir."
10. Bressette, "Subalpine Fir."
11. Helen Macdonald, *Vesper Flights* (New York: Grove Press, 2020).
12. Jennifer S. Holland, "Pining Away? As the Climate Shifts, Porcupines Face a Prickly Future," *National Wildlife Federation* magazine, October 1, 2019, https://www.nwf.org/Magazines/National-Wildlife/2019/Oct-Nov/Conservation/Porcupines.
13. Chesapeake Bay Program, "North American Porcupine," 2022, https://www.chesapeakebay.net/discover/field-guide/entry/north_american_porcupine.
14. Porcupines reach maximum speeds of 2 mph (~3–4 km/hr), as described by Mass Audubon, "Porcupines," 2022, https://www.massaudubon.org/learn/nature-wildlife/mammals/porcupines. Also see Pennsylvania Game Commission, "Porcupine," Pennsylvania Government, 2022, https://www.pgc.pa.gov/Education/WildlifeNotesIndex/Pages/Porcupine.aspx.
15. NPS I&M Northeast Temperate Network, "NETN Species Spotlight - Fisher," National Park Service, August 15, 2021, https://www.nps.gov/articles/netn-species-spotlight-fisher.htm.
16. Hinterland Who's Who, "Porcupine," Environment and Climate Change Canada and the Canadian Wildlife Federation, 1993, https://www.hww.ca/en/wildlife/mammals/porcupine.html.
17. Miche Genest's Boreal Gourmet Sourdough Bootcamp can be found here: https://www.borealgourmet.com/post/sourdough-bootcamp.
18. Thanks to Cath Archbould for your generosity in this and so much else!

NOTES

19. For those not prepared to commit to the multiday process of developing or the ongoing care of nurturing a sourdough starter, but who had a little yeast tucked away in the cupboard, other options for bread-making circulated on online venues. Around this time, I tried out a *"no-knead"* bread recipe shared by the *New York Times*; already popular, it gained new traction during those early days of the pandemic. Not only did the recipe sidestep the strenuous kneading of bread baking, but it also used only a quarter teaspoon of yeast—where most recipes used six to eight times that much for the same amount of flour. The trade-off? Time. A full day, at least, or two, since bakers are instructed to leave the dough for up to 18 hours, stretch it a little, and leave it again for a few more. The *NYT* no-knead bread recipe is available here: https://cooking.nytimes.com/recipes/11376-no-knead-bread.
20. The labour conditions of the pandemic were of course particularly devastating for migrant farm workers and tightly packed factory labourers, for personal care health workers and custodial staff and grocery clerks, all those with "front line" and "essential service" responsibilities, often highly exposed and painfully underpaid.
21. Kristin Granero, "25 Time-Saving Hacks That Will Add Hours Back to Your Week," NBC News, August 12, 2019, https://www.nbcnews.com/better/lifestyle/25-time-saving-hacks-will-add-hours-back-your-week-ncna1041011.
22. Livia Gershon, "How Advertisers Sold Housework to Housewives," *JStor Daily*, January 4, 2016, https://daily.jstor.org/advertisers-sold-housework-housewives/. This article is based on research from Bonnie J. Fox, "Selling the Mechanized Household: 70 Years of Ads in *Ladies Home Journal*," *Gender and Society* 4, no. 1 (1990): 25–40.
23. Fox, "Selling the Mechanized Household."
24. Bathsheba Demuth, *Floating Coast: An Environmental History of the Bering Strait* (New York: Norton, 2019).
25. Paul Wapner, "Forum—Planetary Disasters: Wildness and the Perennial Struggle for Control," *Global Environmental Politics* 21, no. 1 (2021): 3–12.
26. There is an extensive literature on ideas of wildness as "self-willed." For some discussion, see Paul Wapner, *Is Wildness Over?* (Cambridge, UK: Polity Press, 2020), 15. See also an interview with David Foreman

(an environmentalist perhaps best known for his role in founding EarthFirst!): Bioneers, "The Will of The Land: Dave Foreman on Aldo Leopold," 2000, https://bioneers.org/the-will-of-the-land-dave-foreman-on-aldo-leopold/.
27. Wapner, *Is Wildness Over?*, 16.
28. Ibid.
29. Wapner, "Forum—Planetary Disasters."
30. For a probing analysis of the debates over inequality, see David Graeber and David Wengrow, *The Dawn of Everything: A New History of Humanity* (New York: Macmillan, 2021). Graeber and Wengrow argue that searching for the origins of inequality is asking the wrong question, and instead offer a sweeping look at a diversity of forms of human governance and social organization over time.
31. Ministry of Environment and Natural Resources, "Subalpine Fir," Government of the Northwest Territories, https://www.gov.nt.ca/ecc/sites/ecc/files/fact_sheets/subalpine_fir.pdf.
32. Arne Naess' writings reprinted in Alan Drengson and Bill Devall, eds., *The Ecology of Wisdom: Writings by Arne Naess* (Berkeley, CA: Counterpoint LLC, 2010).
33. Gretel Ehrlich, "A River's Route," *Harper's Magazine*, December 1988, 35–36.
34. Don McKay, "Astonished," in *Strike/Slip* (Toronto: McClelland & Stewart, 2006).
35. Rebecca Solnit, *Savage Dreams: A Journey into the Hidden Wars of the American West* (Berkeley: University of California Press, 2014), 47.
36. Simon Morley, "A Short History of the Sublime," *The MIT Press Reader*, 2021, https://thereader.mitpress.mit.edu/a-short-history-of-the-sublime/.
37. Wapner, *Is Wildness Over?*, 31.

CHAPTER V

1. We still don't really know how salmon navigate to their spawning grounds of origin. There is evidence for magnetism and for smell, while others suggest a series of interlinked navigational strategies. See, for instance, Sarah Zielinski, "Animal Magnetism: How Salmon Find Their Way Back Home," NPR, February 7, 2013, https://www.npr.org/

sections/thesalt/2013/02/07/171384063/animal-magnetism-how-salmon-find-their-way-back-home; USGS, "How Do Salmon Know Where Their Home Is When They Return from the Ocean?" US Department of the Interior, https://www.usgs.gov/faqs/how-do-salmon-know-where-their-home-when-they-return-ocean; and Megan McPhee, "How Do Spawning Fish Navigate Back to the Very Same Stream Where They Were Born?" *Scientific American*, January 2, 2009, https://www.scientificamerican.com/article/how-do-spawning-fish-navigate-back/.
2. Anne Carson, "Kinds of Water," *Grand Street* 6, no. 4 (1987): 201.
3. Emily Silber, "Why a Painted Bunting Landed in Brooklyn," National Audubon Society, December 7, 2015, https://www.audubon.org/news/why-painted-bunting-landed-brooklyn.
4. Theories of why birds end up off-course and far from usual flyways and ranges include storms, stowing away on boats, and a mix-up in the magnetic compass of their navigational systems that sends them in the wrong direction. On navigation by birds, see, for instance, Peter J. Hore and Henrik Mouritsen, "How Migrating Birds Use Quantum Effects to Navigate," *Scientific American*, April 1, 2022, https://www.scientificamerican.com/article/how-migrating-birds-use-quantum-effects-to-navigate/.
5. Rebecca Solnit, *A Field Guide to Getting Lost* (New York: Viking, 2005), 6.
6. There are over 280 species of trees in the park. These can be explored through the "Trees of Prospect Park" mapping tool: https://prospectparkny.treekeepersoftware.com/index.cfm?deviceWidth=1280.
7. Details about the boathouse are available from Suzanne Spellen, "The Gleaming Beaux Arts Boathouse of Prospect Park," *Brownstoner*, September 6, 2017, https://www.brownstoner.com/architecture/prospect-park-boathouse-brooklyn-architecture-park-slope/. Spellen explains how the boathouse is linked to bird conservation, observing: "In 1999, a $5 million restoration was done to the entire building, in the process, creating the Audubon Nature Center, the first urban nature center of its kind."
8. Solnit, *A Field Guide*, 6.
9. James Kearney, "Idleness," in *Cultural Reformations: Medieval and Renaissance in Literary History*, eds. James Simpson and Brian Cummings (Oxford: Oxford University Press, 2010), 579–81.

NOTES

10. Andrew Lyndon Knighton, "The Line of Productiveness: Fear at the Frontiers," in *Idle Threats: Men and the Limits of Productivity in 19th-Century America*, chapter 3 (New York: New York University Press, 2012), 103–4.
11. Elaine Clark, "Institutional and Legal Responses to Begging in Medieval England," *Social Science History* 26, no. 3 (2002): 449.
12. J. M. Coetzee, "Idleness in South Africa," *Social Dynamics* 8, no. 1 (1982): 1–13, DOI: 10.1080/02533958208458311. A warning note for those turning to the original source, Coetzee uses an offensive term for the Khoikhoi people in his paper.
13. Ibid., 3.
14. Shino Konishi, "Idle Men: The Eighteenth-Century Roots of the Indigenous Indolence Myth," in *Passionate Histories: Myth, Memory and Indigenous Australia*, eds. Frances Peters-Little, Ann Curthoys, and John Docker, chapter 5, 99–122 (Canberra: ANU Press, 2010), 99.
15. Ibid., 99–100.
16. See information on homelessness in New York from The Bowery Mission: https://www.bowery.org/homelessness/facts-homelessness/.
17. State Assembly of New York, "S. 67" (BILL NO S00067A, same as A00341-A), State of New York, https://nyassembly.gov/leg/?default_fld=&leg_video=&bn=S.+67&term=2001&Summary=Y&Actions=Y&-Floor%26nbspVotes=Y&Memo=Y&Text=Y.
18. New York Civil Liberties Union's opposition to Bill S.67/A.341 is available here, NYCLU, "Legislative Memo: Loitering and Aggressive Begging," January 1, 2001, https://www.nyclu.org/en/legislation/legislative-memo-loitering-and-aggressive-begging. In New York, there is currently legislation in place against "certain forms of aggressive solicitation," as specified in the New York City Administrative Code, "§10-136 Prohibition Against Certain Forms of Aggressive Solicitation," New York City, https://codelibrary.amlegal.com/codes/newyorkcity/latest/NYCadmin/0-0-0-6354.
19. NYCLU, "Legislative Memo."
20. Lisa W. Foderaro, "The Parks That Made the Man Who Made Central Park," *New York Times*, October 30, 2019, https://www.nytimes.com/2019/10/30/travel/footsteps-frederick-law-olmsted-parks.html.
21. Michael Sperber, "Frederick Law Olmsted," *Harvard Magazine*,

July–August 2007, https://www.harvardmagazine.com/2007/07/frederick-law-olmsted.html.

22. Nathaniel Rich, "When Parks Were Radical," *The Atlantic*, September 2016, https://www.theatlantic.com/magazine/archive/2016/09/better-than-nature/492716/.
23. Charles E. Beveridge, "Frederick Law Olmsted Sr.: Landscape Architect, Author, Conservationist (1822–1903)," *Natural Association for Olmsted Parks*, 2000, https://www.olmsted.org/the-olmsted-legacy/frederick-law-olmsted-sr.
24. Sperber, "Frederick Law Olmsted."
25. Roxi Thoren, "Deep Roots: Foundations of Forestry in American Landscape Architecture," *Scenario Journal* 4 (Spring 2014), https://scenariojournal.com/article/deep-roots/.
26. Sperber, "Frederick Law Olmsted."
27. Rich, "When Parks Were Radical."
28. Michelle Nijhuis, "Don't Cancel John Muir—But Don't Excuse Him Either," *The Atlantic*, April 12, 2021, https://www.theatlantic.com/ideas/archive/2021/04/conservation-movements-complicated-history/618556/. Also see Jedediah Purdy, "Environmentalism's Racist History," *The New Yorker*, August 13, 2015, https://www.newyorker.com/news/news-desk/environmentalisms-racist-history.
29. J. Drew Lanham, "What Do We Do About John James Audubon?" *Audubon Magazine*, Spring 2021, https://www.audubon.org/magazine/spring-2021/what-do-we-do-about-john-james-audubon. Also see Gregory Nobles, "The Myth of John James Audubon," *National Audubon Society*, July 31, 2020, https://www.audubon.org/news/the-myth-john-james-audubon.
30. Olmsted worked closely with the forester Gifford Pichot, who left his own legacy of conservation punctuated—or perhaps defined—by racism: a champion of scientific forest management; an advisor to the American Eugenics Society; a defender of utilitarian assessments of forests for their value to humans, over many generations. See Purdy, "Environmentalism's Racist History," and Thoren, "Deep Roots."
31. The park is not necessarily a safe and welcoming place for all visitors; anti-loitering laws persist and are enforced in public parks, among other punitive social restrictions for those who are unhoused. Also, racism can

also lead to danger for those frequenting the park, often from police and other authorities; in a particularly vivid encounter that was highly publicized, a white woman was eventually charged after calling the police with a false accusation of being endangered by a Black man out birdwatching, as reported by Sarah Maslin Nir, "How 2 Lives Collided in Central Park, Rattling the Nation," *New York Times*, June 14, 2020, https://www.nytimes.com/2020/06/14/nyregion/central-park-amy-cooper-christian-racism.html.

32. Central Park Conservancy, "Before Central Park: The Story of Seneca Village," January 18, 2018, https://www.centralparknyc.org/articles/seneca-village.

33. Brent Staples, "The Death of the Black Utopia," *New York Times*, November 28, 2019, https://www.nytimes.com/2019/11/28/opinion/seneca-central-park-nyc.html.

34. Paul Tukker, "Retreating Yukon Glacier Makes River Disappear," CBC News, June 17, 2016, https://www.cbc.ca/news/canada/north/slims-river-dries-yukon-kluane-glacier-1.3639472.

35. Maura Forrest, "The Curious Case of the Vanishing River," *Yukon News*, June 22, 2016, https://www.yukon-news.com/business/the-curious-case-of-the-vanishing-river/.

36. Ibid. See also Ainslie Cruickshank, "A River Ran Through It," *Toronto Star*, June 24, 2019, https://projects.thestar.com/climate-change-canada/yukon/.

37. Ellen Meloy, *The Last Cheater's Waltz: Beauty and Violence in the Desert Southwest* (Tucson: University of Arizona Press, 1997), 113.

38. Ibid.

39. Carmen Wong, Kate Ballegooyen, Lawrence Ignace, Mary Jane (Gùdia) Johnson, and Heidi Swanson, "Towards Reconciliation: 10 Calls to Action to Natural Scientists Working in Canada," *FACETS* 5 (2020): 769–83, doi:10.1139/facets- 2020-0005. See especially p. 776.

40. Tukker, "Retreating Yukon Glacier."

41. David James Duncan, *The River Why* (Boston: Back Bay Books, 1983).

42. Forrest, "The Curious Case."

43. Kearney, "Idleness," 578.

44. Cruickshank, "A River."

45. Rebecca Lindsey and Luann Dahlman, "Climate Change:

Global Temperature," NOAA, June 28, 2022, https://www.climate.gov/news-features/understanding-climate/climate-change-global-temperature.
46. Sissi De Flaviis, "Whitehorse Records Snowiest December Since 1980, Says Environment Canada," CBC News, January 1, 2022, https://www.cbc.ca/news/canada/north/whitehorse-records-snowiest-december-since-1980-says-environment-canada-1.6300135.
47. Lyrics to Grand Coulee Dam are available here: https://www.woodyguthrie.org/Lyrics/Grand_Coulee_Dam.htm.
48. Library of Congress, "Folk Singers, Social Reform, and the Red Scare," https://www.loc.gov/item/ihas.200197399.
49. Aaron J. Leonard, "Newly Released FBI Files Expose Red-Baiting of Woody Guthrie," *TruthOut*, August 14, 2018, https://truthout.org/articles/newly-released-fbi-files-expose-red-baiting-of-woody-guthrie/. The Library of Congress, "Folk Singers," article says: "The Almanac Singers were a target of these fears and were branded a seditious group by the FBI."
50. See the Woody Guthrie website for details: https://store.woodyguthrie.org/products/columbia-river-collection-cd and https://www.woodyguthrie.org/biography/biography5.htm.

    On songwriting for the BPA, the site indicates: "In 1941, Woody, age 28, was hired by the Bonneville Power Administration in Portland, Oregon to write music for a film about the Columbia River and public power. This collection presents all known recordings of Woody singing his Columbia River songs, including recordings lost 40 years ago. Among the classic songs are Roll on Columbia, The Biggest Thing That Man Has Done, and Grand Coulee Dam, for a total of 17 songs."

    On his belief in the public value of cheap electricity, the site describes that: "To Woody, poet of the rain-starved Dust Bowl, this mighty stream of cool, clear water, coursing through evergreen forests, verdant meadows, and high deserts was like a vision of paradise. He saw the majestic Grand Coulee Dam as the creation of the common man to harness the river for the common good – work for the jobless, power to ease household tasks, power to strengthen Uncle Sam in his fight against world fascism."
51. Bonneville Power Administration, "History," https://www.bpa.gov/

news/AboutUs/History/Pages/default.aspx.

52. Peter Bosshard, "China Dams the World," *World Policy Journal* 26, no. 4 (2009). In 2009, Bosshard, then-policy director of the nonprofit International Rivers, wrote that "Hydropower dams generate about one-fifth of the world's electricity." A decade later, this estimate seems to hold. In 2019, the International Renewable Energy Agency relayed that "In the aggregate, renewables account for around a quarter of global electricity generation" and, in spite of growth in wind and solar, confirmed that "Hydropower is the world's largest source of renewable electricity." IRENA, "A New World: The Geopolitics of the Energy Transformation," 2019, www.geopoliticsofrenewables.org.

53. Power Technology, "The 10 Biggest Hydroelectric Power Plants in the World," October 14, 2013, updated July 27, 2020, https://www.power-technology.com/features/feature-the-10-biggest-hydroelectric-power-plants-in-the-world/.

54. Power Technology, "Three Gorges Dam Hydro Electric Power Plant, China," February 21, 2020, https://www.power-technology.com/projects/gorges/. On the Three Gorges Dam, the article notes: "Its output is estimated at 85TW/h a year, which is close to one-tenth of current Chinese requirements."

55. George Ledec and Juan David Quintero, "Good Dams and Bad Dams: Environmental Criteria for Site Selection of Hydroelectric Projects," Latin America and the Caribbean Region, World Bank, Sustainable Development Working Paper No. 16. (November 2003): 12.

56. Norwegian Refugee Council, "Case Study Series: Dam Displacement," April 2017, https://www.internal-displacement.org/publications/case-study-series-dam-displacement.

57. Carolyn Cowan, "Tigers, Jaguars Under Threat from Tropical Hydropower Projects: Study," *Mongabay News*, December 9, 2021, https://news.mongabay.com/2021/12/tigers-jaguars-under-threat-from-tropical-hydropower-projects-study/. The news story reports on this study by Ana Filipa Palmeirim and Luke Gibson, "Impacts of Hydropower on the Habitat of Jaguars and Tigers," *Communications Biology* 4 (2021): 1358, https://www.nature.com/articles/s42003-021-02878-5.

58. US Energy Information Administration, "Hydropower Explained: Hydropower and the Environment," November

7, 2022, https://www.eia.gov/energyexplained/hydropower/hydropower-and-the-environment.php.
59. Many news sources reported on this event, including: Lauren Frayer, "Scores Are Feared Dead in India After Himalayan Glacier Breaks Away," NPR, February 7, 2021, https://www.npr.org/2021/02/07/965046888/scores-are-feared-dead-in-india-after-himalayan-glacier-breaks-away; and Reuters, "India Glacier Avalanche Leaves 18 Dead, More Than 200 Missing," February 8, 2021, https://www.reuters.com/business/environment/india-glacier-avalanche-leaves-18-dead-more-than-200-missing-2021-02-08/.
60. Jamie Workman, at a keynote lecture at a conference on large dams at Yale University in 2006 (personal notes).
61. Zuzanna Ladyga, *The Labour of Laziness in Twentieth-Century American Literature* (Edinburgh: Edinburgh University Press, 2019), iii.
62. Ibid., x.
63. O'Connor, *Idleness*, 36. O'Connor is quoting Robert Burton; the text of Burton's book can be found in edited form here: Robert Burton, *The Anatomy of Melancholy* (Project Gutenberg, 1621, reprint 2004), https://www.gutenberg.org/files/10800/10800-h/10800-h.htm.
64. O'Connor, *Idleness*, 35.
65. Kearney, "Idleness," 576.
66. Anna Tsing, "Unruly Edges: Mushrooms as Companion Species (for Donna Haraway)," *Environmental Humanities* 1 (2012): 141–54.
67. Abrahm Lustgarten, "Use It or Lose It Laws Worsen Western U.S. Water Woes," *Scientific American*, June 9, 2015, https://www.scientificamerican.com/article/use-it-or-lose-it-laws-worsen-western-u-s-water-woes/.
68. Tim Vanderpool, "The Colorado River Delta is Proof of Nature's Resiliency," NRDC, June 28, 2018, https://www.nrdc.org/onearth/colorado-river-delta-proof-natures-resiliency.
69. Lustgarten, "Use It or Lose It Laws."
70. Ibid.
71. S. Hockaday and K. J. Ormerod, "Western Water Law: Understanding the Doctrine of Prior Appropriation," Extension, University of Nevada, Reno, IP-20-01, 2020, https://extension.unr.edu/publication.aspx?PubID=3750.
72. Luke Runyon, "When It Comes to Water Rights, This Once-a-Decade

List Details Who Will 'Use It or Lose It,'" KUNC, June 22, 2020, https://www.kuer.org/2020-06-22/when-it-comes-to-water-rights-this-once-a-decade-list-details-who-will-use-it-or-lose-it.
73. Lustgarten, "Use It or Lose It Laws."
74. Adell L. Amos and Christopher R. Swensen, "Evaluating Instream Flow Programs: Innovative Approaches and Persistent Challenges in the Western United States," in *The Proceedings of the 61st Annual Rocky Mountain Mineral Law Institute*, chapter 22 (Rocky Mountain Mineral Law Foundation, 2015), 22–23.
75. Ibid.
76. Ibid., 22–24 and 22–25.
77. Sandra Postel and Lesli Allison, "Western Water Strategy Shifting from 'Use It or Lose It,' to 'Waste Not, Want Not,'" *The Hill*, June 14, 2018, https://thehill.com/opinion/energy-environment/392341-western-water-strategy-shifting-from-use-it-or-lose-it-to-waste.
78. Gary D. Libecap, "The State of Water Rights and Western US Water Markets," Free Market Forum, 2008, https://www.hillsdale.edu/wp-content/uploads/2016/02/FMF-2008-The-State-of-Water-Rights.pdf. Libecap writes (emphasis added), "A key advantage of markets is that the sale or other exchange of property rights releases valuable information regarding alternative uses and opportunity costs *that promote efficiency* in resource allocation and application. This is especially important for water, where in the past there has been little information to guide its wise use."
79. Ben Ryder Howe, "Wall Street Eyes Billions in the Colorado's Water," *New York Times*, January 3, 2021, https://www.nytimes.com/2021/01/03/business/colorado-river-water-rights.html. On the belief of at least some government officials in private investment in water markets, Howe writes, "Most of the water in the 1,450-mile-long river comes from Colorado, and as that state's top water official from 2013 to 2017, James Eklund directed the creation of a comprehensive long-term plan to address climate change, the first by a state in the West. He believes that the last best hope against the drought is a market-based solution, one that allows private investors seeking a profit a significant hand in redrawing the map of water distribution in the West."
80. Postel and Allison, "Western Water Strategy."

NOTES

81. Rebecca Solnit, "The Most Radical Thing," *Orion*, November/December 2008, https://orionmagazine.org/issue/november-december-2008/.
82. Ibid.
83. Ibid.
84. Ibid.

CHAPTER VI

1. Schneider is quoted in George W. Argus, *A Guide to the Identification of Salix (Willow) in Alaska, the Yukon Territory and Adjacent Regions*, 2004, https://www.naturebob.com/sites/default/files/GuideSalixAK-YT11May05.pdf.
2. iNaturalist Network, "Willow Ptarmigan (*Lagopus lagopus*)," California Academy of Sciences and the National Geographic Society, https://inaturalist.ca/taxa/931-Lagopus-lagopus. See also Hinterland Who's Who, "Ptarmigan," Environment and Climate Change Canada and the Canadian Wildlife Federation, 1994, https://www.hww.ca/en/wildlife/birds/ptarmigan.html
3. Hinterland Who's Who, "Ptarmigan."
4. iNaturalist Network, "Willow Ptarmigan (*Lagopus lagopus*)." See also S. Morland, "*Lagopus Lagopus: Willow Grouse; Red Grouse (also Willow Ptarmigan)*," Animal Diversity Web, University of Michigan, 2011, https://animaldiversity.org/accounts/Lagopus_lagopus/.
5. Art Martell, "Willow Ptarmigan," in *The Atlas of the Breeding Birds of British Columbia, 2008–2012*, eds. P. J. A. Davidson, R. J. Cannings, A. R. Couturier, D. Lepage, and C. M. Di Corrado (Delta, BC: Bird Studies Canada, 2015), http://www.birdatlas.bc.ca/accounts/speciesaccount.jsp?sp=WIPT&lang=en.
6. Cornell Lab, "Willow Ptarmigan," All About Birds, Cornell University, 2023, https://www.allaboutbirds.org/guide/Willow_Ptarmigan/overview.
7. iNaturalist Network, "Willow Ptarmigan (*Lagopus lagopus*)."
8. On the classification of species—and alternate ways of delineating differences in the biotic world—see, for instance, Carol Kaesuk Yoon, *Naming Nature: The Clash Between Instinct and Science* (New York: W. W. Norton, 2010).

NOTES

9. The ministry names and divisions have changed several times since I worked for them. At present, in Ontario it is the "Ministry of Northern Development, Mines, Natural Resources and Forestry."
10. Thames River Clear Water Revival, "The Thames River (Deshkan Ziibi) Shared Waters Approach to Water Quality and Quantity," 2019, https://www.thamesrevival.ca/wp-content/uploads/2020/05/SharedWatersApproach-Dec2019finaldraft.pdf.
11. Courtney Mann, "Restoring and Promoting the Health of Deshkan Ziibi," *The Gazette*, October 22, 2018, https://westerngazette.ca/culture/restoring-and-promoting-the-health-of-deshkan-ziibi/article_1093364e-d414-11e8-9d74-6fa89001b899.html. See also Thames River Clear Water Revival, "Antler River Guardians from the 4 Directions," Steering Committee, https://www.thamesrevival.ca/home/first-nations/first-nations-youth-engagement/.
12. The London, Ontario, city land acknowledgement is available at https://london.ca/city-london-land-acknowledgement. As of January 17, 2023, the acknowledgement reads:

"We acknowledge that we are gathered today on the traditional lands of the Anishinaabek, Haudenosaunee, Lūnaapéewak and Attawandaron. We acknowledge all the treaties that are specific to this area: the Two Row Wampum Belt Treaty of the Haudenosaunee Confederacy/Silver Covenant Chain; the Beaver Hunting Grounds of the Haudenosaunee NANFAN Treaty of 1701; the McKee Treaty of 1790, the London Township Treaty of 1796, the Huron Tract Treaty of 1827, with the Anishinaabeg, and the Dish with One Spoon Covenant Wampum of the Anishnaabek and Haudenosaunee.

This land continues to be home to diverse Indigenous people (First Nations, Métis and Inuit) whom we recognize as contemporary stewards of the land and vital contributors to society. We hold all that is in the natural world in our highest esteem and give honor to the wonderment of all things within Creation. We bring our minds together as one to share good words, thoughts, feelings and sincerely send them out to each other and to all parts of creation. We are grateful for the natural gifts in our world, and we encourage everyone to be faithful to the natural laws of Creation.

The three Indigenous Nations that are neighbours to London are the Chippewas of the Thames First Nation; Oneida Nation of the Thames;

and the Munsee-Delaware Nation who all continue to live as sovereign Nations with individual and unique languages, cultures and customs.

This Land Acknowledgement is a first step towards reconciliation. Awareness means nothing without action. It is important that everyone takes the necessary steps towards decolonizing practices. We encourage everyone to be informed about the traditional lands, Treaties, history, and cultures of the Indigenous people local to their region."

13. Ministry of Natural Resources and Forestry, "American Chestnut," Government of Ontario, 2014 (updated 2021), https://www.ontario.ca/page/american-chestnut. Also see Ministry of the Environment, Conservation and Parks, "American Chestnut," Government of Ontario, 2014 (updated 2021), https://www.ontario.ca/page/american-chestnut-species-risk.

14. Ngũgĩ wa Thiong'o, *Re-membering Africa* (New York: Basic Civitas Books, 2009). In *Re-membering Africa*, Ngũgĩ writes: "When Europe contemplated Africa through the prism of its bourgeois desire to conquer and dominate, it saw nothing but uninhabited lands. A uniform rationale for European settlements in Kenya, Zimbabwe, and South Africa was that the land was empty of human beings. Where inhabited, it was by hordes of savages virtually indistinguishable from nature—an integral part of the gloom that Conrad depicts in *Heart of Darkness*, contact with which could cause a fairly enlightened European to degenerate into primitivity." He also recalls, "All those places had names before – names that pointed to other memories, older memories."

15. Wade Davis, "The Light at the Edge of the World," Inter-American Development Bank and Wade Davis, 2001: 1, https://publications.iadb.org/publications/english/document/The-Light-at-the-Edge-of-the-World.pdf.

16. Ibid., 1–2.

17. Robert Macfarlane, "The Word-Hoard," *The Guardian*, February 27, 2015, http://www.theguardian.com/books/2015/feb/27/robert-macfarlane-word-hoard-rewilding-landscape. On these themes, also see Robert Macfarlane, *Landmarks* (London: Hamish Hamilton, 2015).

18. Macfarlane, "The Word-Hoard."

19. Harvey Locke, "Nature Needs Half: A Necessary and Hopeful New

Agenda for Protected Areas," *The George Wright Forum* 31, no. 3 (2014): 359–71. (The article notes that it is an adapted version, with a previous version published in 2013 in *Parks* 19, no. 2).
20. The UN Convention on Biological Diversity Aichi Biodiversity Targets are listed here: https://www.cbd.int/sp/targets/. Note that the Aichi Targets specify "at least 17 per cent of terrestrial and inland water, and 10 per cent of coastal and marine areas" (so "land" and "oceans" are not exactly accurate, but they are indicative of the commitments).
21. Patrick Greenfield, "World Fails to Meet a Single Target to Stop Destruction of Nature – UN Report," *The Guardian,* September 15, 2020, https://www.theguardian.com/environment/2020/sep/15/every-global-target-to-stem-destruction-of-nature-by-2020-missed-un-report-aoe. Greenfield reports: "Six targets have been partially achieved, including those on protected areas and invasive species. While governments did not manage to protect 17% of terrestrial and inland water areas and 10% of marine habitats, 44% of vital biodiverse areas are now under protection, an increase from 29% in 2000. About 200 successful eradications of invasive species on islands have also taken place."
22. Locke, "Nature Needs Half."
23. Among many articles on this, see Helen Kopnina, "Half the Earth for People (or More)? Addressing Ethical Questions in Conservation," *Biological Conservation* 203 (2016): 176–85.
24. The "Half-Earth Project" is run by the E. O. Wilson Biodiversity Foundation, with details here: https://www.half-earthproject.org/. The project team describes it this way: "With science at its core and our transcendent moral obligation to the rest of life at its heart, the Half-Earth Project is working to conserve half the land and sea to safeguard the bulk of biodiversity, including ourselves."
25. The network Nature Needs Half has details here: https://natureneedshalf.org/. The WILD Foundation launched its Nature Needs Half vision in 2009 in Mexico, and further committed to the concept in Spain in 2013, as described in the Earth Negotiations Bulletin, "WILD Bulletin: A Summary Report of the Tenth World Wilderness Congress (WILD10)," International Institute for Sustainable Development 215, no. 1 (October 13, 2013), http://www.iisd.ca/wild/wild10/.
26. This is described in many mining operations and sectors. See, for

instance, Ministry of Coal, "Overburden Removal," Government of India, 2023, https://coal.gov.in/en/major-statistics/obr.
27. Laura Zinke, "Geomorphology: Plants Hold Back Rivers," *Nature Reviews: Earth & Environment*, December 17, 2019, https://doi.org/10.1038/s43017-019-0016-3. In the article, Zinke is writing about the research reported by A. N. Ielpi and M. G. A. Lapôtre, "A Tenfold Slowdown in River Meander Migration Driven by Plant Life," *Nature Geoscience*, 2019, https:// doi.org/10.1038/s41561-019-0491-7.
28. Bram Büscher, Robert Fletcher, Dan Brockington, Chris Sandbrook, William M. Adams, Lisa Campbell, Catherine Corson, Wolfram Dressler, Rosaleen Duffy, Noella Gray, George Holmes, Alice Kelly, Ellizabeth Lunstrum, Maano Ramutsindela, and Kartik Shanker, "Half-Earth or Whole Earth? Radical Ideas for Conservation, and their Implications," *Oryx* 51, no. 3 (2017): 407–10.
29. Ibid.
30. There is extensive academic work on exclusionary conservation and its related dynamics of dispossession; among other sources, see Toshio Meguro, Chihiro Ito, and Kariuki Kirigia, eds., *'African Potentials' for Wildlife Conservation and Natural Resource Management: Against the Image of 'Deficiency' and Tyranny* (Bamenda, Cameroon: African Books Collective, 2021); Dan Brockington and James Igoe, "Eviction for Conservation: A Global Overview," *Conservation and Society* 4, no. 3 (2006): 424–70; and Mark Dowie, *Conservation Refugees: The Hundred-Year Conflict Between Global Conservation and Native Peoples* (Cambridge, MA: MIT Press, 2009).
31. Büscher et al., "Half-Earth or Whole Earth?," 409.
32. Robin Wall Kimmerer, *Braiding Sweetgrass: Indigenous Wisdom, Scientific Knowledge, and the Teachings of Plants* (Minneapolis, MN: Milkweed, 2013), 6.
33. Toby McLeod, "Biodiversity Thrives on Indigenous Sacred Lands," Sacred Land Film Project, November 27, 2019, https://sacredland.org/biodiversity-thrives-on-indigenous-sacred-lands/.
34. Among many examples of work that documents the flourishing of biodiversity in areas of Indigenous governance, see UNESCO, "Indigenous Peoples: Informed Custodians of Biodiversity," 2021, https://en.unesco.org/courier/2021-3/indigenous-people

s-informed-custodians-biodiversity; Jason Vermes, "'You Protect What You Love': Why Biodiversity Thrives on Indigenous-Managed Lands," CBC Radio, August 12, 2019, https://www.cbc.ca/radio/checkup/are-we-doing-enough-to-protect-canada-s-wildlife-1.5240848/you-protect-what-you-love-why-biodiversity-thrives-on-indigenous-managed-lands-1.5243547; and IUCN, "IUCN Director General's Statement on International Day of the World's Indigenous Peoples," August 9, 2019, https://www.iucn.org/news/secretariat/201908/iucn-director-generals-statement-international-day-worlds-indigenous-peoples-2019.
35. Jamaica Kincaid, "In History," in *Colors of Nature: Culture, Identity and the Natural World*, eds. Alison H. Deming and Lauret E. Savoy, 18–27 (Minneapolis, MN: Milkweed Editions, 2011), 19.
36. Macfarlane, "The Word-Hoard."
37. Kincaid, "In History," 19.
38. Rachel Carson, "Help Your Child to Wonder," *Women's Home Companion*, July 1956, 24–27, 46–48. The article was published in 1956, even as Carson was beginning work on *Silent Spring*, only eight years before her death. The article offered a guide of sorts for adults, especially as they raised children. This piece was later expanded and published posthumously: Rachel Carson, *The Sense of Wonder* (New York: HarperCollins, 1965).
39. Deagan Miller, "Silent Spring & Other Writings on the Environment by Rachel Carson," *Bookforum* magazine, April 3, 2018, https://www.bookforum.com/culture/silent-spring-other-writings-on-the-environment-by-rachel-carson-19477.
40. Ibid.
41. Macfarlane, "The Word-Hoard."
42. Barry Lopez, *Arctic Dreams: Imagination and Desire in a Northern Landscape* (New York: Charles Scribner's Sons, 1986), 34.
43. I've learned much from Rebecca Solnit's terrific and probing look at the myths of solitude and the realities of social embeddedness in Thoreau's life and work. This specific fact is from Rebecca Solnit, "Mysteries of Thoreau, Unsolved: On the Dirtiness of Laundry and the Strength of Sisters," *Orion*, May/June (2013), 19.
44. Macfarlane, "The Word-Hoard."
45. Cornell Lab, "Willow Ptarmigan." In the description, the birds are noted

for their playful behaviour, although with an effort to link this to survival and fitness: "Willow Ptarmigan tend to play with one another when in groups. One bird often starts the play by extending and bobbing the head, then jumping around willy-nilly, flapping the wings alternately. Other birds join in, doing similar antics, which may sharpen motor skills or increase cohesion of the social group, as it does in some mammals."

46. Morland, "*Lagopus Lagopus*," describes frolicking in this way: "Frolicking is a form of play that occurs in willow ptarmigan family groups, or sometimes entire flocks. The birds crouch low to the ground and jump around erratically while flapping their wings." Among the sources cited by Morland on this are: A. Andreev, "Winter Adaptations in the Willow Ptarmigan," *Arctic* 44, no. 2 (1991): 106–14; Francis E. Schwab, Neal P. P. Simon, and Sherri Nash, "Age and Sex Segregation of Wintering Willow Ptarmigan in Labrador," *Northeastern Naturalist* 12, no. 1 (2005): 113–18. I have never observed this phenomenon in person.

47. Brian O'Connor, *Idleness: A Philosophical Essay* (Princeton, NJ: Princeton University Press, 2018), 12. O'Connor explains Hume's account of hedonism from the text "The Epicurean" to explore how the Scottish philosopher considers idleness within the search for the "good life"— O'Connor says: "The essay takes as its enemy a philosophical claim that living according to certain 'rules of reason' can generate a distinctive form of happiness, one that supposedly amounts to 'a new pleasure.' Hume voices the objection that the 'original frame and structure' of human beings is not designed for such an unnatural variety of enjoyment. Rather, what pleases it is 'ease, contentment, repose.' This languid mode contrasts with the disagreeable regime of 'watchfulness, care, and fatigue,' which the proponents of a purely regulated life would inflict on us." But he continues (p. 13), that for Hume: "Pleasure should, it transpires, be controlled by 'virtue,' obscurely identified as its 'sister.' Pleasure checked by virtue will restore 'to the rose its hue, and to the fruit its flavour.' Through this partnership the 'mind,' as Hume carefully puts it, can keep 'pace with the body.' The wisdom we possess when in a state of virtuous pleasure can enable us both to repel 'the barbarous dissonance of Bacchus' and to see through the absurdity of a life dedicated to the pursuit of glory at the expense of pleasure."

48. Kate Soper, *Post-Growth Living: For an Alternative Hedonism* (New York:

Verso, 2020).
49. Michael Maniates and John M. Meyer, eds., *The Environmental Politics of Sacrifice* (Cambridge, MA: MIT Press, 2010).
50. Cheryl Hall, "Freedom, Values, and Sacrifice: Overcoming Obstacles to Environmentally Sustainable Behavior," in *The Environmental Politics of Sacrifice*, eds. Michael Maniates and John M. Meyer, chapter 4, 61–86 (Cambridge, MA: MIT Press, 2010).
51. Paul Gallant, "Deliberate Degrowth," Canadian Index of Wellbeing, August 6, 2020, https://this.org/2020/08/06/deliberate-degrowth/.
52. Kimmerer, *Braiding Sweetgrass*, 339.
53. Arthur C. Brooks, "How to Want Less," *The Atlantic*, March 2022, https://www.theatlantic.com/magazine/archive/2022/03/why-we-are-never-satisfied-happiness/621304/.
54. Hall, "Freedom, Values, and Sacrifice."

CHAPTER VII

1. R. J. Cannings, "Great Horned Owl," in *The Atlas of the Breeding Birds of British Columbia, 2008–2012*, eds. P. J. A. Davidson, R. J. Cannings, A. R. Couturier, D. Lepage, and C. M. Di Corrado (Delta, BC: Bird Studies Canada, 2015), http://www.birdatlas.bc.ca/accounts/speciesaccount.jsp?sp=GHOW&lang=en.
2. Wislawa Szymborska, "Could Have," in *View with a Grain of Sand: Selected Poems*, trans. Stanislaw Baranczak and Clare Cavanagh (New York: Harcourt Brace, 1995).
3. Hinterland Who's Who, "Great Horned Owl," Environment and Climate Change Canada and the Canadian Wildlife Federation, 1986, https://www.hww.ca/en/wildlife/birds/great-horned-owl.html.
4. Sian Lewis and Lloyd Llewellyn-Jones, *The Culture of Animals in Antiquity: A Sourcebook with Commentaries* (London: Routledge, 2018), 493 and 497.
5. Nikita Banerjee, "3 Maa Lakshmi's Owl Remedies for Diwali," *Times of India*, October 28, 2016, https://timesofindia.indiatimes.com/religion/rituals-puja/3-maa-lakshmis-owl-remedies-for-diwali/articleshow/68206628.cms.
6. Helen Frisby, "'Them Owls Know': Portending Death in Later

Nineteenth- and Early Twentieth-Century England," *Folklore* 126, no. 2 (2015): 196–214, DOI: 10.1080/0015587X.2015.1047176. In China, owls have birthed dynasties and adorned tombs, been worshipped and feared, connected life and death. See, for instance, Shuxian Ye, "Xuan Bird from Heaven: The Owl Archetype Theory," in *A Mythological Approach to Exploring the Origins of Chinese Civilization*, trans. Hui Jia and Jing Hua, chapter 17 (New York: Springer, 2022).

7. Lewis and Llewellyn-Jones, *The Culture of Animals*, 493.

8. On the geologic legacy of human activities, see, for instance, David Farrier and Aeon, "How the Concept of Deep Time is Changing," *The Atlantic*, October 31, 2016, https://www.theatlantic.com/science/archive/2016/10/aeon-deep-time/505922/. As Farrier writes, "The planet's carbon and nitrogen cycles, ocean chemistry and biodiversity—each one the product of millions of years of slow evolution—have been radically and permanently disrupted by human activity." See also, among others, Phoebe Weston, "Top Scientists Warn of 'Ghastly Future of Mass Extinction' and Climate Disruption," *The Guardian*, January 13, 2021, https://www.theguardian.com/environment/2021/jan/13/top-scientists-warn-of-ghastly-future-of-mass-extinction-and-climate-disruption-aoe.

9. On possible markers of human activity as a geologic force, see the Anthropocene Working Group of the International Commission on Stratigraphy: http://quaternary.stratigraphy.org/working-groups/anthropocene/. See also, among others: Heather Davis and Zoe Todd, "On the Importance of a Date, or Decolonizing the Anthropocene," *ACME: An International Journal for Critical Geographies* 16, no. 4 (2017): 761–80; and Donna Haraway and Martha Kenney, "Anthropocene, Capitalocene, Chthulhocene," in *Art in the Anthropocene: Encounters Among Aesthetics, Politics, Environments and Epistemologies*, eds. Heather Davis and Etienne Turpin, 255–70 (London: Open Humanities Press, 2015). On nuclear testing in Bikini Atoll, see Peter Dauvergne, *The A to Z of Environmentalism* (Lanham, MD: Scarecrow Press, 2009).

10. For a collection of terms and references on the Anthropocene, see Yadvinder Malhi, "The Concept of the Anthropocene," *Annual Review of Environment and Resources* 42 (2017): 77–104. See also Haraway and Kenney, "Anthropocene, Capitalocene, Chthulhocene"; J. W. Moore, *Anthropocene or Capitalocene? Nature, History, and the*

Crisis of Capitalism (Oakland, CA: PM Press, 2016); Jairus Grove, "Response to Jedediah Purdy," in Forum: The New Nature, *Boston Review*, January 11, 2016, https://bostonreview.net/forum_response/jairus-grove-response-nature-anthropocene/; Alf Hornborg, "The Political Ecology of the Technocene: Uncovering Ecologically Unequal Exchange in the World-System," in *The Anthropocene and the Global Environmental Crisis: Rethinking Modernity in a New Epoch*, eds. Clive Hamilton, François Gemenne, and Christophe Bonneuil (London: Routledge, 2015); and Kate Raworth, "Must the Anthropocene be a Manthropocene?" *The Guardian*, October 20, 2014, https://www.theguardian.com/commentisfree/2014/oct/20/anthropocene-working-group-science-gender-bias.

11. On the concept of deep time, see Farrier and Aeon, "How the Concept of Deep Time." As Farrier recounts, "The concept of 'deep time' was first described in 1788 by the Scottish geologist James Hutton, although only coined as a term 200 years later, by the American author John McPhee. Hutton posited that geological features were shaped by cycles of sedimentation and erosion, a process of lifting up then grinding down rocks that required timescales much grander than those of prevailing Biblical narratives. This dizzying Copernican shift threw both God and man into question. 'The mind seemed to grow giddy by looking so far back into the abyss of time,' was how John Playfair, a scientist who accompanied Hutton on several crucial expeditions, described the effect of looking over the stratified promontory of Siccar Point in Scotland."

12. Peter Brannan, "The Anthropocene is a Joke," *The Atlantic*, August 13, 2019, https://www.theatlantic.com/science/archive/2019/08/arrogance-anthropocene/595795/.

13. Jan Zwicky and Robert Bringhurst, *Learning to Die: Wisdom in the Age of Climate Change* (Regina, Saskatchewan: University of Regina Press, 2018).

14. This quotation is from philosopher Glenn Albrecht, which I first encountered in Rebecca Elliott, "The Sociology of Climate Change as a Sociology of Loss," *European Journal of Sociology* 59, no. 3 (2018): 311. The original source is Glenn Albrecht, "The Age of Solastalgia," *The Conversation*, August 7, 2012, https://theconversation.com/the-age-of-solastalgia-8337.

15. Reprinted here, https://robertpinsky.wordpress.com/tag/

walter-savage-landor/, and also discussed in a *Washington Post* article by Robert Pinsky, "That Time Flies is a Cliché," *Washington Post*, January 30, 2005.
16. Susan T. Stevens, "Charon's Obol and Other Coins in Ancient Funerary Practice," *Phoenix* 45, no. 3 (1991): 215–29.
17. On Hass's and Hillman's poetic styles, see Angela Hume, "Imagining Ecopoetics: An Interview with Robert Hass, Brenda Hillman, Evelyn Reilly, and Jonathan Skinner," *Interdisciplinary Studies in Literature and Environment* 19, no. 4 (2012): 751–66.
18. From KQED Public Media for Northern CA – Forum: http://www.kqed.org/a/forum/R201401291000.
19. Pinsky, "That Time Flies."
20. Lesley Evans Ogden, "The Silent Flight of Owls, Explained," *Audubon*, July 28, 2017, https://www.audubon.org/news/the-silent-flight-owls-explained.
21. Ibid.
22. Daniel Pauly, *Vanishing Fish: Shifting Baselines and the Future of Global Fisheries* (Vancouver: Greystone Books, 2019).
23. J. B. MacKinnon, *The Once and Future World: Nature As It Was, As It Is, As It Could Be* (n.p.: Random House Canada, 2013).
24. Cannings, "Great Horned Owl."
25. Cornell Lab "Great Horned Owl," All About Birds, Cornell University, 2023, https://www.allaboutbirds.org/guide/Great_Horned_Owl/id.
26. Hinterland Who's Who, "Great Horned Owl."
27. Ibid.
28. Mark Doty, *Still Life with Oysters and Lemon* (Boston: Beacon Press, 2001), 67.
29. Helen Macdonald, *H is for Hawk* (London: Jonathan Cape, 2014), 13.
30. Doty, *Still Life*, 68.
31. Simone Weil, *Gravity and Grace* (London: Routledge, 2002), 170.
32. Robert Hass, "Measure," in *Field Guide* (New Haven, CT: Yale University Press, 1973), also available online at: https://www.poetryfoundation.org/poems/48852/measure.
33. Deborah Bird Rose, "Shimmer: When All You Love Is Being Trashed," in *Arts of Living on a Damaged Planet: Ghosts and Monsters of the Anthropocene*, eds. Anna Lowenhaupt Tsing et al., G51–G64 (University

of Minnesota Press, 2017).
34. Pam Houston, "What Has Irony Done for Us Lately," *About Place Journal*, 2018, http://aboutplacejournal.org/issues/political-landscapes/political/pam-houston/.
35. This point from E. O. Wilson is explored in an aching and beautiful essay by Meera Subramanian, "The Age of Loneliness," *Guernica: A Magazine of Art and Politics*, September 15, 2015, https://www.guernicamag.com/features/the-age-of-loneliness.
36. Siegfried Wenzel, "Acedia and Related Terms in Medieval Thought with Special Emphasis on Middle English Literature" (PhD diss., Ohio State University, 1960), 74.
37. Ibid., 7–14.
38. Ibid., 7.
39. Ibid., 22.
40. Ibid., 91–93.
41. Ibid., 103–4.
42. Ibid., 103–4.
43. Ibid., 103–4.
44. Ibid., 17–35.
45. Ibid., 87.
46. Juliana Spahr, *This Connection of Everyone with Lungs: Poems* (Berkeley: University of California Press, 2005), 10.
47. Houston, "What Has Irony."
48. Barry Lopez, "The Invitation," *Granta*, no. 133 (2015), https://granta.com/invitation/.
49. Henry Barrett Hinckley, "Science and Folk-Lore in the Owl and the Nightingale," *Publications of the Modern Language Association of America (PMLA)* 47, no. 2 (June 1932): 305.
50. Anna Lowenhaupt Tsing, *The Mushroom at the End of the World: On the Possibility of Life in Capitalist Ruins* (Princeton, NJ: Princeton University Press, 2015).
51. Hinckley, "Science and Folk-Lore," 308.
52. Rebecca Solnit, "The Blue of Distance," *Harper's Magazine*, July 2005, 15. This is an excerpt from Rebecca Solnit, *A Field Guide to Getting Lost* (New York: Viking, 2005).
53. Ibid., 15.

54. Tess Gallagher, "Choices," in *Midnight Lantern: New and Selected Poems* (Minneapolis, MN: Graywolf Press, 2011), also available online at https://www.poetryfoundation.org/poems/48950/choices.
55. Tomas Tranströmer, "Vermeer," in *The Half-Finished Heaven: The Best Poems of Tomas Tranströmer*, chosen and translated by Robert Bly, 87–88 (Minneapolis, MN: Graywolf Press, 2001).

CONCLUSIONS

1. Merriam-Webster, "Petrichor," https://www.merriam-webster.com/dictionary/petrichor. The definition says petrichor is "a distinctive, earthy, usually pleasant odor that is associated with rainfall especially when following a warm, dry period and that arises from a combination of volatile plant oils and geosmin released from the soil into the air and by ozone carried by downdrafts."
2. M. Prunier, "Petrichor: The Smell of Rain," American Chemical Society, https://www.acs.org/content/dam/acsorg/education/students/highschool/chemistryclubs/infographics/petrichor-the-smell-of-rain.pdf.
3. Anne Michaels, *The Winter Vault* (Toronto: McClelland & Stewart, 2009). This is a novel on memory, loss, and love.
4. Conchitina Cruz, *Dark Hours* (Quezon City: University of the Philippines Press, 2005). Part of the poem reads:
   3. Landscape
   When we were children, you didn't care for words, you only filled pages with wide vertical lines. Beyond the page, the bite marks at the tip of your pencil, bare knees, a scrawny cat sleeping at your feet. We lived in the city and I thought you drew lampposts, telephone lines, the long, rusty rods scattered in construction sites. Your voice insisting, no, no, these are trees.

   Thanks to Chingbee for her abundant generosity when I found myself in Manila, overwhelmed by the lampposts and long, rusty rods, looking for trees.
5. Statius, "The Thebaid," trans. John Henry Mozley (Loeb Classical Library edition, 1928), the Theoi Project (2000–2017), https://www.theoi.com/Daimon/Hypnos.html and https://www.theoi.com/Daimon/Aergia.html.
6. Hyginus, "Fabulae," in *The Myths of Hyginus*, ed. and trans. Mary

Grant (Lawrence: University of Kansas Press, 1960), https://topostext.org/work/206.
7. Don McKay, "As If," in *Paradoxides: Poems* (Toronto: McClelland and Stewart, 2012).
8. Ibid.
9. Barry Lopez, "The Invitation," *Granta*, no. 133 (2015), https://granta.com/invitation/.
10. Annie Dillard, "The Wreck of Time," *Harper's Magazine*, 1998, 51–56.
11. Ibid.
12. Cara New Daggett, *The Birth of Energy: Fossil Fuels, Thermodynamics, and the Politics of Work* (Durhan, NC: Duke University Press, 2019), 22. Daggett quotes these lines from Lucretius, *Lucretius: The Way Things Are: The De Rerum Natura of Titus Lucretius Carus*, trans. Rolfe Humphries (Bloomington: Indiana University Press, 1968), 170 (lines 369–74).
13. Daggett, *The Birth of Energy*, 22.
14. Ibid., 22.
15. This passage from Lucretius is quoted by David Simpson, from one of several translations that he consults, as noted in David Simpson, "Lucretius," https://iep.utm.edu/lucretiu/.
16. Deveron Projects, "Walking and Søren Kierkegaard," The Walking Institute, https://www.deveron-projects.com/the-walking-institute/temp/reference/soren-kierkegaard/. There is a wide range of writing and thinking on walking as part of relationships with place and the nonhuman world, and in environmental philosophy. On such themes, I am indebted to, among others: Dianne Chisholm, "The Nomadic Experiment of a Steppe Land Flâneuse," *Wagadu* 7 (Fall 2009): 1–25; Jabr Ferris, "Why Walking Helps Us Think," *The New Yorker*, September 3, 2014, https://www.newyorker.com/tech/annals-of-technology/walking-helps-us-think; Rebecca Solnit, *Wanderlust: A History of Walking* (New York: Penguin Random House, 2000); and H. D. Thoreau, "Walking," 1862 (reprinted in *The Atlantic*), https://www.theatlantic.com/magazine/archive/1862/06/walking/304674/.
17. Merriam-Webster, "Sabbatical," https://www.merriam-webster.com/dictionary/sabbatical. Also see https://www.etymonline.com/word/sabbatical.
18. Cooper Brinson, "History of May Day!" Civil Liberties Defense Center,

May 1, 2018, https://cldc.org/history-of-may-day/. Also see UE Union, "May Day: The Forgotten Labor Day," United Electrical, Radio, and Machine Workers of America, April 30, 2007, https://www.ueunion.org/ue-news/2007/may-day-the-forgotten-labor-day.
19. Benjamin Fong, "Inventing the Weekend," *Jacobin Magazine*, July 2018, https://www.jacobinmag.com/2018/07/leisure-time-holidays-religion-weekend.
20. Ibid.
21. Eric Chase, "The Brief Origins of May Day," Industrial Workers of the World, 1993, https://archive.iww.org/history/library/misc/origins_of_mayday/.
22. PBS, "The Rise of Labor," Picture History and Educational Broadcasting Corporation, 2002, https://www.thirteen.org/wnet/historyofus/web09/segment6_p.html.
23. Labour disruptions need not be as stark as those that led up to the Haymarket Incident to still be powerful. In research initially focused on class relations in a Malaysian village in the 1980s, political scientist James Scott documented strategies of resistance undertaken by those with the fewest resources. He tracked the more covert ways that people, unable to risk the penalties of outright rebellion, use to resist exploitation: desertion, feigned ignorance, sabotage, pilfering, and foot-dragging among them. The latter, foot-dragging, is a strategy of subversive slowness, involving technical compliance but at such a reduced pace that it compromises the work. James C. Scott, *Weapons of the Weak: Everyday Forms of Peasant Resistance* (New Haven, CT: Yale University Press, 1985).
24. PBS, "The Rise of Labor."
25. Chase, "The Brief Origins of May Day."
26. Cooper, "History of May Day!"
27. On conflicting accounts, see PBS, "The Anarchists and the Haymarket Square Incident," article featured with Chicago: City of the Century, January 13, 2003, https://www.pbs.org/wgbh/americanexperience/features/chicago-anarchists-and-haymarket-square-incident/. See also Chase, "The Brief Origins of May Day."
28. PBS, "The Rise of Labor," Picture History and Educational Broadcasting Corporation, 2002, https://www.thirteen.org/wnet/historyofus/web09/segment6_p.html. See also Chase, "The Brief Origins of May Day."

NOTES

29. PBS, "The Rise of Labor" and Chase, "The Brief Origins of May Day."
30. UE Union, "May Day," and PBS, "The Rise of Labor."
31. Several sources informed this section including PBS, "The Anarchists," and UE Union, "May Day." See also Jonathan Garlock, "Knights of Labor History and Geography 1869–1899," University of Washington Civil Rights and Labor History Consortium, 2015, https://depts.washington.edu/moves/knights_labor_map.shtml.
32. Steven Heighton, "On Hope and Embracing the Smallest Life You Can Love," *The Star*, September 19, 2020, https://www.thestar.com/entertainment/books/2020/09/19/steven-heighton-on-hope-and-embracing-the-smallest-life-you-can-love.html.
33. Heighton, "On Hope."
34. Don McKay, "The Bushtits' Nest," in *Thinking and Singing: Poetry and the Practice of Philosophy*, ed. Tim Lilburn (Toronto: Cormorant, 2002).
35. Barks writes this in the introduction to *Birdsong*, a book of translations of poems by Rumi.
    Rumi, *Birdsong: Fifty-Three Short Poems*, trans. Coleman Barks (n.p.: Maypop Books, 1993).
36. Rumi, *The Book of Love: Poems of Ecstasy and Longing*, trans. Coleman Barks (n.p.: Deckle Edge, 2003).
37. Tim Lilburn, *Living in the World As If It Were Home* (n.p.: Corbel Stone Press, 1999, reprint 2016).
38. Michaels, *The Winter Vault*.
39. Ibid.
40. Dillard, *The Writing Life*, chapter 2.

REFERENCES

I've drawn on wide-ranging materials in these essays—while I've noted intellectual debts along the way through notes and citations, it is worth pointing to a few sources that have had outsized influence on my thinking, even if they are not directly cited. Among them: Mark Slouka's compelling *Harper's* essay "Quitting the Paint Factory"; Jenny Odell's querying look at autonomy and freedom in *How to Do Nothing: Resisting the Attention Economy*; Ellen Meloy's stunning *The Anthropology of Turquoise: Reflections on Desert, Sea, Stone, and Sky*; Meghan O'Gieblyn's recorded workshop on the familiar essay, and her brilliant essays in *Interior States*; Rebecca Solnit's astonishing range of essays and books that so often make me reconsider what I know and how I see things, and whose work on hope, in particular, through *Hope in the Dark*, has had such sustaining power; and Bathsheba Demuth's powerful essay in *Emergence Magazine* "Living in the Bones." My stylistic choice to begin each essay with a list of thematic words borrows from journal sketch essays by Virginia Woolf, which I found in S. P. Rosenbaum's *The Bloomsbury Group: Collection of Memoirs and Commentary*.

Albrecht, Glenn. "The Age of Solastalgia." *The Conversation*, August 7, 2012. https://theconversation.com/the-age-of-solastalgia-8337.

Alexander, Thomas. "The Fourth World of American Philosophy: The Philosophical Significance of Native American Culture." *Transactions of the Charles S. Peirce Society* 32, no. 3 (1996): 375–402.

REFERENCES

Amos, Adell L., and Christopher R. Swensen. "Evaluating Instream Flow Programs: Innovative Approaches and Persistent Challenges in the Western United States." In *The Proceedings of the 61st Annual Rocky Mountain Mineral Law Institute*, chapter 22. Westminster, CO: Rocky Mountain Mineral Law Foundation, 2015.

Andreev, A. "Winter Adaptations in the Willow Ptarmigan." *Arctic* 44, no. 2 (1991): 106–14.

Argus, George W. *A Guide to the Identification of Salix (Willows) in Alaska, the Yukon Territory and Adjacent Regions*, 2004. https://www.nature-bob.com/sites/default/files/GuideSalixAK-YT11May05.pdf.

Awad, Marwa. "South Sudanese Struggle to Survive Climate Change Effects." *Newsweek*, February 10, 2022. https://www.newsweek.com/south-sudanese-struggle-surviv e-climate-change-effects-opinion-1677714.

Ayto, John. *Oxford Dictionary of English Idioms*. Oxford: Oxford University Press, 2010.

Backhouse, Frances. "Rethinking the Beaver." *Canadian Geographic*, December 1, 2013. https://www.canadiangeographic.ca/article/rethinking-beaver.

Bakker, Karen. *The Sounds of Life: How Digital Technology Is Bringing Us Closer to the Worlds of Animals and Plants*. Princeton, NJ: Princeton University Press, 2022.

Baron, Nancy. "Salmon Trees." *Hakai Magazine*, April 22, 2015. https://hakaimagazine.com/features/salmon-trees/.

Begazo, A., ed. "Peru Aves: Black Metaltail (*Metallura phoebe*)." Lima, Peru: CORBIDI, 2022. https://www.peruaves.org/trochilidae/black-metaltail-metallura-phoebe/.

Benanav, Aaron. *Automation and the Future of Work*. New York: Verso, 2020.

Berggrun, Chase. "Mostly His Apocalyptic Star Glitters Wondrously." *Poetry* magazine, November 2, 2020. https://www.poetryfoundation.org/poetrymagazine/articles/154451/mostly-his-apocalyptic-star-glitters-wondrously.

Beston, Henry. *The Outermost House*. Garden City, NY: Doubleday and Doran, 1928.

Beveridge, Charles E. "Frederick Law Olmsted Sr.: Landscape Architect,

Author, Conservationist (1822–1903)." Natural Association for Olmsted Parks, 2000. https://www.olmsted.org/the-olmsted-legacy/frederick-law-olmsted-sr.

Bierce, Ambrose. *Fantastic Fables*. New York and London: G. P. Putnam's Sons, 1899.

Biggs, Thomas. "Contesting *Cunctatio*: Livy 22.14, Fabius Maximus, and the Problem of Pastoral." *The Classical Journal* 111, no. 3 (2016): 281–301.

Bioneers. "The Will of the Land: Dave Foreman on Aldo Leopold." 2000. https://bioneers.org/the-will-of-the-land-dave-foreman-on-aldo-leopold/.

Bird Rose, Deborah. "Shimmer: When All You Love is Being Trashed." In *Arts of Living on a Damaged Planet: Ghosts and Monsters of the Anthropocene*, edited by Anna Lowenhaupt Tsing et al., G51–G64. Minneapolis: University of Minnesota Press, 2017.

Boldyrev, Oleg. "Belarus: Silent Protests Frighten Regime." BBC News, June 30, 2011. https://www.bbc.com/news/world-europe-13975788.

Bosshard, Peter. "China Dams the World." *World Policy Journal* 26, no. 4 (2009).

Brannan, Peter. "The Anthropocene Is a Joke." *The Atlantic*, August 13, 2019. https://www.theatlantic.com/science/archive/2019/08/arrogance-anthropocene/595795/.

Bressette, Dana Kelley. "Subalpine Fir." *Native Plants PNW*, March 19, 2014. http://nativeplantspnw.com/subalpine-fir-abies-lasiocarpa/.

Brinson, Cooper. "History of May Day!" Civil Liberties Defense Center, May 1, 2018. https://cldc.org/history-of-may-day/.

Brockington, Dan, and James Igoe. "Eviction for Conservation: A Global Overview." *Conservation and Society* 4, no. 3 (2006): 424–70.

Brooks, Aaron. "19 Productivity Hacks to Get More Done in 2022." Venture Harbour Ltd. December 9, 2021. https://www.ventureharbour.com/productivity-hacks/.

Brooks, Arthur C. "How to Want Less." *The Atlantic*, 2022. https://www.theatlantic.com/magazine/archive/2022/03/why-we-are-never-satisfied-happiness/621304/.

Burgin, Shelley. "BioBanking: An Environmental Scientist's View of the Role of Biodiversity Banking Offsets in Conservation." *Biodiversity and*

Conservation 17 (2008): 807–16.

———. "'Mitigation Banks' for Wetland Conservation: A Major Success or an Unmitigated Disaster?" *Wetlands Ecology and Management* 18 (2010): 49–55.

Burton, Robert. *The Anatomy of Melancholy*. Project Gutenberg, 1621, reprint 2004. https://www.gutenberg.org/files/10800/10800-h/10800-h.htm.

Büscher, Bram, Robert Fletcher, Dan Brockington, Chris Sandbrook, William M. Adams, Lisa Campbell, Catherine Corson, Wolfram Dressler, Rosaleen Duffy, Noella Gray, George Holmes, Alice Kelly, Ellizabeth Lunstrum, Maano Ramutsindela, and Kartik Shanker. "Half-Earth or Whole Earth? Radical Ideas for Conservation, and Their Implications." *Oryx* 51, no. 3 (2017): 407–10.

Busher, Peter E., and Paul J. Lyons. "Long-Term Population Dynamics of the North American Beaver, *Castor canadensis*, on Quabbin Reservation, Massachusetts, and Sagehen Creek, California." In *Beaver Protection, Management, and Utilization in Europe and North America*, edited by Busher and Dzieciolowski, 147–60. New York: Kluwer Academic/Plenum Publishers, 1999.

California Native Plant Society. "Species: *Abies lasiocarpa* (Hook.) Nutt. var. *lasiocarpa*, Subalpine Fir." *CNPS Rare Plant Inventory*, October 5, 2021. https://rareplantfiles.cnps.org/scc/AbiesLasiocarpaVarLasiocarpaSpAcctSCC20211005.pdf.

Cannings, R. J. "Great Horned Owl." In *The Atlas of the Breeding Birds of British Columbia, 2008–2012*, edited by P. J. A. Davidson, R. J. Cannings, A. R. Couturier, D. Lepage, and C. M. Di Corrado. Delta, BC: Bird Studies Canada, 2015. http://www.birdatlas.bc.ca/accounts/speciesaccount.jsp?sp=GHOW&lang=en.

Carroll, Lewis. *Through the Looking Glass and What Alice Found There*. Los Angeles, CA: Enhanced Media Publishing, 1871, reprint 2017.

Carson, Anne. "Kinds of Water." *Grand Street* 6, no. 4 (1987): 177–212.

Carson, Rachel. "Help Your Child to Wonder." *Women's Home Companion*, July 1956, 24–27 and 46–48. https://rachelcarsoncouncil.org/wp-content/uploads/2019/08/whc_rc_sow_web.pdf.

———. *The Sense of Wonder*. New York: HarperCollins, 1965.

———. "Silent Spring–I." *The New Yorker*, June 1962. https://www.

newyorker.com/magazine/1962/06/16/silent-spring-part-1.

Castrodeza, C. "Non-Progressive Evolution, the Red Queen Hypothesis, and the Balance of Nature." *Acta Biotheoretica* 28, no. 1 (1979): 11–18.

Celan, Paul. *Selected Poems and Prose of Paul Celan*, translated by John Felstiner. New York: W. W. Norton, 2001.

Celan, Paul, and Nelly Sachs. *Correspondence*, translated by Christopher Clark. Riverdale-on-Hudson, NY: The Sheep Meadow Press, 1998.

Central Park Conservancy. "Before Central Park: The Story of Seneca Village." January 18, 2018. https://www.centralparknyc.org/articles/seneca-village.

Central Yukon Species Inventory Project (CYSIP). "*Abies lasiocarpa*: Subalpine Fir." http://www.flora.dempstercountry.org/0.Site.Folder/Species.Program/Species.php?species_id=Abi.lasi.

Cep, Casey. "Songs of the Cicada." *The New Yorker*, June 6, 2013. https://www.newyorker.com/books/page-turner/songs-of-the-cicada.

Chase, Eric. "The Brief Origins of May Day." *Industrial Workers of the World*, 1993. https://archive.iww.org/history/library/misc/origins_of_mayday/.

Chesapeake Bay Program. "North American Porcupine." 2022. https://www.chesapeakebay.net/discover/field-guide/entry/north_american_porcupine.

Chisholm, Dianne. "The Nomadic Experiment of a Steppe Land Flâneuse." *Wagadu* 7 (Fall 2009): 1–25.

Clark, Elaine. "Institutional and Legal Responses to Begging in Medieval England." *Social Science History* 26, no. 3 (2002): 447–73.

Coetzee, J. M. "Idleness in South Africa." *Social Dynamics* 8, no. 1 (1982): 1–13. DOI: 10.1080/02533958208458311.

Committee of Appropriations. "The Department of the Interior and Related Agencies Appropriations for Fiscal Year 1998: Hearings before a Subcommittee of the Committee on Appropriations." United States Senate, Hearing 105-374 (1998). https://www.govinfo.gov/content/pkg/CHRG-105shrg39858/pdf/CHRG-105shrg39858.pdf.

Confederated Salish and Kootenai Tribes and Montana Fish, Wildlife & Parks. *Flathead Subbasin Plan: Part I: Flathead River Subbasin Assessment*. Portland, OR: Northwest Power and Conservation Council, 2004.

REFERENCES

Coulthard, Glen S. *Red Skin, White Masks: Rejecting the Colonial Politics of Recognition*. Minneapolis: University of Minnesota Press, 2014.

Cowan, Carolyn. "Tigers, Jaguars Under Threat from Tropical Hydropower Projects: Study." *Mongabay News*, December 9, 2021. https://news.mongabay.com/2021/12/tigers-jaguars-under-threat-from-tropical-hydropower-projects-study/.

Cox, Sarah. "Canada's Forgotten Rainforest." *The Narwhal*, July 27, 2019. https://thenarwhal.ca/canadas-forgotten-rainforest/.

Cronon, William. "Landscape and Home: Environmental Traditions in Wisconsin." Madison Civics Club lecture, *Wisconsin Magazine of History* 74 (Winter 1990/1991).

Cruickshank, Ainslie. "A River Ran Through It." *Toronto Star*, June 24, 2019. https://projects.thestar.com/climate-change-canada/yukon/.

Cruz, Conchitina. *Dark Hours*. Quezon City: University of the Philippines Press, 2005.

Cunningham, J. *An Essay on Trade and Commerce*. London: S. Hooper, 1770.

D'Erasmo, Stacey. "The Uses of Doubt." *Ploughshares* 28, no. 4 (2002/2003): 24–34.

Dagg, Joachim L. "How Counterfactuals of Red-Queen Theory Shed Light on Science and Its Historiography." *Studies in History and Philosophy of Biological and Biomedical Sciences* 64 (2017): 53–64.

Daggett, Cara New. *The Birth of Energy: Fossil Fuels, Thermodynamics, and the Politics of Work*. Durham, NC: Duke University Press, 2019.

Dale-Harris, Luke. "How the Brown Bear Became Public Enemy Number One in Rural Romania." *The Guardian*, November 22, 2017. https://www.theguardian.com/environment/2017/nov/22/how-the-brown-bear-became-public-enemy-number-one-in-rural-romania.

Dauvergne, Peter. *The A to Z of Environmentalism*. Lanham, MD: Scarecrow Press, 2009.

Davies, Matt. "Romania's Brown Bears." *Mossy Earth*, 2021. https://mossy.earth/rewilding-knowledge/romanias-brown-bears.

Davis, Heather, and Zoe Todd. "On the Importance of a Date, or Decolonizing the Anthropocene." *ACME: An International Journal for Critical Geographies* 16, no. 4 (2017): 761–80.

Davis, Wade. *The Light at the Edge of the World*. Inter-American

Development Bank and Wade Davis, 2001. https://publications.iadb.org/publications/english/document/The-Light-at-the-Edge-of-the-World.pdf.

De Flaviis, Sissi. "Whitehorse Records Snowiest December Since 1980, Says Environment Canada." CBC News, January 1, 2022. https://www.cbc.ca/news/canada/north/whitehorse-records-snowiest-december-since-1980-says-environment-canada-1.6300135.

Demuth, Bathsheba. *Floating Coast: An Environmental History of the Bering Strait*. New York: Norton, 2019.

———. "Living in the Bones." *Emergence Magazine*, September 16, 2021. https://emergencemagazine.org/essay/living-in-the-bones/

Denchak, Melissa. "Want to Fight Climate Change? Stop Clearcutting our Carbon Sinks." NRDC, December 13, 2017. https://www.nrdc.org/stories/stop-clearcutting-carbon-sinks.

DePaoli, Neill. "Beaver, Blankets, Liquor, and Politics: Pemaquid's Fur Trade, 1614–1760." *Maine History* 33, no. 3 (1994): 166–201.

Dillard, Annie. "The Wreck of Time." *Harper's Magazine*, 1998, 51–56.

———. *The Writing Life*. New York: Harper & Row, 1989.

Doty, Mark. *Still Life with Oysters and Lemon*. Boston: Beacon Press, 2001.

Dowie, Mark. *Conservation Refugees: The Hundred-Year Conflict Between Global Conservation and Native Peoples*. Cambridge, MA: MIT Press, 2009.

Doyle, Brian. "Joyas Voladoras." *The American Scholar*, June 12, 2012. https://theamericanscholar.org/joyas-volardores/.

Drengson, Alan, and Bill Devall, eds. *The Ecology of Wisdom: Writings by Arne Naess*. Berkeley, CA: Counterpoint LLC, 2010.

Duncan, David James. *The River Why*. Boston: Back Bay Books, 1983.

Earle, Chris. *"Abies lasiocarpa* var. *bifolia*/Western Subalpine Fir." American Conifer Society, 2013. https://conifersociety.org/conifers/abies-lasiocarpa-bifolia/.

———. "The Gymnosperm Database: *Abies lasiocarpa*." 2021. https://www.conifers.org/pi/Abies_lasiocarpa.php.

Earth Negotiations Bulletin. "WILD Bulletin: A Summary Report of the Tenth World Wilderness Congress (WILD10)." International Institute for Sustainable Development (IISD) and The WILD Foundation, October 13, 2013. http://www.iisd.ca/wild/wild10/.

REFERENCES

Edōsdi, Judith Charlotte Thompson. *Hedekeyeh Hots'ih K!hidi – "Our Ancestors Are in Us": Strengthening Our Voices Through Language Revitalization from a Tahltan Worldview*. PhD thesis, University of Victoria, 2012. http://www.malsmb.ca/docs/thompson-judith-phd-2012.pdf.

Ehrlich, Gretel. "A River's Route." *Harper's Magazine*, December 1988, 35–36.

Elliott, Rebecca. "The Sociology of Climate Change as a Sociology of Loss." *European Journal of Sociology* 59, no. 3 (2018): 301–37.

Entrepreneur Media. "101 Efficiency Hacks for Busy Entrepreneurs." *Entrepreneur*, November 10, 2016. https://www.entrepreneur.com/article/284768.

Farrier, David, and Aeon. "How the Concept of Deep Time is Changing." *The Atlantic*, October 31, 2016. https://www.theatlantic.com/science/archive/2016/10/aeon-deep-time/505922/.

Felstiner, John. "Paul Celan Translating Others." *World Literature Today*, November 11, 2014. https://www.worldliteraturetoday.org/blog/translation/paul-celan-translating-others.

Fischer, Molly. "David Graeber's Possible Worlds." *NYMag Intelligencer*, November 9, 2021. https://nymag.com/intelligencer/2021/11/david-graeber-dawn-of-everything.html.

Foderaro, Lisa W. "The Parks that Made the Man Who Made Central Park." *New York Times*, October 30, 2019. https://www.nytimes.com/2019/10/30/travel/footsteps-frederick-law-olmsted-parks.html.

Fong, Benjamin. "Inventing the Weekend." *Jacobin* magazine, July 2018. https://www.jacobinmag.com/2018/07/leisure-time-holidays-religion-weekend.

Forrest, Maura. "The Curious Case of the Vanishing River." *Yukon News*, June 22, 2016. https://www.yukon-news.com/business/the-curious-case-of-the-vanishing-river/.

Fox, Bonnie J. "Selling the Mechanized Household: 70 Years of Ads in Ladies Home Journal." *Gender and Society* 4, no. 1 (1990): 25–40.

Franklin, Ruth. "How Paul Celan Reconceived Language for a Post-Holocaust World." *The New Yorker*, November 16, 2020. https://www.newyorker.com/magazine/2020/11/23/how-paul-celan-reconceived-language-for-a-post-holocaust-world.

REFERENCES

Frayer, Lauren. "Scores Are Feared Dead in India After Himalayan Glacier Breaks Away." NPR, February 7, 2021. https://www.npr.org/2021/02/07/965046888/scores-are-feared-dead-in-india-after-himalayan-glacier-breaks-away.

Frisby, Helen. "'Them Owls Know': Portending Death in Later Nineteenth- and Early Twentieth-Century England." *Folklore* 126, no. 2 (2015): 196–214. DOI: 10.1080/0015587X.2015.1047176.

Gallagher, Tess. *Midnight Lantern: New and Selected Poems*. Minneapolis, MN: Graywolf Press, 2011.

Gallant, Paul. "Deliberate Degrowth." Canadian Index of Wellbeing, August 6, 2020. https://this.org/2020/08/06/deliberate-degrowth/.

Garlock, Jonathan. "Knights of Labor History and Geography 1869–1899." *University of Washington Civil Rights and Labor History Consortium*, 2015. https://depts.washington.edu/moves/knights_labor_map.shtml.

Geography Open Textbook Collective. "Chapter 6: Forestry in British Columbia—History of Commercial Logging." In *British Columbia in a Global Context*, BCcampus, 2014. https://opentextbc.ca/geography/chapter/7-3-history-of-commercial-logging/#:~:text=Commercial%20logging%20in%20British%20Columbia,Island%20and%20the%20Burrard%20Inlet.

Gershon, Livia. "How Advertisers Sold Housework to Housewives." *JStor Daily*, January 4, 2016. https://daily.jstor.org/advertisers-sold-housework-housewives/.

Goldfarb, Ben, and BioGraphic. "The Re-Beavering of the American West." *The Atlantic*, December 4, 2018. https://www.theatlantic.com/science/archive/2018/12/relocating-beavers-save-salmon-washington-state-tulalip-tribe/576916/.

Goldman, Emma. "Anarchism: What It Really Stands For." In *Emma Goldman, Anarchism and Other Essays*, 3rd rev. ed., chapter 1. New York: Mother Earth Publishing Association, 1917. https://theanarchistlibrary.org/library/emma-goldman-anarchism-and-other-essays#toc3.

González-Bernardo, Enrique, Luca Francesco Russo, Esther Valderrábano, Ángel Fernández, and Vincenzo Penteriani. "Denning in Brown Bears." *Ecology and Evolution* 10 (2020): 6844–62.

Government of British Columbia. "Subalpine Fir." https://www2.gov.

REFERENCES

bc.ca/gov/content/industry/forestry/managing-our-forest-resources/silviculture/tree-species-selection/tree-species-compendium-index/subalpine-fir.

Graeber, David. "On the Phenomenon of Bullshit Jobs: A Work Rant." *STRIKE! Magazine*, no. 3 (August 2013). https://www.strike.coop/bullshit-jobs/.

Graeber, David, and David Wengrow. *The Dawn of Everything: A New History of Humanity*. New York: Macmillan, 2021.

Granero, Kristin. "25 Time-Saving Hacks That Will Add Hours Back to Your Week." *NBC News*, August 12, 2019. https://www.nbcnews.com/better/lifestyle/25-time-saving-hacks-will-add-hours-back-your-week-ncna1041011.

Greenfield, Patrick. "World Fails to Meet a Single Target to Stop Destruction of Nature – UN Report." *The Guardian*, September 15, 2020. https://www.theguardian.com/environment/2020/sep/15/every-global-target-to-stem-destruction-of-nature-by-2020-missed-un-report-aoe.

Grove, Jairus. "Response to Jedediah Purdy." *Boston Review*, January 11, 2016. http://bostonreview.net/forum/new-nature/jairus-grove-jairus- grove-response-jedediah-purdy.

Hall, Cheryl. "Freedom, Values, and Sacrifice: Overcoming Obstacles to Environmentally Sustainable Behavior." In *The Environmental Politics of Sacrifice*, edited by Michael Maniates and John M. Meyer, chapter 4, 61–86. Cambridge, MA: MIT Press, 2010.

Haraway, Donna, and Martha Kenney. "Anthropocene, Capitalocene, Chthulhocene." In *Art in the Anthropocene: Encounters Among Aesthetics, Politics, Environments and Epistemologies*, edited by Heather Davis and Etienne Turpin, 255–70. London: Open Humanities Press, 2015.

Harding, Luke. "'We Are a Huge Amount of Ants': The United Front of Ukrainian Volunteers." *The Guardian*, March 2, 2022. https://www.theguardian.com/world/2022/mar/02/ukrainian-volunteers-united-front-against-russia-invasion.

Hass, Robert. *Field Guide*. New Haven, CT: Yale University Press, 1973.

Hawgood, John A. "Review of H. A. Innis' *The Fur Trade in Canada: An Introduction to Canadian Economic History*." *The Economic History Review* 4, no. 3 (1933): 369–71. https://www.jstor.org/stable/2590659.

REFERENCES

Heighton, Steven. "On Hope and Embracing the Smallest Life You Can Love." *The Star*, September 19, 2020. https://www.thestar.com/entertainment/books/2020/09/19/steven-heighton-on-hope-and-embracing-the-smallest-life-you-can-love.html.

Hersey, Tricia. *Rest Is Resistance: A Manifesto*. Boston: Little, Brown Spark, 2022.

Hesiod. *Works and Days, Theogony, and the Shield of Heracles*, translated by Hugh G. Evelyn-White. Mineola, NY: Dover Publications Inc., 2006.

Hicks, Lucy. "To Survive Frigid Nights, Hummingbirds Cool Themselves to Record-Low Temperatures." *Science*, September 8, 2020. https://www.science.org/content/article/survive-frigid-nights-hummingbirds-cool-themselves-record-low-temperatures.

Hinckley, Henry Barrett. "Science and Folk-Lore in the Owl and the Nightingale." *Publications of the Modern Language Association of America (PMLA)* 47, no. 2 (June 1932): 303–14.

Hinterland Who's Who. "Great Horned Owl." Environment and Climate Change Canada and the Canadian Wildlife Federation, 1986. https://www.hww.ca/en/wildlife/birds/great-horned-owl.html.

———. "Porcupine." Environment and Climate Change Canada and the Canadian Wildlife Federation, 1993. https://www.hww.ca/en/wildlife/mammals/porcupine.html.

———. "Ptarmigan." Environment and Climate Change Canada and the Canadian Wildlife Federation, 1994. https://www.hww.ca/en/wildlife/birds/ptarmigan.html.

Hockaday, S., and K. J. Ormerod. "Western Water Law: Understanding the Doctrine of Prior Appropriation." Extension, University of Nevada, Reno, IP-20-01, 2020. https://extension.unr.edu/publication.aspx?PubID=3750.

Holland, Jennifer S. "Pining Away? As the Climate Shifts, Porcupines Face a Prickly Future." *National Wildlife Federation Magazine*, October 1, 2019. https://www.nwf.org/Magazines/National-Wildlife/2019/Oct-Nov/Conservation/Porcupines.

Hore, Peter J., and Henrik Mouritsen. "How Migrating Birds Use Quantum Effects to Navigate." *Scientific American*, April 1, 2022. https://www.scientificamerican.com/article/how-migrating-birds-use-

REFERENCES

quantum-effects-to-navigate/.

Hornborg, Alf. "The Political Ecology of the Technocene: Uncovering Ecologically Unequal Exchange in the World-System." In *The Anthropocene and the Global Environmental Crisis: Rethinking Modernity in a New Epoch*, edited by Clive Hamilton, François Gemenne, and Christophe Bonneuil. London: Routledge, 2015.

Houston, Pam. "What Has Irony Done for Us Lately." *About Place Journal*, 2018. http://aboutplacejournal.org/issues/political-landscapes/political/pam-houston/.

Housty, Jess ('Cúagilákv). "Winter Is for Regeneration. The Garden's — and Yours, Too." *The Tyee*, December 14, 2021. https://thetyee.ca/Culture/2021/12/14/Winter-Regeneration-Garden-Yours-Too/.

Howe, Ben Ryder. "Wall Street Eyes Billions in the Colorado's Water." *New York Times*, January 3, 2021. https://www.nytimes.com/2021/01/03/business/colorado-river-water-rights.html.

Hume, Angela. "Imagining Ecopoetics: An Interview with Robert Hass, Brenda Hillman, Evelyn Reilly, and Jonathan Skinner." *Interdisciplinary Studies in Literature and Environment* 19, no. 4 (2012): 751–66.

Hyginus. "Fabulae." In *The Myths of Hyginus*, edited and translated by Mary Grant. Lawrence: University of Kansas Press, 1960. https://topostext.org/work/206.

Ielpi, A. N., and M. G. A. Lapôtre. "A Tenfold Slowdown in River Meander Migration Driven by Plant Life." *Nature Geoscience*, 2019. https://doi.org/10.1038/s41561-019-0491-7.

Innis, H. A. *The Fur Trade in Canada: An Introduction to Canadian Economic History*. New Haven, CT: Yale University Press, 1930.

International Renewable Energy Agency (IRENA). "A New World: The Geopolitics of the Energy Transformation." 2019. www.geopoliticsofrenewables.org.

IUCN. "IUCN Director General's Statement on International Day of the World's Indigenous Peoples." August 9, 2019. https://www.iucn.org/news/secretariat/201908/iucn-director-generals-statement-internatio nal-day-worlds-indigenous-peoples-2019.

Jabr, Ferris (with photographs by Brendan George Ko). "The Social Life of Forests." *New York Times*, December 2, 2020. https://www.nytimes.

REFERENCES

com/interactive/2020/12/02/magazine/tree-communication-mycorrhiza.html.

———. "Why Walking Helps Us Think." *The New Yorker*, September 3, 2014. https://www.newyorker.com/tech/annals-of-technology/walking-helps-us-think.

James, Thomas. *Æsop's Fables: A New Version, Chiefly from Original Sources*. London: John Murray, 1848.

Jones, V. S. Vernon. Æsop's Fables, *A New Translation*. London: William Heinemann, and New York: Doubleday, Page, and Company, 1912 (reprint 1916).

Kagge, Erling. *Silence in the Age of Noise*. New York: Pantheon, 2017.

Kaminsky, Ilya, and Katherine Towler. "Introduction." In *A God in the House: Poets Talk About Faith*, edited by Ilya Kaminsky and Katherine Towler. North Adams, MA: Tupelo Press, 2012.

Kanngieser, Anja, and Zoe Todd. "From Environmental Case Study to Environmental Kin Study." *History and Theory* 59, no. 3 (September 2020): 385–93.

Kearney, James. "Idleness." In *Cultural Reformations: Medieval and Renaissance in Literary History*, edited by James Simpson and Brian Cummings. Oxford, UK: Oxford University Press, 2010.

Keay, Jerey A., Charles T. Robbins, and Sean D. Farley. "Characteristics of a Naturally Regulated Grizzly Bear Population." *The Journal of Wildlife Management* 82, no. 4 (2018): 789–801, https://doi.org/10.1002/jwmg.21425.

Kelly, Robert. "A Love Affair with Silence." *New York Times*, November 9, 1986. https://www.nytimes.com/1986/11/09/books/a-love-affair-with-silence.html.

Kenkō, Yoshida. *Essays in Idleness: The Tsurezuregusa of Kenko*, translated by Donald Keene. 2nd paperback ed. New York: Columbia University Press, 1998.

Khurshudyan, Isabelle, Siobhán O'Grady, and Loveday Morris. "'Weapons to Anyone': Across Ukraine, Militias Form as Russian Forces Near." *Washington Post*, February 26, 2022. https://www.washingtonpost.com/world/2022/02/26/ukraine-russia-militias/.

Kimmerer, Robin Wall. *Braiding Sweetgrass: Indigenous Wisdom, Scientific Knowledge, and the Teachings of Plants*. Minneapolis, MN: Milkweed

Editions, 2013.

———. "Returning the Gift." *Minding Nature* 7, no. 2 (2014), republished by the Network for Grateful Living. https://gratefulness.org/resource/returning-the-gift/.

———. "The Serviceberry: An Economy of Abundance." *Emergence Magazine*, 2020. https://emergencemagazine.org/story/the-serviceberry/.

Kincaid, Jamaica. "In History." In *Colors of Nature: Culture, Identity and the Natural World*, edited by Alison H. Deming and Lauret E. Savoy, 18–27. Minneapolis, MN: Milkweed Editions, 2011.

Knighton, Andrew Lyndon. "The Line of Productiveness: Fear at the Frontiers." In *Idle Threats: Men and the Limits of Productivity in 19th-Century America*, chapter 3. New York: New York University Press, 2012.

Komlosy, Andrea. *Work: The Last 1,000 Years*. London and New York: Verso, 2014 [translation 2018].

Konishi, Shino. "Idle Men: The Eighteenth-Century Roots of the Indigenous Indolence Myth." In *Passionate Histories: Myth, Memory and Indigenous Australia*, edited by Frances Peters-Little, Ann Curthoys, and John Docker, chapter 5, 99–122. Canberra: ANU Press, 2010.

Kopnina, Helen. "Half the Earth for People (or More)? Addressing Ethical Questions in Conservation." *Biological Conservation* 203 (2016): 176–85.

Kramer, Andrew E. "'Everybody in Our Country Needs to Defend.'" *New York Times*, February 26, 2022. https://www.nytimes.com/2022/02/26/world/europe/ukraine-russia-civilian-military.html.

Kreider, Tim. "The 'Busy' Trap." *New York Times*, June 30, 2012.

Kroskrity, Paul V. "Narrative Reproductions: Ideologies of Storytelling, Authoritative Words, and Generic Regimentation in the Village of Tewa." *Journal of Linguistic Anthropology* 19, no. 1 (2009): 40–56.

Kureishi, Hanif. "The Art of Writing." *The Independent*, March 4, 2011. https://www.independent.co.uk/arts-entertainment/books/features/the-art-of-writing-hanif-kureishi-reveals-how-to-succeed-in-the-worlds-of-fiction-and-film-2231223.html.

L'Estrange, Roger. *Fables of Æsop and Other Eminent Mythologists, with*

REFERENCES

Morals and Reflections. London: R. Sare et al., 1692.

Ladyga, Zuzanna. *The Labour of Laziness in Twentieth-Century American Literature*. Edinburgh: Edinburgh University Press, 2019.

Lafargue, Paul. *The Right to Be Lazy*, translated by Charles Kerr. Charles Kerr and Co., Co-operative, 1883 (reprint 2000), accessed through The Anarchist Library, Anti-Copyright, online version from the Lafargue Internet Archive, https://www.marxists.org/archive/lafargue/1883/lazy.

Lambert, Jonathan. "This Hummingbird Survives Cold Nights by Nearly Freezing Itself Solid." *ScienceNews*, September 8, 2020. https://www.sciencenews.org/article/hummingbirds-black-metaltail-cold-torpor.

Lanham, J. Drew. "What Do We Do About John James Audubon?" *Audubon Magazine*, Spring 2021. https://www.audubon.org/magazine/spring-2021/what-do-we-do-about-john-james-audubon.

LeBaron, Genevieve. *Combatting Modern Slavery: Why Labour Governance is Broken and What We Can Do About It*. Cambridge, UK: Polity Press, 2020.

LeBaron, Genevieve, and Jane Lister. "The Hidden Costs of Global Supply Chain Solutions." *Review of International Political Economy*, 2021. DOI: 10.1080/09692290.2021.1956993.

Ledec, George, and Juan David Quintero. *Good Dams and Bad Dams: Environmental Criteria for Site Selection of Hydroelectric Projects*. Latin America and the Caribbean Region, Sustainable Development Working Paper No. 16 (November). World Bank, 2003.

Leonard, Aaron J. "Newly Released FBI Files Expose Red-Baiting of Woody Guthrie." *TruthOut*, August 14, 2018. https://truthout.org/articles/newly-released-fbi-files-expose-red-baiting-of-woody-guthrie/.

Lewis, Sian, and Lloyd Llewellyn-Jones. *The Culture of Animals in Antiquity: A Sourcebook with Commentaries*. London: Routledge, 2018.

Libecap, Gary D. "The State of Water Rights and Western US Water Markets." *Free Market Forum*, 2008. https://www.hillsdale.edu/wp-content/uploads/2016/02/FMF-2008-The-State-of-Water-Rights.pdf.

Library of Congress. "Folk Singers, Social Reform, and the Red Scare." https://www.loc.gov/item/ihas.200197399.

Lilburn, Tim. *Living in the World As If It Were Home*. n.p.: Corbel Stone

Press, 1999, reprint 2016.

Lindsey, Rebecca, and Luann Dahlman. "Climate Change: Global Temperature." NOAA, June 28, 2022. https://www.climate.gov/news-features/understanding-climate/climate-change-global-temperature.

Linnitt, Carol. "In Photos: See Old-Growth Go from Stand to Stump on B.C.'s Vancouver Island." *The Narwhal*, December 10, 2020. https://thenarwhal.ca/bc-old-growth-forest-vancouver-island-caycuse/.

Lionni, Leo. *Frederick*. New York: Pantheon, 1967.

Locke, Harvey. "Nature Needs Half: A Necessary and Hopeful New Agenda for Protected Areas." *The George Wright Forum* 31, no. 3 (2014): 359–71.

Lopez, Barry. *Arctic Dreams: Imagination and Desire in a Northern Landscape*. New York: Charles Scribner's Sons, 1986.

———. "The Invitation." *Granta*, no. 133 (2015). https://granta.com/invitation/.

López-Alfaro, Claudia, Charles T. Robbins, Andreas Zedrosser, and Scott E. Nielsen. "Energetics of Hibernation and Reproductive Trade-Offs in Brown Bears." *Ecological Modelling* 270 (December 2013): 1–10.

Lucretius. *Lucretius: The Way Things Are: The De Rerum Natura of Titus Lucretius Carus*, translated by Rolfe Humphries, 170, v. 369–74. Bloomington: Indiana University Press, 1968.

Lustgarten, Abraham. "Use It or Lose It Laws Worsen Western U.S. Water Woes." *Scientific American*, June 9, 2015. https://www.scientificamerican.com/article/use-it-or-lose-it-laws-worsen-western-u-s-water-woes/.

Macdonald, Helen. *H is for Hawk*. London: Jonathan Cape, 2014.

———. *Vesper Flights*. New York: Grove Press, 2020.

MacKay, Jory. "10 Email Canned Responses That Will Save You Hours Each Week." Rescue Time Blog, August 2, 2018. https://blog.rescuetime.com/canned-responses-gmail/.

MacKinnon, J. B. *The Once and Future World: Nature As It Was, As It Is, As It Could Be*. n.p.: Random House Canada, 2013.

Macfarlane, Robert. *Landmarks*. London: Hamish Hamilton, 2015.

———. "The Word-Hoard." *The Guardian*, February 27, 2015. http://www.theguardian.com/books/2015/feb/27/robert-macfarlane-word-hoard-rewilding-landscape.

Malhi, Yadvinder. "The Concept of the Anthropocene." *Annual Review of Environment and Resources*, 42 (2017): 77–104.

Maniates, Michael, and John M. Meyer, eds. *The Environmental Politics of Sacrifice*. Cambridge, MA: MIT Press, 2010.

Mann, Courtney. "Restoring and Promoting the Health of Deshkan Ziibi." *The Gazette*, October 22, 2018. https://westerngazette.ca/culture/restoring-and-promoting-the-health-of-deshkan-ziibi/article_1093364e-d414-11e8-9d74-6fa89001b899.html.

Marom, Yotam. "What to Do When the World is Ending." *Medium*, March 3, 2022. https://medium.com/@YotamMarom/what-to-do-when-the-world-is-ending-99eea2e1e2e7.

Martell, Art. "Willow Ptarmigan." In *The Atlas of the Breeding Birds of British Columbia, 2008–2012*, edited by P. J. A. Davidson, R. J. Cannings, A. R. Couturier, D. Lepage, and C. M. Di Corrado. Delta, BC: Bird Studies Canada, 2015. http://www.birdatlas.bc.ca/accounts/speciesaccount.jsp?sp=WIPT&lang=en.

Martin, Sarah. "The Political Economy of Distillers' Grains and the Frictions of Consumption." *Environmental Politics* 29, no. 2 (2019): 297–316. DOI: 10.1080/09644016.2019.1565461.

Mass Audubon. "Porcupines." 2022. https://www.massaudubon.org/learn/nature-wildlife/mammals/porcupines.

McGranahan, Carole. "Theorizing Refusal: An Introduction." *Cultural Anthropology* 31, no. 3 (2016): 319–25.

McKay, Don. "The Bushtits' Nest." In *Thinking and Singing: Poetry and the Practice of Philosophy*, edited by Tim Lilburn. Toronto: Cormorant, 2002.

———. *Paradoxides: Poems*. Toronto: McClelland and Stewart, 2012.

———. *Strike/Slip*. Toronto: McClelland & Stewart, 2006.

McKenzie, Liz. (Photography by Richard Nelson.) "Beaver - Ecology." *Encounters North*, August 2017. https://www.encountersnorth.org/beaver-summary/2017/8/2/beaver-ecology.

McLeod, Toby. "Biodiversity Thrives on Indigenous Sacred Lands." Sacred Land Film Project, November 27, 2019. https://sacredland.org/biodiversity-thrives-on-indigenous-sacred-lands/.

McNeil, Alex. "What's in a 'Nym'? Pseudonyms, Heteronyms, and the

Remarkable Case of Fernando Pessoa." *Shakespeare Oxford Fellowship*, September 9, 2002. https://shakespeareoxfordfellowship.org/whats-in-a-nym/.

McPhee, Megan. "How Do Spawning Fish Navigate Back to the Very Same Stream Where They Were Born?" *Scientific American*, January 2, 2009. https://www.scientificamerican.com/article/how-do-spawning-fish-navigate-back/.

Medler, Louis. "Villefranche, Fabuliste Catholique (1829–1904)." *Le Sel de la Terre*, no. 70 (Autumn 2009): 165–83. https://isidore.co/misc/Res%20pro%20Deo/Sel%20de%20la%20Terre/Sdt%20N%C2%B0070/42%20PLM-Villefranche-(fini).pdf.

Meguro, Toshio, Chihiro Ito, and Kariuki Kirigia, eds. *'African Potentials' for Wildlife Conservation and Natural Resource Management: Against the Image of 'Deficiency' and Tyranny*. Bamenda, Cameroon: African Books Collective, 2021.

Meloy, Ellen. *The Anthropology of Turquoise: Reflections on Desert, Sea, Stone, and Sky*. n.p.: Vintage, 2003.

———. *The Last Cheater's Waltz: Beauty and Violence in the Desert Southwest*. Tucson: University of Arizona Press, 1997.

Merwin, W. S. "Unchopping a Tree." In *The Miner's Pale Children*. New York: Atheneum, 1970. [Reprinted in Merwin, W. S. *The Book of Fables*, 72–74. Port Townsend, WA: Copper Canyon Press, 2007.]

Meyer, John R. "Orthoptera." In the *Index to the Compendium of Hexapod Classes and Orders*, 2020. https://projects.ncsu.edu/cals/course/ent425/library/compendium/orthoptera.html.

Michaels, Anne. *The Winter Vault*. Toronto: McClelland & Stewart, 2009.

Miller, Daegan. "Silent Spring & Other Writings on the Environment by Rachel Carson." *Bookforum*, April 3, 2018. https://www.bookforum.com/culture/silent-spring-other-writings-on-the-environment-by-rachel-carson-19477.

Ministry of Environment and Natural Resources. "Subalpine Fir." Government of the Northwest Territories. https://www.gov.nt.ca/ecc/sites/ecc/files/fact_sheets/subalpine_fir.pdf.

Ministry of Natural Resources and Forestry. "American Chestnut." Government of Ontario, 2014 (updated 2021). https://www.ontario.ca/page/american-chestnut.

REFERENCES

Ministry of the Environment, Conservation and Parks. "American Chestnut." Government of Ontario, 2014 (updated 2021). https://www.ontario.ca/page/american-chestnut-species-risk.

Montaigne, Michel de. *Volume I: The Essays of Montaigne*, translated by George B. Ives. Cambridge, MA: Harvard University Press, 1925.

Moore, J. W. *Anthropocene or Capitalocene? Nature, History, and the Crisis of Capitalism*. Oakland, CA: PM Press, 2016.

Morland, S. "*Lagopus Lagopus*: Willow Grouse; Red Grouse (also Willow Ptarmigan)." Animal Diversity Web, University of Michigan, 2011. https://animaldiversity.org/accounts/Lagopus_lagopus/.

Morley, Simon. "A Short History of the Sublime." *The MIT Press Reader*, 2021. https://thereader.mitpress.mit.edu/a-short-history-of-the-sublime/.

Motlagh, Jason. "In Belarus, Clapping Can be Subversive." *The Atlantic*, July 21, 2011. https://www.theatlantic.com/international/archive/2011/07/in-belarus-clapping-can-be-subversive/242271/.

Mouzykantskii, Ilya. "In Belarus, Just Being Can Prompt an Arrest." *New York Times*, July 29, 2011. https://www.nytimes.com/2011/07/30/world/europe/30belarus.html.

Nancy, Jean-Luc. *After Fukushima: The Equivalence of Catastrophes*, translated by Charlotte Mandell. New York: Fordham University Press, 2015.

Nancy, Jean-Luc, and John Paul Ricco. "The Existence of the World Is Always Unexpected—Jean-Luc Nancy in Conversation with John Paul Ricco, translated by Jeffrey Malecki." In *Art in the Anthropocene: Encounters Among Aesthetics, Politics, Environments and Epistemologies*, edited by Heath Davis and Etienne Turpin, 85–92. London: Open Humanities Press, 2015.

National Forest Service. "Subalpine Fir." US Department of Agriculture. https://www.srs.fs.usda.gov/pubs/misc/ag_654/volume_1/abies/lasiocarpa.htm.

Nechepurenko, Ivan, and Andrew Higgins. "Belarus Says Longtime Leader Is Re-Elected in Vote Critics Call Rigged." *New York Times*, August 9, 2020. https://www.nytimes.com/2020/08/09/world/europe/belarus-election-lukashenko.html.

Neruda, Pablo. *Extravagaria: A Bilingual Edition*, translated by Alastair

Reid. New York: Farrar, Straus and Giroux, 1972 (reprint 2001).

New York City Administrative Code. "§10-136 Prohibition Against Certain Forms of Aggressive Solicitation." New York City. https://codelibrary.amlegal.com/codes/newyorkcity/latest/NYCadmin/0-0-0-6354.

New York Civil Liberties Union (NYCLU). "Legislative Memo: Loitering and Aggressive Begging." Opposition to Bill S.67/A.341, January 1, 2001. https://www.nyclu.org/en/legislation/legislative-memo-loitering-and-aggressive-begging.

Ngũgĩ wa Thiong'o. *Re-Membering Africa*. New York: Basic Civitas Books, 2009.

Nijhuis, Michelle. "Don't Cancel John Muir—But Don't Excuse Him Either." *The Atlantic*, April 12, 2021. https://www.theatlantic.com/ideas/archive/2021/04/conservation-movements-complicated-history/618556/.

Nir, Sarah Maslin. "How 2 Lives Collided in Central Park, Rattling the Nation." *New York Times*, June 14, 2020. https://www.nytimes.com/2020/06/14/nyregion/central-park-amy-cooper-christian-racism.html.

Nobles, Gregory. "The Myth of John James Audubon." *National Audubon Society*, July 31, 2020. https://www.audubon.org/news/the-myth-john-james-audubon.

Northwest Conifers Connections. "Focus on Subalpine Fir." January 13, 2018. nwconifers.blogspot.com/2018/01/focus-on-subalpine-fir.html.

Norton, Thomas Elliot. *The Fur Trade in Colonial New York, 1686–1776*. PhD thesis, University of Tennessee, 1972.

Norwegian Refugee Council. "Case Study Series: Dam Displacement." April 2017. https://www.internal-displacement.org/publications/case-study-series-dam-displacement.

NPS I&M Northeast Temperate Network. "NETN Species Spotlight – Fisher." National Park Service, August 15, 2021. https://www.nps.gov/articles/netn-species-spotlight-fisher.htm.

O'Connor, Brian. *Idleness: A Philosophical Essay*. Princeton, NJ: Princeton University Press, 2018.

Odell, Jenny. *How to Do Nothing: Resisting the Attention Economy*. New York: Penguin Random House, 2019.

REFERENCES

Ogden, Lesley Evans. "The Silent Flight of Owls, Explained." *Audubon*, July 28, 2017. https://www.audubon.org/news/the-silent-flight-owls-explained.

O'Gieblyn, Meghan. *Interior States*. New York: Penguin Random House, 2018.

Pablo, Carlito. "B.C. has Highest Proportion of Renters in Canada Spending over 50 Percent of Income on Housing." *Georgia Straight*, May 8, 2018. https://www.straight.com/news/1071531/bc-has-highest-proportion-renters-canada-spending-over-50-percent-income-housing.

Palmeirim, Ana Filipa, and Luke Gibson. "Impacts of Hydropower on the Habitat of Jaguars and Tigers." *Communications Biology* 4 (2021): 1358. https://www.nature.com/articles/s42003-021-02878-5.

Paul, Trina. "Interested in Retiring Early? 3 Lessons from People Who Retired in Their 30s." CNBC, December 8, 2021. https://www.cnbc.com/select/lessons-from-people-who-retired-in-their-30s/.

Pauly, Daniel. *Vanishing Fish: Shifting Baselines and the Future of Global Fisheries*. Vancouver: Greystone Books, 2019.

PBS. "The Anarchists and the Haymarket Square Incident." Article featured with Chicago: City of the Century, January 13, 2003. https://www.pbs.org/wgbh/americanexperience/features/chicago-anarchists-and-haymarket-square-incident/.

——. "The Rise of Labor," Picture History and Educational Broadcasting Corporation, 2002. https://www.thirteen.org/wnet/historyofus/web09/segment6_p.html.

Pennsylvania Game Commission. "Porcupine." Pennsylvania Government, 2022. https://www.pgc.pa.gov/Education/WildlifeNotesIndex/Pages/Porcupine.aspx.

Pessoa, Fernando. *A Little Larger Than the Entire Universe: Selected Poems*, edited and translated by Richard Zenith. London: Penguin Classics, 2006.

Pigeon, Karine E., Gordon Stenhouse, and Steeve D. Côté. "Drivers of Hibernation: Linking Food and Weather to Denning Behaviour of Grizzly Bears." *Behavioral Ecology and Sociobiology* 70 (2016): 1745–54.

Pinsky, Robert. "That Time Flies is a Cliche." *Washington Post*, January 30, 2005.

REFERENCES

Plato. *Phaedrus*, translated by Benjamin Jowett. Available from The Internet Classics Archive. http://classics.mit.edu/Plato/phaedrus.html.

Postel, Sandra, and Lesli Allison. "Western Water Strategy Shifting from 'Use It or Lose It,' to 'Waste Not, Want Not.'" *The Hill*, June 14, 2018. https://thehill.com/opinion/energy-environment/392341-western-water-strategy-shifting-from-use-it-or-lose-it-to-waste.

Power Technology. "The 10 Biggest Hydroelectric Power Plants in the World." October 14, 2013, updated July 27, 2020. https://www.power-technology.com/features/feature-the-10-biggest-hydroelectric-power-plants-in-the-world/.

———. "Three Gorges Dam Hydro Electric Power Plant, China." February 21, 2020. https://www.power-technology.com/projects/gorges/.

Prunier, M. "Petrichor: The Smell of Rain." American Chemical Society. https://www.acs.org/content/dam/acsorg/education/students/highschool/chemistryclubs/infographics/petrichor-the-smell-of-rain.pdf.

Purdy, Jedediah. "Environmentalism's Racist History." *The New Yorker*, August 13, 2015. https://www.newyorker.com/news/news-desk/environmentalisms-racist-history.

Raworth, Kate. "Must the Anthropocene be a Manthropocene?" *The Guardian*, October 20, 2014. https://www.theguardian.com/commentisfree/2014/oct/20/anthropocene-working-group-science-gender-bias.

Reuters. "India Glacier Avalanche Leaves 18 Dead, More Than 200 Missing." February 8, 2021. https://www.reuters.com/business/environment/india-glacier-avalanche-leaves-18-dead-more-than-200-missing-2021-02-08/.

Reynolds, Jesse L. "Governing New Biotechnologies for Biodiversity Conservation: Gene Drives, International Law, and Emerging Politics." *Global Environmental Politics* 20, no. 3 (2020): 28–48.

Rich, Nathaniel. "When Parks Were Radical." *The Atlantic*, September 2016. https://www.theatlantic.com/magazine/archive/2016/09/better-than-nature/492716/.

Robbins, Charles T., Claudia Lopez-Alfaro, Karyn D. Rode, Øivind Tøien, and O. Lynne Nelson. "Hibernation and Seasonal Fasting in Bears: The Energetic Costs and Consequences for Polar Bears." *Journal of Mammalogy* 93, no. 6 (2012): 1493–1503. https://doi.

org/10.1644/11-MAMM-A-406.1.

Roberts, Strother, E. *Colonial Ecology, Atlantic Economy*. Philadelphia: University of Pennsylvania Press, 2019.

Robertson, Morgan M. "The Neoliberalization of Ecosystem Services: Wetland Mitigation Banking and Problems in Environmental Governance." *Geoforum* 35, no. 3 (2004): 361–73.

Roche, John P. "The Origin of Grasshoppers, Katydids, and Crickets: A New Study Resolves the Evolutionary Tree of the Orthoptera." *Entomology Today*, April 8, 2015. https://entomologytoday.org/2015/04/08/the-origin-of-grasshoppers-katydids-and-crickets-a-new-study-resolves-the-evolutionary-tree-of-the-orthoptera/.

Rose, Julie L. *Free Time*. Princeton, NJ: Princeton University Press, 2016.

Rosenbaum, S. P. *The Bloomsbury Group: Collection of Memoirs and Commentary*. Toronto: University of Toronto Press, 1995.

Runyon, Luke. "When It Comes to Water Rights, This Once-a-Decade List Details Who Will 'Use It or Lose It.'" KUNC, June 22, 2020. https://www.kuer.org/2020-06-22/when-it-comes-to-water-rights-this-once-a-decade-list-details-who-will-use-it-or-lose-it.

Russell, Bertrand. "In Praise of Idleness." *Harper's Magazine*, October 1932. https://harpers.org/archive/1932/10/in-praise-of-idleness/.

Rustad, Harley. "Big Lonely Doug." *The Walrus*, September 19, 2016, https://thewalrus.ca/big-lonely-doug/.

———. *Big Lonely Doug: The Story of One of Canada's Last Great Trees*. Toronto: House of Anansi Press, 2018.

Salmón, Enrique. "Kincentric Ecology: Indigenous Perceptions of the Human-Nature Relationship." *Ecological Applications* 10, no. 5 (October 2000): 1327–32. https://www.fws.gov/nativeameri-can/pdf/tek-salmon-2000.pdf.

Sands, Leo. "Pakistan Floods: One Third of Country Is Under Water – Minister." BBC, August 30, 2022. https://www.bbc.com/news/world-europe-62712301.

Schollenberger, Piotr. "Idleness and Contemporary Art. On Taking One's Time." *Art Inquiry* 12 (2010): 71–90.

Schwab, Francis E., Neal P. P. Simon, and Sherri Nash. "Age and Sex Segregation of Wintering Willow Ptarmigan in Labrador." *Northeastern Naturalist* 12, no. 1 (2005): 113–18.

REFERENCES

Schwartz, Charles C., Sterling D. Miller, and Mark A. Haroldson. "Grizzly Bear (*Ursus arctos*)." In *Wild Mammals of North America: Biology, Management, and Conservation*, 2nd ed., edited by G. A. Feldhamer, B. C. Thompson, and J. A. Chapman, chapter 26, 556–86. Baltimore, MD: Johns Hopkins University Press, 2003.

Scott, James C. *Seeing Like a State: How Certain Schemes to Improve the Human Condition Have Failed*. New Haven, CT: Yale University Press, 1998.

———. *Two Cheers for Anarchism: Six Easy Pieces on Autonomy, Dignity, and Meaningful Work and Play*. Princeton, NJ: Princeton University Press, 2012.

———. *Weapons of the Weak: Everyday Forms of Peasant Resistance*. New Haven, CT: Yale University Press, 1985.

Segal, Corinne, and Ocean Vuong. "Ocean Vuong on Taking the Time You Need to Write." *Literary Hub*, April 8, 2022. https://lithub.com/ocean-vuong-on-taking-the-time-you-need-to-write/.

Seiter, Courtney. "The Science of Taking Breaks at Work." *Buffer*, August 21, 2014. https://buffer.com/resources/science-taking-breaks-at-work/.

Sierra Club. "About Clearcutting." 2022. https://www.sierraclub.org/grassroots-network/stop-clearcutting-ca/about-clearcutting.

Silber, Emily. "Why a Painted Bunting Landed in Brooklyn." *National Audubon Society*, December 7, 2015. https://www.audubon.org/news/why-painted-bunting-landed-brooklyn.

Simpson, Leanne Betasamosake. "A Short History of the Blockade: Giant Beavers, Diplomacy, and Regeneration in Nishnaabewin." *CLC Kriesel Lecture Series*, Edmonton, University of Alberta Press, 2021.

Simpson, Leanne Betasamosake, and Dionne Brand. "'Temporary Spaces of Joy and Freedom': Leanne Betasamosake Simpson in Conversation with Dionne Brand." *Literary Review Canada—A Journal of Ideas*, June 2018. https://reviewcanada.ca/magazine/2018/06/temporary-spaces-of-joy-and-freedom/.

Sitrin, Marina. "The Anarchist Spirit." *Dissent* 62, no. 4 (2015): 84–86.

Slouka, Mark. "Quitting the Paint Factory." *Harper's Magazine*, November 2004, 57–65.

Solnit, Rebecca. "The Blue of Distance." *Harper's Magazine*, July 2005.

———. *A Field Guide to Getting Lost*. New York: Viking, 2005.

REFERENCES

———. *Hope in the Dark: Untold Histories, Wild Possibilities.* Chicago: Haymarket Books, 2004 (reprint 2016).
———. "'Hope Is an Embrace of the Unknown': Rebecca Solnit on Living in Dark Times." *The Guardian*, July 15, 2016. https://www.theguardian.com/books/2016/jul/15/rebecca-solnit-hope-in-the-dark-new-essay-embrace-unknown.
———. "The Most Radical Thing." *Orion*, 2008. https://orionmagazine.org/article/the-most-radical-thing-you-can-do/.
———. "Mysteries of Thoreau, Unsolved: On the Dirtiness of Laundry and the Strength of Sisters." *Orion*, May/June 2013, 18–23.
———. *Savage Dreams: A Journey into the Hidden Wars of the American West.* Berkeley: University of California Press, 2014.
———. *Wanderlust: A History of Walking.* New York: Penguin Random House, 2000.
Soper, Kate. *Post-Growth Living: For an Alternative Hedonism.* New York: Verso, 2020.
Spahr, Juliana. *This Connection of Everyone with Lungs: Poems.* Berkeley: University of California Press, 2005.
Spellen, Suzanne. "The Gleaming Beaux Arts Boathouse of Prospect Park." *Brownstoner*, September 6, 2017. https://www.brownstoner.com/architecture/prospect-park-boathouse-brooklyn-architecture-park-slope/.
Spence, Austin R., Erin E. Wilson Rankin, and Morgan W. Tingley. "DNA Metabarcoding Reveals Broadly Overlapping Diets in Three Sympatric North American Hummingbirds." *Ornithology* 139, no. 1 (2022): ukab074, https://doi.org/10.1093/ornithology/ukab074.
Sperber, Michael. "Frederick Law Olmsted." *Harvard Magazine*, July–August 2007. https://www.harvardmagazine.com/2007/07/frederick-law-olmsted.html.
Standing, Guy. "Why a Basic Income Is Necessary for a Right to Work." *Basic Income Studies* 7, no. 2 (2013): 19–40.
Staples, Brent. "The Death of the Black Utopia." *New York Times*, November 28, 2019. https://www.nytimes.com/2019/11/28/opinion/seneca-central-park-nyc.html.
Stark, Heidi Kiiwetinepinesiik. "Respect, Responsibility, and Renewal: The Foundations of Anishinaabe Treaty Making with the United

REFERENCES

States and Canada." *American Indian Culture and Research Journal* 34, no. 2 (2010): 145–64.

State Assembly of New York. "S. 67" (BILL NO S00067A, same as A00341-A), State of New York. https://nyassembly.gov/leg/?default_fld=&leg_video=&bn=S.+67&term=2001&Summary=Y&Actions=Y&Floor%26nbspVotes=Y&Memo=Y&Text=Y.

Statistics Canada. "Section 2—Forests and the Forest Sector in Canada." In *Human Activity and the Environment 2017: Forests in Canada*, 2018. https://www150.statcan.gc.ca/n1/pub/16-201-x/2018001/sec-2-eng.htm.

Statius. "The Thebaid," translated by John Henry Mozley. Loeb Classical Library edition, 1928, the Theoi Project (2000–2017). https://www.theoi.com/Daimon/Hypnos.html and https://www.theoi.com/Daimon/Aergia.html.

Steingraber, Sandra. "The Fracking of Rachel Carson." *Orion*, September/October 2012. https://orionmagazine.org/article/the-fracking-of-rachel-carson/.

Stern, David. "Belarus's Alexander Lukashenko Begins Fourth Term." BBC News, January 21, 2011. https://www.bbc.com/news/world-europe-12247664.

Stevens, Susan T. "Charon's Obol and Other Coins in Ancient Funerary Practice." *Phoenix* 45, no. 3 (1991): 215–29.

Stickney, J. H. *Aesop's Fables: A Version for Young Readers*. 1915. Available from Project Gutenberg at https://www.gutenberg.org/ebooks/49010.

Straka, Martin, Ladislav Paule, Jozef Štofík, Ovidiu Ionescu, and Michal Adamec. "Genetic Differentiation of Carpathian Brown Bear (*Ursus arctos*) Populations Reflects the Human Caused Isolation." *Beitrage zur Jagd-und Wildforschung* 36 (2011): 77–86.

Stronge, Will, and Kyle Lewis. *Overtime: Why We Need a Shorter Working Week*. New York: Verso, 2021.

Subramanian, Meera. "The Age of Loneliness." *Guernica: A Magazine of Art and Politics*, September 15, 2015. https://www.guernicamag.com/features/the-age-of-loneliness.

Szymborska, Wislawa. *View with a Grain of Sand: Selected Poems*, translated by Stanislaw Baranczak and Clare Cavanagh. New York: Harcourt Brace, 1995.

REFERENCES

Taylor, Astra. "Against Activism." *The Baffler* 20 (March 2016). https://thebaffler.com/salvos/against-activism.

Thames River Clear Water Revival. "Antler River Guardians from the 4 Directions," Steering Committee. https://www.thamesrevival.ca/home/first-nations/first-nations-youth-engagement/.

———. "The Thames River (Deshkan Ziibi) Shared Waters Approach to Water Quality and Quantity." 2019. https://www.thamesrevival.ca/wp-content/uploads/2020/05/SharedWatersApproach-Dec2019finaldraft.pdf.

The Care Collective. *The Care Manifesto: The Politics of Interdependence.* New York: Verso, 2020.

Thompson, Mitchell. "Is the Canada Recovery Benefit a 'Workfare' Program in Disguise?" *Canadian Dimension*, June 8, 2021. https://canadiandimension.com/articles/view/is-the-canada-recovery-benefit-a-workfare-program-in-disguise.

Thoren, Roxi. "Deep Roots: Foundations of Forestry in American Landscape Architecture." *Scenario Journal* 4 (Spring 2014). https://scenariojournal.com/article/deep-roots/.

Topol, Sarah A. "The Battle for the Mural — and the Future of Belarus." *New York Times*, March 30, 2022. https://www.nytimes.com/2022/03/30/magazine/belarus-mural.html.

Tranströmer, Tomas. "Vermeer." In *The Half-Finished Heaven: The Best Poems of Tomas Tranströmer*, chosen and translated by Robert Bly, 87–88. Minneapolis, MN: Graywolf Press, 2001.

Tsing, Anna. "Unruly Edges: Mushrooms as Companion Species (for Donna Haraway)." *Environmental Humanities* 1 (2012): 141–54.

Tsing, Anna Lowenhaupt. *The Mushroom at the End of the World: On the Possibility of Life in Capitalist Ruins.* Princeton, NJ: Princeton University Press, 2015.

Tukker, Paul. "Retreating Yukon Glacier Makes River Disappear." CBC News, June 17, 2016. https://www.cbc.ca/news/canada/north/slims-river-dries-yukon-kluane-glacier-1.3639472.

UNESCO. "Indigenous Peoples: Informed Custodians of Biodiversity." 2021. https://en.unesco.org/courier/2021-3/indigenous-peoples-informed-custodians-biodiversity.

US Energy Information Administration. "Hydropower

REFERENCES

Explained: Hydropower and the Environment." November 7, 2022. https://www.eia.gov/energyexplained/hydropower/hydropower-and-the-environment.php.

USGS. "How Do Salmon Know Where Their Home Is When They Return from the Ocean?" US Department of the Interior. https://www.usgs.gov/faqs/how-do-salmon-know-where-their-home-when-they-return-ocean.

Vanderpool, Tim. "The Colorado River Delta is Proof of Nature's Resiliency." NRDC, June 28, 2018. https://www.nrdc.org/onearth/colorado-river-delta-proof-natures-resiliency.

van Wees, Hans. "The Economy." In *A Companion to Archaic Greece*, edited by Kurt A. Raaflaub and Hans van Wees, chapter 23, 444–67. Hoboken, NJ: Blackwell Publishing Ltd., 2009.

Venkiteswaran, Rajesh Trichur. "Food Grains Rot in India While Millions Live with Empty Stomachs." Lowy Institute, November 16, 2018. https://www.lowyinstitute.org/the-interpreter/food-grains-rot-india-while-millions-live-empty-stomachs.

Vermes, Jason. "'You Protect What You Love': Why Biodiversity Thrives on Indigenous-Managed Lands." CBC Radio, August 12, 2019. https://www.cbc.ca/radio/checkup/are-we-doing-enough-to-protect-canada-s-wildlife-1.5240848/you-protect-what-you-love-why-biodiversity-thrives-on-indigenous-managed-lands-1.5243547.

Waida, Manabu. "Birds in the Mythology of Sacred Kingship." *East and West* 28, 1/4 (December 1978): 283–89.

Waldie, Paul. (Photography by Anna Liminowicz.) "Too Precious to Leave Behind." *The Globe and Mail*, March 4, 2022. https://www.theglobeandmail.com/world/article-ukrainians-fleeing-war-with-russia-share-the-items-they-couldnt-leave/.

Wanberg, Kyle. "Echoes of the Ant People: Vocal Traces and Writing Practices in a Translation of 'O'odham Orature." *Canadian Review of Comparative Literature* 40, no. 3 (2013): 271–88.

Wapner, Paul. "Forum—Planetary Disasters: Wildness and the Perennial Struggle for Control." *Global Environmental Politics* 21, no. 1 (2021): 3–12.

———. *Is Wildness Over?* Cambridge, UK: Polity Press, 2020.

Watts, Vanessa. "Indigenous Place-Thought and Agency Amongst

REFERENCES

Humans and Non-humans: First Woman and Sky Woman Go on a European Tour!" *Decolonization: Indigeneity, Education & Society* 2, no. 1 (2013): 20–34.

Weil, Simone. *Gravity and Grace*. London: Routledge, 2002.

Wenzel, Siegfried. *Acedia and Related Terms in Medieval Thought with Special Emphasis on Middle English Literature*. PhD diss., Ohio State University, 1960.

Whetung, Madeline. "(En)gendering Shoreline Law: Nishnaabeg Relational Politics Along the Trent Severn Waterway." *Global Environmental Politics* 19, no. 3 (2019): 16–32. https://doi.org/10.1162/glep_a_00513.

Wien, Thomas. "Selling Beaver Skins in North America and Europe, 1720–1760: The Uses of Fur-Trade Imperialism." *Journal of the Canadian Historical Association* 1, no. 1 (1990): 293–317. https://doi.org/10.7202/031021ar.

Wolf, Blair O., Andrew E. McKechnie, C. Jonathan Schmitt, Zenon J. Czenze, Andrew B. Johnson, and Christopher C. Witt. "Extreme and Variable Torpor Among High-Elevation Andean Hummingbird Species." *Biology Letters* 16 (2020): 20200428. http://dx.doi.org/10.1098/rsbl.2020.0428.

Wong, Carmen, Kate Ballegooyen, Lawrence Ignace, Mary Jane (Gùdia) Johnson, and Heidi Swanson. "Towards Reconciliation: 10 Calls to Action to Natural Scientists Working in Canada." *FACETS* 5 (2020): 769–783. doi:10.1139/facets- 2020-0005.

Woolf, Virginia. *To the Lighthouse*. London: Hogarth Press, 1927. [Note: the full text of *To the Lighthouse* is available from Project Gutenberg: https://gutenberg.net.au/ebooks01/0100101h.html.]

———. *The Waves*. London: Hogarth Press, 1931. [Note: the full text of *The Waves* is available from Project Gutenberg: https://gutenberg.ca/ebooks/woolfv-thewaves/woolfv-thewaves-00-h.html.]

Ye, Shuxian. *A Mythological Approach to Exploring the Origins of Chinese Civilization*, translated by Hui Jia and Jing Hua. New York: Springer, 2022.

Yong, Ed. "Plants Can Hear Animals." *The Atlantic*, January 10, 2019. https://www.theatlantic.com/science/archive/2019/01/plants-use-flowers-hear-buzz-animals/579964/.

REFERENCES

Yoon, Carol Kaesuk. *Naming Nature: The Clash Between Instinct and Science.* New York: W. W. Norton, 2010.

Young, Pariesa. "'Hello from Ukraine': Volunteers Make Molotov Cocktails to Counter Russian Assault." *France24*, February 28, 2022. https://observers.france24.com/en/europe/20220228-citizen-volunteers-ukraine-russia-invasion-molotov-cocktails.

Zarter, C. Ryan, Barbara Demmig-Adams, Volker Ebbert, Iwona Adamska, William W. Adams III. "Photosynthetic Capacity and Light Harvesting Efficiency During the Winter-to-Spring Transition in Subalpine Conifers." *New Phytologist* 172, no. 2 (2006): 283–92. https://doi.org/10.1111/j.1469-8137.2006.01816.x.

Zielinski, Sarah. "Animal Magnetism: How Salmon Find Their Way Back Home." NPR, February 7, 2013. https://www.npr.org/sections/thesalt/2013/02/07/171384063/animal-magnetism-how-salmon-find-their-way-back-home.

Zinke, Laura. "Geomorphology: Plants Hold Back Rivers." *Nature Reviews: Earth & Environment*, 2019 (December 17). https://doi.org/10.1038/s43017-019-0016-3.

Zwicky, Jan, and Robert Bringhurst. *Learning to Die: Wisdom in the Age of Climate Change.* Regina, Saskatchewan: University of Regina Press, 2018.

INDEX

Ä'äy Chù, 84–85, 88, 100
absence, 123, 127–28
abstemiousness, 101
abundance, 14, 37
accumulation: and abundance, 37; and food security, 35; through investment, 32, 33; work and, 31
acedia, 123–24
activism / activist, 63–64, 172n56
Aergia, 133
Aesop, 22, 26
Alarm, The, 137, 138
anarchism / anarchy, 11–13, 15
Anthropocene, 114–16
ants, 21–22, 30, 31, 34, 36, 37–38
art, outcomes versus processes of, 24. *See also* creativity
assessment, overconfidence in, 100–101, 104
Atlin Lake, 56–57, 65–66, 142
attention, 113–29
audiobooks, 42
authoritarianism / authoritarian regime, 11, 62–64

bark, sent to Sachs from Celan, 50–51
Barks, Coleman, 140
Bashō, 156n9
bears, 40–41, 44–46, 48, 49, 164n26/28
beavers, 53, 56–60, 61–62, 63–64, 66, 169n26
bedrock, 85
bee, benevolent, 34, 36
begging, 83, 178n18
bereavement, 120. *See also* grief
Beston, Henry, 19–20, 154n54
Big Lonely Doug, 54, 65
biodiversity, 101–2
Bird Rose, Deborah, 121–22, 124
birds: birdsong, absent, 47–48; and breathing, 140; conservation of, 177n7; eiders, 133; frolicking in, 108, 190nn45–46; migration, 177n4; off-course, 80, 177n4; owls and loss, 114, 117–19; swallow nests, 6; unseen nests, 127–28. *See also* bunting, off-course; great horned owl; hummingbirds; owls; ptarmigan, willow
Bonneville Power Administration, 87, 181n50
bread, 71–72, 175n19
breaks, 43
breathing, 72, 124–25
Bringhurst, Robert, 115–16
buckbrush, 100–101
bunting, off-course, 80, 84

INDEX

Campania, 14
carbon, 72
Carson, Rachel, 47–48, 103–4, 190n38
Celan, Paul, 48–49, 50–51, 166n48
cell phones, abstaining from using, 104–7, 109–10
Central Park, 83, 84, 179n31
cicadas, 26
Cicero, 14
clear-cutting, 53–55, 167n7
climate change, 13, 34, 92–94
coercion, 12, 110
Colorado River, 90–91
colours, 23
Columbia River, 181n50
competition, 36–37
complex systems, 16
conservation, 101, 104, 177n7
consumption, "frictions" of, 34–35
conveniences, modern, 74–76
creative work, 21–23, 24
creativity, 20–38
Cruz, Conchitina, 132, 197n4

dams, 87–88, 181n50, 182n52. *See also* beavers
Dark Hours (Cruz), 132
decay, 5–6, 16
deep time, 193n8, 194n11
degrowth, 110
Demuth, Bathsheba, 75, 170n29
deterioration, 5–6, 16
detours, 79–94
dignity, work as, 28
Dillard, Annie, 26–27, 135–36, 141
Doty, Mark, 119, 120
doubt, 18

early retirement, 31–33
efficiency, 42–44, 74–76
energy, 10
Eremozoic, 123
evergreen, as economic model, 77
evolution, 36, 193n8
exploitation, 27, 30
exposure, 77

feeling, 103–4
Financial Independence; Retire Early (F.I.R.E), 31–33, 36
fir trees, 54, 65, 67–68, 77
fire, 33, 69
fish: as casualties of hydropower dams, 88; counted at a weir, 88; and habitat created by beavers, 57; salmon migrations, 79–80. *See also* salmon
flash mobs, and political resistance in Belarus, 62–63
floods, 34
food security, 35
foot-dragging, 199n23
forests: clear-cutting, 53–55, 167n7; replanting, 15–16
forgetting, 117
Frederick (Lionni), 22–23, 24
freedom: and doing nothing, 89; in work, 28
frolicking, in birds, 108, 190nn45–46
fulfillment, in retirement, 32–33
fur trade, 60–62; and imperialism, 61

Gallagher, Tess, 127–28
gardens, shifts in occupancy of, 6–7
generosity, 37
geological features, shaping of, 194n11

INDEX

gig economy, 28. *See also* precarity; zero-hour contracts
"going to seed," 5, 6, 8
Goldman, Emma, 11–12
Graeber, David, 13, 19, 154n52, 176n30
Grand Coulee Dam, 181n50
"Grasshopper and the Ants," 21–22, 30, 34, 35, 160n47
grasshopper(s), 21–22, 26, 30, 35
great horned owl, 113–14, 118–19
grief, 117–18, 120, 122
Guthrie, Woody, 86–87, 181n50

"Half-Earth." *See* Nature Needs Half
Hass, Robert, 117, 121
Haymarket Incident (1886), 138–39
hedonism, 108–9, 136, 191n47
Hesiod, 9, 30–31, 150n13
heteronyms, of Fernando Pessoa, 25
hibernation, 40–41, 45, 46
holding back. *See* restraint
hope, 66
houses / housing: affordable, 159n46; shifts in occupancy of, 5–7
Houston, Pam, 122, 125
hummingbirds, 41–42
hunting and trapping. *See* fur trade
hydropower dams, 87–88, 181n50, 182n52

idleness: as anarchic, 10, 13; antonyms, 132; blurred divide between work and, 132–33; as exploitative, 27; importance of, 43–44; negative perceptions of, 9; politics of, 19; as regulated, 82; Slouka on, 10–11; synonyms, 9; as unsettling political figures, 13–14. *See also* laziness
idling, 19, 22, 59, 62–63. *See also* loitering
imagination, 10, 66, 132
Indigenous blockades, 64
Indigenous lands, 99, 186n12
Indigenous peoples, resisting labour exploitation, 81–82
inequality, searching for origins of, 176n30
information intake, 42, 43
interaction, interspecies, 36–37, 90, 110–11, 154n54
investment, 32, 33

joblessness, 28–29

Kaskawulsh Glacier, 84–85, 88
Kenkō, 9, 13, 151n31, 152n33
Keynes, John Maynard, 7
Kimmerer, Robin Wall, 37, 102, 111

labour. *See* work
labour disruptions, 137–39, 199n23
Lafargue, Paul, 7, 29, 32, 149n9, 158nn29/31/32
Landor, Walter Savage, 116, 117
languages, lost, 99–100
law-breaking, 12
laziness, 9, 29, 81–82, 89, 123, 132
legibility, 15
logging, 53–55, 60–61, 66
loitering, 83, 179n31. *See also* idling
loneliness, 123
loons, 125
Lopez, Barry, 47, 104, 125–26, 135
loss: and Anthropocene, 114–15; grief

and, 117–18, 120, 122
love, and loss, 117–18, 120
Lucretius, 136

Macdonald, Helen, 69, 120
Macfarlane, Robert, 100, 103, 107
MacKinnon, J. B., 118
management: and forest regeneration, 15–16, 153n43; of lands under Indigenous governance, 102; as oversight of others' labour, 30–31
Mandelstam, Osip, 49
Manila, 139
Marom, Yotam, 64
materialism, 109
May Day, 138–39
McKay, Don, 78, 133, 140
media intake, 42, 43
meditation, 18, 121
Meloy, Ellen, 41, 85
meritocracy, 27
Merwin, W. S., 55, 56, 66
metamorphosis, 26
mice, 4–5, 22–24
Michaels, Anne, 132, 141
mining, 102
mobility: and mandated work, 81–82; and river piracy, 85–86
modern conveniences, 74–76
Montaigne, Michel de, 44–45, 150n15
morality/moralizing: of accumulation, 30; appeals to, as strategy for increasing labour demands, 27, 137; equated with work, 10
movement, 92–94
mushrooms, 90
mycorrhizal networks, 65
mythology: and fables, 22, 25–26, 34, 55; Greek and Roman gods and goddesses, 30, 114, 116–17, 126, 132–33; and Muses, 26

Nakina River, 39–40, 51–52
names / naming, 99, 100, 103–4
Nanda Devi Glacier, 88
narwhal, 47
Nature Needs Half, 101–2, 111, 123, 188n24
Neruda, Pablo, 49–50, 52
no-knead bread, 175n19

occupancy, shifts in, 5–7
Olmsted, Frederick Law, 83–84, 179n30
other nations, 20
otium, 14
outsourcing, 74–76
overburden, 102
owls, 113–14, 117, 118–19, 126–27, 192n6

painted bunting, off-course, 80, 84
painting: and eternity, 128; and a single second of pigment, 141; still life, 119–21
pandemic, Covid-19, 71–73, 93–94, 106–7, 175n20
paradox, 131–42
Pessoa, Fernando, 25, 156n15
petrichor, 131–32, 197n1
phones, abstaining from using, 104–7, 109–10
pilgrims, 79–80
plants: importance of, 19–20; sounds of, 46–47
play, 108, 110, 190nn45–46

INDEX

pleasure, 108–9, 110–11, 191n47
Pliny, 14, 45, 114
poetry: and blurred lines between idleness and work, 133; as requiring silence, 51
porcupine(s), 69–71, 174n14
power: asymmetry of, 28; legibility as condition for, 15
precarity, in labour conditions, 19, 27, 32, 94
production, 24
productivity, 42–44, 57, 59, 74–76, 89–90
progress, 15, 58–59, 75
Prospect Park, 83, 177n7
protests, in Belarus, 62–63, 64
ptarmigan, willow, 96–97, 103, 107–8, 190–91nn45–46

quill pigs, 70. *See also* porcupine(s)

racism, and conservation movements and public space, 179nn30–31
red foxes, 118
refuge, 50–51
refusal, versus resistance, 63
relocation, forcible, 93–94
resin, 67
resistance, 53–66
responsibility, 115, 139–41
rest, 43, 136–37
restraint, 95–111
retirement, early, 31–33
River Lethe, 116–17
rivers: names of, 99–100, 142; piracy, 85–86; rerouting of, 84–86. *See also* Colorado River; Columbia River; dams; Nakina River; River Lethe; Thames River / Deshkan Ziibi; T'ooch' Héeni; weir
Roman Empire, 13–14
Rumi, 140
Russell, Bertrand, 7, 27

sabbatical, 136–37
Sachs, Nelly, 49, 50–51
sacrifice, 109–10. *See also* restraint
salmon, 39–40, 79–94, 176n1
sand mandalas, 24–25
saplings, 15–16, 54, 65, 127–28
Saskatoon berry, 37
Scott, James, 12, 15, 16, 199n23
screens, abstaining from, 104–7, 109–10
self-determination, 13
serviceberry, 37
shifting baselines, 118
shimmer, concept of, 121–22, 124
silence, 46–49, 51, 127–28
Silent Spring (Carson), 47–48
Simard, Suzanne, 65, 153n43
Simpson, Leanne Betasamosake, 63–64
Sisyphus, 55–56. *See also* mythology
slash, 53–54
Slim's River, 84–85, 88. *See also* Ä'äy Chù
Slouka, Mark, 10–11, 13, 42
slowness, 67–78
Socrates, 25–26
solastalgia, 116
solitude, 45
Solnit, Rebecca, 66, 78, 80, 92–94, 127, 190n43
sorrow, 120, 122–23, 126–27
sourdough bread, 71–72, 175n19

235

INDEX

speed, 42–43
Stark, Heidi Kiiwetinepinesiik, 60
stillness, 59–60, 121
strikes / striking, 137–39, 199n23
subalpine fir trees, 54, 65, 67–68, 77
sublime, 78
Szymborska, Wisław, 113

Taku River, 39
technology, 7, 74–76, 104–7, 109–10
Thames River / Deshkan Ziibi, 99, 100
theft, 30
Three Gorges Dam, 88
Through the Looking-Glass, and What Alice Found There (Carroll), 58, 59
time, 10–11, 13, 24, 43, 74, 105–8, 115–18, 136–37, 149–50n11, 194n11
toads, 5, 41
T'ooch' Héeni, 141
torpor, 41–42
To the Lighthouse (Woolf), 5–7, 16, 153nn46/48
transform / transformation, 25, 78, 80, 111. *See also* metamorphosis
Tranströmer, Tomas, 128
travail, 20
Tsing, Anna, 90, 126

uncertainty, 18, 66, 75, 96
unemployment, 28–29
unhoused people, 83, 178n18, 179n31
United Nations Declaration of Human Rights, 28
United Nations International Covenant on Economic, Social and Cultural Rights, 28

"unplugging," 104–7, 109–10
unruliness, 89

vagrants / vagrancy, 80–81, 83, 84
Vermeer, Jan, 128
Vuong, Ocean, 23, 156n9

Wapner, Paul, 75, 78
war, 49–51
water rights, 90–92, 184nn78–79
watershed, 3–4, 39–40, 79
Waves, The (Woolf), 44
Weil, Simone, 120–21
weir, 39–40, 51–52
"Whole Earth." *See* Nature Needs Half
wildfires, 69
wildness, 75–76, 77–78
willows, 95–96, 103
Wilson, E. O., 101, 123
women, and increased productivity through technology, 74–75
wonder, 103–4, 111
Woolf, Virginia, 5–7, 16, 44, 133, 153nn46/48
work, 7–10; against beavers, 58–59; benefits of, 18; blurred divide between idleness and, 132–33; as coerced, 28; critiques of meaningful, 154n52; defining, 132; as dignity, 28; displacement of, 18; freedom in, 28; and loitering, 83; mobility and mandated, 81–82; as necessary, 18–19; of nonhuman entities, 14–15, 16; outsourcing, 74–76; politics of, 19; re-devotion to, 124; rethinking pace and distribution of, 77; Russell on types of,

27; standards concerning hourly, 137–38; and staving off deterioration, 16; undervalued or ignored, 90; unequal outcomes from, 31; vagrants and shortage of, 81; value attached to, 28–29; and worker unrest, 138–39
work-life balance, 73–74
Works and Days (Hesiod), 9

yeast, 71, 175n19
Yolngu, 121–22, 124, 141

zero-hour contracts, 28
Zwicky, Jan, 115–16

Kate J. Neville is an associate professor in the Department of Political Science and the School of the Environment at the University of Toronto, where she studies global resource politics, energy transitions and technologies, and community resistance. When not in the city, Kate can be found in an off-grid cabin in the woods.

Author photo by Kate Harris